Reading Nietzsche at the Margins

Reading Nietzsche at the Margins

Steven V. Hicks and Alan Rosenberg

Purdue University Press / West Lafayette, Indiana

Printed in the United States of America.

ISBN 978-1-55753-451-4

Library of Congress Cataloging-in-Publication Data

Reading Nietzsche at the margins / edited by Steven V. Hicks and Alan Rosenberg.
    p. cm.
    Includes bibliographical references and index.
    ISBN-13: 978-1-55753-451-4 (alk. paper)
    1. Nietzsche, Friedrich Wilhelm, 1844–1900. I. Hicks, Steven V., 1956–
II. Rosenberg, Alan, 1939–
    B3317.R36 2008
    193—dc22   2008003485

Contents

About the Contributors

CHRISTA DAVIS ACAMPORA is Associate Professor of Philosophy at Hunter College of the City University of New York. She is the editor of Nietzsche's "On the Genealogy of Morals": Critical Essays (2006), coeditor of A Nietzschean Bestiary: Animality Beyond Docile and Brutal (2004), and the author of numerous articles on Nietzsche. Her other research projects include a manuscript on the relation between imagination and social and political philosophy, several articles on aesthetics and philosophy of sport, and a book on Nietzsche's conception of competition. She is currently the executive editor of the Journal of Nietzsche Studies.

DAVID B. ALLISON is Professor of Philosophy at the State University of New York at Stony Brook. He is the editor of the groundbreaking anthology The New Nietzsche (1977) and the author of Reading the New Nietzsche (2001).

STUART ELDEN is a Lecturer in Political Geography at the University of Durham, UK. He is the author of Mapping the Present: Heidegger, Foucault, and the Project of a Spatial History (2001) and Henri Lefebvre: A Critical Introduction (2004), and the coeditor of Henri Lefebvre: Key Writings (2003).

LAWRENCE J. HATAB is Professor of Philosophy at Old Dominion University, Norfolk, Virginia. His published works include Myth and Philosophy: A Contest of Truths (1990), A Nietzschean Defense of Democracy: An Experiment in Postmodern Politics (1999), Ethics and Finitude: Heideggerian Contributions to Moral Philosophy (2000), and Nietzsche's Life Sentence: Coming to Terms with Eternal Recurrence (2005).

STEVEN V. HICKS is Professor and Chair of Philosophy at Queens College of the City University of New York. He is the author of International Law and the Possibility of a Just World Order (1999) and the coeditor of Mythos and Logos: How to Regain the Love of Wisdom (2004) and The Challenges of Globalization: Rethinking Nature, Culture, and Freedom (2007). He has published numerous articles and book chapters on Hegel, Nietzsche, and nineteenth-century German philosophy and literature. From 2001 to 2004 he served on the board of editorial consultants for the History of Philosophy Quarterly, and he is currently the editor of the special book series Universal Justice of Editions Rodopi.

KATHLEEN MARIE HIGGINS is Professor of Philosophy at the University of Texas at Austin. Her main areas of research are continental philosophy and aesthetics, particularly musical aesthetics. She has published a number of books, including *Comic Relief: Nietzsche's Gay Science* (2000), *What Nietzsche Really Said* (with Robert C. Solomon, 2000), *A Passion for Wisdom* (with Robert C. Solomon, 1997), *A Short History of Philosophy* (with Robert C. Solomon, 1996), *The Music of Our Lives* (1991), and *Nietzsche's Zarathustra* (1987). She has also edited or coedited several other books on such topics as Nietzsche, German Idealism, aesthetics, ethics, erotic love, and non-Western philosophy.

TYLER ROBERTS is Associate Professor of Religious Studies at Grinnell College, Grinnell, Iowa. He is author of *Contesting Spirit: Nietzsche, Affirmation, Religion* (1998).

ALAN ROSENBERG is Professor of Philosophy at Queens College of the City University of New York. He has coedited numerous books, including *Echoes from the Holocaust: Philosophical Reflections on a Dark Time* (1990), *Healing Their Wounds: Psychotherapy and Holocaust Survivors* (1989), *Contemporary Portrayals of Auschwitz: Philosophical Challenges* (2000), and *Foucault and Heidegger: Critical Encounters* (2003).

RICHARD SCHACHT is Jubilee Professor of Liberal Arts and Sciences at the University of Illinois, Urbana-Champaign. He is the author of numerous books including *Hegel and After* (1975), *Nietzsche* (1983), and *Nietzsche, Genealogy, Morality* (1994). His interests center on issues relating to human nature, value theory, and social theory. His most recent books include *The Future of Alienation* (1994), *Making Sense of Nietzsche* (1995), and *Nietzsche's Postmoralism* (2000). He is the current executive director of the North American Nietzsche Society.

CHARLES E. SCOTT is Distinguished Professor of Philosophy and Director of the Center for Ethics at Vanderbilt University, Nashville, Tennessee. For many years he was the Edwin Erle Sparks Professor of Philosophy at Pennsylvania State University. He is the author of numerous books including *The Question of Ethics: Nietzsche, Foucault, and Heidegger* (1990) and *The Time of Memory* (1999). His most recent book is *The Lives of Things* (2002).

GARY SHAPIRO is Tucker-Boatwright Professor in the Humanities, Department of Philosophy at the University of Richmond, Richmond, Virginia. He is author of *Alcyone: Nietzsche on Gifts, Noise, and Women* (1991) and *Nietzschean Narratives* (1989).

MICHAEL E. ZIMMERMAN is Professor of Philosophy and Director of the Center for Humanities and the Arts at the University of Colorado, Boulder. For many years he was Professor of Philosophy, Codirector of Environmental Studies, and Codirector of Asian Studies at Tulane University, New Orleans, Louisiana. He has also held the title of Clinical Professor of Psychiatry at the Louisiana State

University Medical School. He is the author of two books on Heidegger (*Eclipse of the Self: The Development of Heidegger's Concept of Authenticity*, 1981, and *Heidegger's Confrontation with Modernity*, 1991) and of many academic articles. He has also published *Contesting Earth's Future: Radical Ecology and Postmodernity* (1997) and coedited *Environmental Philosophy: From Animal Rights to Radical Ecology* (2001). Zimmerman is on the executive committee of the International Association for Environmental Philosophy.

Abbreviations of Nietzsche's Texts

AC   *Der Antichrist* 1888: *The Antichrist*. Translated by Walter Kaufmann in *The Portable Nietzsche*. New York: Viking Penguin, 1954.

AOM   *Vermischte Meinungen und Sprüche* 1879: *Assorted Opinions and Maxims*. Translated by R. J. Hollingdale in part 1 of volume 2 of *Human, All Too Human*. Cambridge: Cambridge University Press, 1986.

BGE   *Jenseits von Gut und Böse* 1886: *Beyond Good and Evil*. Translated by Walter Kaufmann in *Basic Writings of Nietzsche*. New York: Random House (Modern Library), 1968.

BT   *Der Geburt der Tragödie* 1872: *The Birth of Tragedy*. Translated by Walter Kaufmann in *Basic Writings of Nietzsche*.

CW   *Der Fall Wagner* 1888: *The Case of Wagner*. Translated by Walter Kaufmann in *Basic Writings of Nietzsche*.

D   *Morgenröte* 1881: *Dawn*. Translated by R. J. Hollingdale as *Daybreak*. Cambridge: Cambridge University Press, 1982.

EH   *Ecce Homo* 1888. Translated by Walter Kaufmann in *Basic Writings of Nietzsche*.

GM   *Zur Genealogie der Moral* 1887: *On the Genealogy of Morals*. Translated by Walter Kaufmann and R. J. Hollingdale in *Basic Writings of Nietzsche*.

GS   *Die fröhliche Wissenschaft* 1882 (Part 5, 1887): *The Gay Science*. Translated by Walter Kaufmann. New York: Random House (Vintage), 1974.

HAH   *Menschliches, Allzumenschliches* 1878: *Human, All Too Human*. Translated by R. J. Hollingdale. Cambridge: Cambridge University Press, 1986.

HL   *On the Uses and Disadvantages of History for Life*. Translated by R. J. Hollingdale. Cambridge: Cambridge University Press, 1983.

NC   *Nietzsche contra Wagner* 1888. Translated by Walter Kaufmann, in *The Portable Nietzsche*.

PPP   *The Pre-Platonic Philosophers.* Translated and edited by Greg Whitlock. Urbana and Chicago: University of Illinois Press, 2001.

PTG   *Die Philosophie im tragischen Zeitalter der Griechen* 1873: *Philosophy in the Tragic Age of the Greeks.* Translated by Marianne Cowen. Washington, D.C.: Regnery Publishing, 1962.

SW   *Sämtliche Werke. Kritische Studienausgabe in 15 Bänden.* Edited by G. Colli and M. Montinari. Berlin: de Gruyter, 1980.

TI   *Götzen-Dämmerung* 1888: *Twilight of the Idols.* Translated by Walter Kaufmann in *The Portable Nietzsche.*

TL   "Über Wahrheit und Lüge im aussermoralischen Sinne" 1873: "Truth and Lies in an Extra-Moral Sense." Translated by Daniel Breazeale in *Truth and Philosophy: Selections from Nietzsche's Notebooks of the 1870s.* Atlantic Highlands, N.J.: Humanities Press, 1989.

UM   *Unzeitgemässe Betrachtungen* 1873–76: *Untimely Meditations.* Translated by R. J. Hollingdale. Cambridge: Cambridge University Press, 1997.

WP   *Der Wille zur Macht* (Notes from the 1880s): *The Will to Power.* Translated by Walter Kaufmann and R. J. Hollingdale. New York: Vintage Books, 1968.

WS   *Der Wanderer und sein Schatten* 1879: *The Wanderer and His Shadow.* Translated by R. J. Hollingdale in part 2 of volume 2 of *Human, All Too Human.* Cambridge: Cambridge University Press, 1986.

Z   *Also sprach Zarathustra* 1883–85: *Thus Spoke Zarathustra.* Translated by Walter Kaufmann in *The Portable Nietzsche.*

Editorial Introduction

Steven V. Hicks and Alan Rosenberg

I

Over the last two decades, the philosophical world has witnessed an explosion of interest in Nietzsche. There is now a whole scholarly industry devoted to Nietzsche, and the volume of exegesis and interpretation has been so large that one might well wonder whether anything could possibly remain to be said about him.

Actually, however, most of the current work deals with a certain limited set of central, or "canonical," Nietzschean topics: his ideas on "will to power" and "eternal recurrence," his infamous *Übermensch* (superman) doctrine, his critique of morality and religion, his analysis of the "ascetic ideal," and his proposed "perspectivism." In the Anglo-American world, in particular, Nietzsche scholarship has tended to keep to these topics.

What we propose to explore in this volume of essays are certain important issues in Nietzsche that have received little attention in the recent flurry of Nietzsche scholarship. The essays included here will explore ideas in Nietzsche's writings that have been marginalized or slighted precisely because they do not fit neatly into any of the foregoing canonical categories of mainstream Nietzsche scholarship. These seemingly "marginal" ideas can be shown to appear over and over again in Nietzsche's writing and to be essential to Nietzsche's unique view of philosophy as "a way or life" or "in service of life" as opposed to a merely academic undertaking (cf. *UM* II, § 3). For example, there has been little or no attention given to the key Nietzschean notions of "forgetfulness" and "remembering," though they permeate many of his writings. Both notions are at the heart of his attempt to formulate an "intellectual conscience" strong and courageous enough to deflect the dead-end nihilism toward which, as Nietzsche thinks, modernity is heading. Similarly, Nietzsche observes that the prevailing "ascetic ideal" in the

1

West has only certain enemies that are capable of harming it: "the comedians of this ideal, for they alone arouse mistrust of it" (*GM* III, § 27). Few commentators, however, have said much about just who these comedians (these "last satyrs") are or how their "tragic/comic art" might be effective or what its effects could accomplish for a future humanity. Also receiving scant scholarly attention are such key Nietzschean topics as love, friendship, compassion, suffering, convalescence, autocritique, ecology, geophilosophy, war, terrorism, and the conflict of Islam and the West. What can we learn regarding Nietzsche's work by exploring his writings from the perspective of these and other "marginal" topics? Our volume of original essays will explain.

As Bernd Magnus and Kathleen Higgins have pointed out, most philosophers tend to understand Nietzsche in one of two ways: either they view him as offering alternative answers to traditional philosophical questions, or they view him as offering therapeutic notions, rhetorical devices, self-consuming concepts, and so forth intended to make us stop feeling that we should try to answer them.[1] On this latter interpretation, Nietzsche's canonical concepts of will to power, eternal recurrence, and others are intended primarily to help us get past the common idea that there must be a final truth about reality that it is the business of philosophy to discover. By shifting the focus of philosophical analysis away from the canonical topics to "marginal" ones, the essays in this volume will illuminate or reveal alternatives to these two ways of understanding Nietzsche. They will also make a contribution to the recent debates about whether Nietzsche is best to be understood as a literary theorist, as a philologist, as a rhetorician, or as a philosopher.[2] How should one approach the issue of his "multifarious stylings"—the many hyperbolic tropes, the epigrammatic and aphoristic expressions, the numerous metaphorical figures and masks? Some suggest that we should be concerned primarily with tracing out the philosophical import of Nietzsche's thoughts through extended readings and analyses of his diverse styles, tropes, rhetorical strategies, and techniques—in effect, separating philosophical content from literary style. Others suggest that we should view Nietzsche as primarily using literary figures and images to displace traditional philosophy and to transform philosophical discourse into literary or rhetorical discourse. The essays in this volume, for their part, will focus on topics (such as love, laughter, music, and mimesis) that are situated precisely at the interface of philosophy, literature, and rhetoric; thus they will also help to bridge philosophy, literature, and rhetoric, and open up alternatives to viewing style and content in Nietzsche as binary opposites. *Reading Nietzsche at the Margins* will show that the unique features of style and expression in Nietzsche's writings are not easily detachable from the philosophical thoughts that they express. Like Plato's picturesque images and myths, Nietzsche's figures and styles emerge not as literary icing on the conceptual cake but as part and parcel of his philosophical thoughts and values, as indispensable to the direction and development, both intellectually and affectively, of his "philosophy of life."

II

In Part One, titled "Prefacing the Margins: A Beginning at Self-Disclosure," David B. Allison explores the topic of "Resolution and Autocritique in the Late Prefaces." Allison argues that, beginning with the 1886 Prefaces to the second edition of Nietzsche's works, there emerges in Nietzsche a remarkably transfigured sense of his own self-awareness—a "turn" (Kehre) as it were, that is based largely on what Allison sees as Nietzsche's own "autocritique." According to Allison, this autocritique functions as a form of self-theory, "enabling him [Nietzsche] to grasp the really binding purchase" that the social system (i.e., "the whole set of traditions, usage, codes, customs, values, social and cultural assumptions") has on the individual. In submitting himself to this intense autocritique, something personally dramatic occurs to Nietzsche: he is struck by the feeling that many of his formerly revered values and commitments are simply "meaningless, non-sensical, and absurd." As Allison sees it, Nietzsche realizes that "he has himself changed, and this is the first step in his self-liberation." Allison also raises the question of whether Nietzsche's intense autocritique can be generalized beyond the analysis of his own personal moral feelings and extended, as a metacritique, to the very nature of morality itself, effectively serving as a critique of morality. Here Allison argues that, following his "turn," Nietzsche proceeds to "effectuate" his autocritique in a rather complex manner, especially in the detailed metacritical works of the later period (such as Beyond Good and Evil and Genealogy of Morals). In these later works, morality becomes effectively "self-sublimated" into a form of "conscience" governed by Nietzsche's aesthetic sensibilities and perspectively oriented experience. What is truly novel about Allison's reading of Nietzsche is the great weight he attributes to the seemingly marginal role of the prefaces in Nietzsche's own individual quest for autocritique, resoluteness, and self-disclosure.

In her essay "Forgetting the Subject," Christa Davis Acampora also explores the roles of self-disclosure and memory in the formation of the "moral subject" that Nietzsche criticizes in the Genealogy of Morals. In particular, she examines how the opposed forces of remembering and forgetting are analogous to other contesting forces in Nietzsche's other works (such as the Apollinian and Dionysian forces in The Birth of Tragedy). Acampora argues that the conception of human subjectivity that emerges out of the contesting forces of memory and forgetfulness is essential to addressing the important question Nietzsche raises in Beyond Good and Evil (§ 12), in which he considers what might possibly emerge as a refinement of the "soul hypothesis" that he undermines in his critique of the idea of the "substantial self." More specifically, Acampora claims that the significance of forgetting, as well as the role forgetting plays in the formation of the self, has yet to be fully appreciated in Nietzsche's philosophy. While the subject of forgetting has typically been "intentionally marginalized" in the history of Western philosophy, Acampora makes the case that Nietzsche places it at the center of his philosophical concern: Nietzsche describes forgetting not as an absence or lack of memory but, rather, as an active force in its own right (see *GM* II, § 2). Acampora concludes that understanding this active force (i.e., understanding Nietzsche's "forgetting of the subject") is crucial to understanding his account of the development of human psychology and to the possible future he envisions for humanity.

Part Two is titled "Laughing at the Margins: Nietzsche's Tragic/Comic Sense of Life." The essays in this section explore various aspects of Nietzsche's complex response to the pervasiveness and inevitability of human suffering. Kathleen Marie Higgins, in her essay "Suffering in Nietzsche's Philosophy," sets the tone for this section by arguing that the common (albeit misguided) view that Nietzsche is insensitive to human suffering stems from Nietzsche's conclusion that pain is ineliminable from the human condition and that most of the strategies humanity has developed for dealing with suffering (such as pity) actually intensify it. According to Higgins, to the extent that Nietzsche ever resolved his own disturbance over suffering, he advocates confronting it head-on by accepting it and by showing its "indispensable" place within the overall economy of human life. Higgins further argues that Nietzsche's strategy for accepting suffering is to somehow "encompass it within an attitude of joy within life," as opposed to the "otherworldly" (Christian/ascetic) approach that treats suffering as the price of happiness in the hereafter. According to Higgins, Nietzsche consistently sought "to come to terms with what seems objectionable in life, not by defining it away, but by embracing it as an essential element within the whole." Higgins describes this strategy as "Nietzsche's aesthetic approach to theodicy." By contrast, the "hitherto reigning" Christian approach actually promotes a style of moral reasoning (a "morality of pity") within which suffering is treated as an intrinsic "disvalue" and from the perspective of which, therefore, "pity" (and its attendant virtues and behaviors) must be regarded as the obligatory response to any instance of human suffering (see *GM* II, § 24). Nietzsche objects to this style of moral reasoning, arguing that it is a mistake to treat suffering as intrinsically "disvaluable": to do so is to devalue human existence (which is necessarily characterized by suffering); moreover, suffering can sometimes be instrumentally valuable in the context of the creation of other values plausibly to be regarded as intrinsic. Finally, even where a given instance of suffering can be shown to have no direct instrumental value, pity is still a questionable response to it. Nietzsche believes that pity can be shown to be damaging, in a variety of ways, both to the person who pities and to the person who is the object of pity. According to Higgins, Nietzsche's conclusion is that "pity does not ameliorate suffering, but instead increases the amount of suffering in the world (see *AC*, § 7)." What remains to be seen, however, is whether or not one could attempt to "reconstruct" a Nietzschean style of moral reasoning within which a less objectionable version of pity—what Nietzsche at one point terms a "*more manly* brother of pity" (*D*, § 78)—might actually have a role to play in a "joyful," "life-affirming" response to suffering.[3]

In his essay "To Laugh Out of the Whole Truth: Nietzsche as Tragicomic Satyr," Lawrence J. Hatab explores the complex roles of joy and laughter in Nietzsche's thought, and he further examines their special relation to Nietzsche's notion of "tragic truth." As Hatab observes, "in the history of philosophy, perhaps the most marginal phenomenon has been laughter. Philosophers have written about laughter as a subject of study, but simply as one among other human capacities calling for explanation and analysis. Moreover, the affective force and disruptive effects of laughter have generally earned it low esteem in the 'serious business' of philosophy's pursuit of truth." By contrast, Hatab claims that one of the most distinctive features of Nietzsche's thought is a "demarginalization of laughter" unmatched in the history of Western philosophy. Hatab further argues that the "force of joy" is central to Nietzsche's texts, and yet it coexists with the recognition of an abysmal truth: the "terrible inevitability of loss, ruin, and death." Indeed, as Hatab sees it, Nietzsche elevates laughter to a level of philosophical importance so pronounced that it almost becomes "joined with truth." In this context, Hatab examines Nietzsche's many references to ancient Greek culture, and especially to the satyr figure, to help draw out the peculiar blending of comic and tragic excess that Nietzsche wanted to retrieve in his mature philosophy. Hatab argues that "tragic pathos and comic laughter present a primal existential bivalence in the human experience of negative limits" and that for Nietzsche "both phenomena depict an *affirmative negation,* which avoids a pessimistic denial of life and an optimistic fantasy that negative limits can be overcome or resolved in some way." In Hatab's view, Nietzsche comes to emphasize comic laughter as an especially positive "life-affirming" response to tragic suffering, but a response that nonetheless does not overcome or cancel "tragic negativity." Rather than being contrary to serious and even tragic matters, comic laughter can be seen as an "overture" to, and perhaps a consummation of, deeply serious matters. So understood, laughter can be seen as an essential part of Nietzsche's "Dionysian Wisdom," a tragic/comic wisdom that eventually may enable humankind to orient its activities to an alternative ideal to the heretofore dominant "ascetic ideal" and its (life-denying) morality of pity. By exploring the dynamic interplay between seriousness (*Ernst*) and cheerfulness (*Heiterkeit*), Nietzsche distinguishes himself as a "comedian of the ascetic ideal"—one of the "last of the satyrs"—whose role it is to attempt to arouse mistrust of this ideal and to help us gain some measure of freedom from it.

Finally, Tyler Roberts, in his essay "Awaiting Love: Nietzsche's (Com)Passion," examines the agonal tensions and confluences in Nietzsche's thought between different forms of love. Here, Roberts is concerned not just with the love of "friendship" or with the "erotic love" that Nietzsche thinks drives human creativity but also with what Roberts describes as a "joyful love" that (Roberts believes) is at the heart of one of Nietzsche's most canonical concepts, namely "amor fati," or the love of eternity. Roberts concludes his essay by tying together Nietzsche's reflections on love and faith and by suggesting that, despite Nietzsche's radical individualism and his many attacks on the Christian "morality of pity,"

Nietzsche does make a place for a form of love that reaches beyond the self toward others. According to Roberts, this form of love can plausibly be described as "(com)passion," a "joyful love" that is analogous, in many ways, to the Christian concept of *agape*. Perhaps this "Nietzschean love" is the less objectionable, "more manly brother of pity" that Nietzsche thinks still has a philosophically important role to play in our postmoral response to human suffering.

Part Three is entitled "Spirit at the Margins: Mimesis, Music, and the Art of Self-Fashioning." As the title implies, the essays in this section examine various (seemingly marginal) aspects of what Nietzsche has in mind by "spirituality" (*Geistigkeit*). They also explore the "edges" of Nietzsche's "noncomplacent thought" where his "mimetic spirit" (as expressed, e.g., in music, in "soul artistry," and in "the art of living") is most forceful. Charles E. Scott, in his essay "Mimetic Geist," attempts to study the function and content of the concept and images of "indifference" in Nietzsche's descriptive account of *Geist*. As Scott observes, the term *Geistigkeit* can connote multiple identities, none of which completely or adequately defines it. For example, "*Geistigkeit* can mean a harbor and producer of freedom, a site of potential pride and self-confidence as well as of enslavement, self-mockery, and self-mutilation." In particular, Scott is concerned to examine the aspect of spirituality that comes to bear in Nietzsche's account of "the free spirit" (*der freie Geist*). As Scott sees it, Nietzsche's intriguing account of "the free spirit" charts a departure, and also articulates an agency for the departure, from "the traditional prejudices imbedded in western spiritual achievement." According to Scott, Nietzsche's writings embody "a common spiritual lineage" with more traditional spiritual thinkers such as Pascal, but they also embody a unique kind of spirituality that Pascal could not bring to creative expression, namely a "spiritual indifference," or what Scott dubs a strange mimesis of "voided presence," a mimesis with no fixed or final identity to imitate. As Scott sees it, this strange "mimetic indifference" comprises forcefully "the vault of spiritual life" as Nietzsche depicts it. In Scott's words, "Mimetic Geist" produces "differences in a context of overcoming its own formation, points out indirectly a weakness in many forms of western spiritual life as well as in Pascal's . . . [and] expresses a desire for something personal, even human-like, at the outer borders of spiritual agency, something that saves us from the indifference that permeates living events." Scott concludes that by "free spirit" Nietzsche intends a certain quality of mind that in its passionately engaged, critical, and constructive activity nonetheless reflects "a dimension of indifference to most of the images and signs that organized what people have traditionally affirmed as good, evil, and holy." Scott stresses that this reflection also includes an "inscribed indifference" to images of the free spirit's own moral values, and as such, it constitutes a certain autocritical "self-overcoming of morality."

Richard Schacht in his essay "Nietzsche on Music" also explores the margins of Nietzsche's mimetic spirit and its "confluence of powers of formation and deformation." More specifically, Schacht is concerned to examine the thesis that, in his (Nietzsche's) thinking about human life and even about truth and value more generally, Nietzsche is often guided (in the language of the *Birth of Tragedy*) by the "spirit of music" and the paradigm of music and is best understood accordingly. The results of reading Nietzsche in this marginal way, Schacht contends, are both interpretively and philosophically interesting. As opposed to Alexander Nehamas and others who tend to view Nietzsche's philosophical epigraph as being "life as literature," Schacht suggests that the epigraph "life as music" would be closer to the mark. Schacht argues persuasively that Nietzsche drew upon the phenomenon of music as a source of insight with respect to understanding our human reality and possibility and that Nietzsche took music making to be paradigmatic of human spirituality. According to Schacht, music for Nietzsche both expresses and epitomizes the kind of thing human life is and has in it to become. As Schacht reads him, for Nietzsche, the "art of living"— the art of "becoming those we are"— is more akin to the art of "music-being-made" than it is to either plastic arts or works of literature (see *GS*, § 335). Schacht concludes that the ideal of rendering human life more fully and truly "musical" became, in a sense, Nietzsche's "theme song," the elaboration and refinement of which occupied him for the rest of his productive life.

In "Nietzsche and the Transfiguration of Asceticism: An Ethics of Self-Fashioning," Steven V. Hicks and Alan Rosenberg also explore the margins of human spiritual possibilities in Nietzsche's philosophy, the development and expression of which can make a significant difference in the transforming enhancement of human life and in creative efforts to "become those we are" (*GS*, § 335). Like Higgins and Hatab, Hicks and Rosenberg examine Nietzsche's complex response to suffering, especially his attempts to use suffering as a "spur" to human creativity and self-overcoming. In this context, Hicks and Rosenberg also analyze Nietzsche's attempts to "re-naturalize asceticism," and they scrutinize his efforts to "transfigure" traditional ascetic techniques and practices as a means to implementing an alternative (life-affirming) ideal to the "hitherto reigning" ascetic ideal, namely, the ideal of "ethical self-fashioning." As Hicks and Rosenberg argue, it is only by "exploring the creative tension between such transfigured ascetic techniques on the one hand, and aesthetic/artistic procedures on the other, and [only] by utilizing what Nietzsche terms this ascetic 'artists' cruelty'—'this delight in imposing a form upon oneself as a hard, recalcitrant, suffering material . . . this uncanny joyous labor of a soul voluntarily at odds with itself'—[that] Nietzsche hopes to open up a space within which a new, life-affirming 'ethics of self-fashioning' can occur (see *GM* II, §§ 10, 18)." To this end, Hicks and Rosenberg examine Nietzsche's unconventional attempts to use the often marginalized "tools" we have ready to hand—what Nietzsche likes to term the "small everyday things in life," generally considered "matters of complete indifference" to philosophy (*WS*, §§ 5–6)—to change ourselves, educate ourselves against ourselves, and in doing so, to discover new and noble ways of living, as well as creative ways of self-enhancement and self-expression. As Nietzsche sees it, in learning to "master" the "small, everyday matters" that confront us in life, we can (potentially) become "the poets of our life," learn the "artistry of the soul," and "fashion something that was not there before," namely, "a character with style—a grand and rare art" (see *GS*, §§ 290, 299, 301). Hicks and Rosenberg conclude their essay by examining Nietzsche's problematic attempts to link his ethics of self-fashioning with his theory of "eternal recurrence."

Part Four, the final section of the book, is titled "Natural and Cultural Expressions of Marginal Forces: Nietzsche on War, Ecology, and Geophilosophy." The essays here examine Nietzsche's complex and often ignored, misunderstood, or misappropriated views on a variety of natural, political, and cultural topics (such as war, terrorism, environmental degradation, health, and illness). They also analyze and criticize certain contemporary attempts to "naively" apply Nietzsche's philosophy to this or that current social or political problem. Michael E. Zimmerman, in his essay "Nietzsche and Ecology: A Critical Inquiry," argues that Nietzsche cannot accurately be depicted as "reactionary" politically, but rather as a "progressive" thinker who regards most so-called progressive political ideals as blocking the path to higher development. According to Zimmerman, Nietzsche foresees higher humanity as a "friend of the earth," but of an earth inevitably transformed by human capacities and activities that can scarcely be envisioned at this point. While recognizing that Nietzsche was always deeply appreciative of the natural world and that he defined humankind at least partly in terms of naturalistic categories, Zimmerman argues that there are considerable difficulties in the way of any uncritical reading of Nietzsche as a "proto-ecologist." According to Zimmerman, Nietzsche's major concern was how to avoid degeneration and nihilism, not how to avoid environmental destruction and *ecocide*. Having said this, Zimmerman still contends that there are a number of fruitful ways of understanding Nietzsche's pertinence to ecology, and his essay concludes with an attempt to inspire constructive debate on the issue of Nietzsche's relevance to environmentalism.

In his essay "Assassins and Crusaders: Nietzsche after 9/11," Gary Shapiro explores the themes of war, terrorism, and the conflict of Islam and the West in Nietzsche's writing in a geopolitical and geophilosophical perspective. Shapiro also examines Nietzsche's generally favorable references to Islam and uses the more recent conflict of the West and radical/militant Islam as a lens through which to analyze Nietzsche's thoughts about war and his understanding of active nihilism. Shapiro argues that Nietzsche frequently borrowed figures and examples from Europe's conflict with Islam to attempt to make sense of the geopolitical past and future. While cautioning against naive "misappropriations" of Nietzsche (which, in the past, have marginalized him as a thinker), Shapiro argues that we can learn something important about Nietzsche, as well as about "Crusaders and Assassins" past and present, by beginning to examine "the uncanny resonances of these figures that appear at the margins of his texts." Finally, Nietzsche's important concept of "convalescence," and its relation to the notions of "place" and "location," is examined by Stuart Elden in his essay "The Convalescent: Geographies of Health and Illness." Elden argues that Nietzsche's many references to location (both actual and figurative), as well as his carefully constructed emphasis on oppositions between different spatial elements of landscape (sea and mountain, cave and town) and recurrent metaphors of under and over/height and depth, have a range of positive and negative connotations throughout his works. Elden tries to show that "place" is not just a background to Nietzsche's work but is an important feature to his discussion of such topics as health and illness, solitude and silence, convalescence and infirmity, crowds and noise. According to Elden, Nietzsche's "heady mix" of geography and health, history and medicine, demonstrates the importance of philosophy to Nietzsche "as a way of life" and as an "opening up of concrete possibilities."

By "stalking the margins" of Nietzsche's noncomplacent thought and by shifting the focus of philosophical attention away from the standard "canonical" Nietzschean topics to the above mentioned "marginal" ones, the original essays in *Reading Nietzsche at the Margins* help illuminate and reveal alternatives to the usual ways of understanding and interpreting Nietzsche. They will also inspire constructive debate concerning Nietzsche's relevance to a variety of philosophical, political, social, and cultural concerns.[4]

Notes

1. Bernd Magnus and Kathleen Higgins, introduction to *The Cambridge Companion to Nietzsche* (Cambridge: Cambridge University Press, 1996), pp. 1–17.
2. Two recent contributions to this debate are Douglas Thomas, *Reading Nietzsche Rhetorically* (New York and London: The Guilford Press, 1999), and Bernd Magnus, Stanley Stewart, and Jean-Pierre Mileur, *Nietzsche's Case: Philosophy as/and Literature* (New York: Routledge, 1993).
3. We would like to thank Aaron Ridley for bringing this point to our attention.
4. Support for this project was provided by a grant from the City University of New York PSC-CUNY Research Award Program. The editors would like to thank James N. Jordan and Morris Rabinowitz for their helpful comments and suggestions. Alan Rosenberg, in particular, would like to thank Shawn O'Connell for his help in keeping Rosenberg's computer running through thick and thin. Steven Hicks would like to thank Edith Krause for her editorial advice and suggestions concerning translations of German texts. Finally, a special thanks is owed to all of our contributors for their patience and support through numerous editorial revisions and unforeseen delays in the completion of this volume. For the most part, the contributors have followed the standard English translations of Nietzsche's texts listed in the Abbreviations section (xi–xii). Any alterations they have made are usually minor ones.

Part One

Prefacing the Margins:
A Beginning at Self-Disclosure
Nietzsche on Resolution, Memory, and Autocritique

Chapter One

Resolution and Autocritique in the Late Prefaces

David B. Allison

With the appearance of *Zarathustra* and the work immediately following that—particularly, in Book Five of *The Gay Science* and in the 1886 prefaces to the second edition of his works, there emerges a remarkably transformed sense of Nietzsche's own self-awareness, a turn, based on his own autocritique, that basically works as a form of self-therapy—enabling him to grasp the really binding purchase the social symbolic has on the individual. In submitting himself to this autocritique, he first raises the question as to its possibility and then proceeds to effectuate it in a rather complex manner. Ultimately, this opens the way for his finely detailed metacritical works of the later period, especially *Beyond Good and Evil* and *On the Genealogy of Morals*.

I. Nietzsche's Despair in *Zarathustra:* Personalization

In large part due to the self-consciously rhetorical import of his work, the reader of Nietzsche is acutely aware that he is really attending to the witness, the testimony, of a *particular* author, a particular thinker. And of course this complicates matters of interpretation. Certainly, Nietzsche is the *last* philosopher who would hide behind the cloak of anonymity or the authority of tradition. And while an author may well introduce himself and his concerns in the prefaces to his works, this takes on a rather roundabout itinerary in Nietzsche's case—basically, his explicit self-disclosure takes place in *Zarathustra*, and the articulation of this revelation really occurs in the 1886 prefaces. As he wrote to Malwida von Meysenbug:

The long prefaces which I have found necessary for the new edition of my complete works tell with a ruthless honesty some curious things about myself. With these I'll ward off "the many" once and for all ... I've thrown out my hook to "the few" instead, and even with them I'm prepared to be patient.[1]

Of course Nietzsche exhibits a preoccupation with himself early on, clearly betraying a *romantic*, youthful bias in his several autobiographical sketches and his early reflections on religion, fate, and free will. With his writings on culture by the period of *The Birth of Tragedy*, Nietzsche still writes under the influence of Schopenhauer, stressing the role—and the suffering—of the *genius*, the purported defender and savior of traditional culture—the "true" or "superior" culture—faced with what he calls the "universalization" of culture, the "commercial culture" fostered by state and industrial interests. Such an *individual* must suffer isolation and personally carry the burden of cultural enlightenment. In the earliest accounts of this, such a burden is sustained by cultivating the Apollonian-Dionysian *instincts or drives*—and this is most obvious in the Lugano Fragment of early 1871 (*SW* 7: 333–350), and in the lectures "On the Future of Our Educational Institutions" of late 1872 (*SW* 1: 641–752). But a striking change takes place with the revision of the Lugano Fragment into his essay "The Greek State" (*SW* 1: 764–777),[2] whereby the rather romantic, metaphysically suffering *individual* is seen not so much in some *heroic, individual isolation* but rather as a *product* of the *culture's social and political dynamics*. This *cultural subjection* is also paralleled in his revision of the essay "On Music and Words" (*SW* 7: 359–369; 185–190),[3] where Nietzsche explains that the individual's most intensely personal states of Dionysian ecstasy are in fact *induced by* the *actual performance* of the dynamic musical spectacle. This emphasis on the *cultural dynamic* is also seen in his celebrated essay "Homer's Contest" (*SW* 1: 783–792),[4] whereby it is the socially and politically orchestrated *agon* that gives rise to the unique strengths of classical Greek civilization and to the individuals such a *culture* produces. Clearly, it was Jacob Burckhardt who was behind this remarkable *decentering shift* in Nietzsche's concerns, particularly Burckhardt's lectures on "The Agonal Age,"[5] lectures Burckhardt had been working on since as early as 1864 and that were the focus of his many extended conversations with Nietzsche.

In any case, it is the role of the *agon*, the contest or competition, that will, as it were, put Nietzsche's preoccupations with *the individual per se,* back in the box of the social symbolic. And it is from this perspective of Burckhardt's methodology of cultural historiography, that Nietzsche will develop the broad outlines of cultural analysis that stem from *The Birth of Tragedy* itself right to the end of his productive writings. Already, in *The Birth of Tragedy*, we see his preoccupation with the Greek *cultural dynamics* of the "tragic age," the broad cultural motifs of the Apollonian and Dionysian elements, the role of religious cult worship and celebrations, and finally, the Socratic culture itself. "Homer's Contest" sharpens the focus of the underlying *cultural dynamics,* and the *Untimely Meditations* offers us several analyses of his contemporary cultural milieu—perhaps most importantly, his scathing treatment of David Strauss's rational Christian theology. In *The Use and Abuse of History,* he critiques the monumental and antiquarian "great men" historiography and insists on critically understanding what he calls "our historical horizon," that is, the whole set of traditions, usage, codes, customs, values, social and cultural assumptions that constitute our *social symbolic order.* It is this social symbolic order that will be repeatedly articulated through his analyses of our religio-metaphysical tradition as the death of God and its aftermath, the morality of mores, and especially, slave morality, with its remarkable power to induce and to structure our very affects themselves so as to produce a culture of *ressentiment,* guilt, bad conscience, asceticism, shame, and so forth, all pointing the way to his account of a seemingly inevitable decadence and nihilism.

While each of these concerns is treated to one degree or another in *Human, All Too Human* and *Daybreak,* they are perhaps best presented collectively in *The Gay Science,* where Nietzsche carefully lays out a detailed account of the death of God—his avatars of nationalism, modern science, the utilitarian ethics of sympathy and pity, as well as nihilism—and the *antidote* of a de-deified nature, understood under the formulation of the eternal return.

In the first version of *The Gay Science*—that is, the first four books, published in 1882—the penultimate section, § 341, is the only one that deals with the eternal return in any detail whatsoever, and it is only two brief paragraphs long. It poses the question of whether one would be crushed or liberated by the "eternal hourglass of existence" (*GS,* § 341). The preceding section—"The Dying Socrates"—clearly indicates that Socrates was indeed crushed: Nietzsche recalls his dying remark, "O Crito, I owe Asclepius a cock" (*GS,* § 340). The section before that, "Vita Femina," celebrates what he calls "the most powerful magic of life. . . . A veil of beautiful possibilities, sparkling with promise, resistance, bashfulness, mockery, pity, and seduction. Yes, life is a woman" (*GS,* § 339). Since Nietzsche composed this in the presence of Lou Salomé during their retreat to Tautenburg in the early summer of 1882, we may assume that Nietzsche, unlike Socrates, did *not* suffer life as a disease. The final section of the 1882 edition of *The Gay Science* has Zarathustra emerge from his cave, bathed in sunlight, to give his teaching about the eternal return, which will be his undergoing, or rather, his *overcoming* of the old morality, what he will call the "spirit of gravity." This final section, § 342, of *The Gay Science,* is effectively the beginning of Zarathustra's prologue, which will itself issue on the specific, and quite dramatic, motif of *one's own self-overcoming,* in Zarathustra's first speech on "The Three Metamorphoses."

Given a life "sparkling with promise," and presumably already in possession of his own teaching, the question that arises, however, is precisely, "What is there to overcome?"—for Zarathustra himself, who, after all, has *left* Plato's cave, and, much less, does this have anything to do with the *person* of Friedrich Nietzsche, who seemed so blissfully happy in Tautenburg? In *The Gay Science*, the *textual distance* between the eternal return and Zarathustra's prologue, presciently entitled "Incipit Tragoedia," is *one section number*, but between *The Gay Science* and *Zarathustra's* completion, there is a distance of some *three years*. What accounts for *this* distance? What happened? Quite simply, Nietzsche's world completely fell apart. His break with Wagner was sealed in stone by the spring of 1878, when Wagner accused him of suffering from an excessive preoccupation with onanism. This was revealed to Nietzsche by his physician, Dr. Otto Eiser, who, as president of the Frankfurt Wagner Circle, also circulated Wagner's charge about Nietzsche's alleged misbehavior to the assembled festival celebrants at Bayreuth. Nietzsche was humiliated and forcibly had to remove himself from perhaps the single group of educated and cultivated figures with whom he would have enjoyed public contact and recognition. But by the spring of 1882, he had met—and fallen passionately in love with—Lou Salomé. At once he found the love of his life, to compensate for his loneliness, and an intellectual peer, whom he also thought of as his closest disciple. While she rejected his three marriage proposals, Nietzsche nonetheless pursued her avidly, thinking their four weeks in Tautenburg, vacationing in a country home secluded in the forest, would bring her around to his affections. Unfortunately, she dropped Nietzsche for Paul Rée, who was infinitely more pliable than Nietzsche, was emotionally stable—if somewhat dull at times—but who was nonetheless wealthy, his family having extensive land and property holdings in Pomerania and East Prussia. When Nietzsche met the two for an afternoon in Leipzig in October of 1882, he realized that all his hopes for Lou had been irretrievably crushed. He never saw either of the two again; he was devastated by what he thought was Rée's deception, and he was cast completely alone, bereft of any emotional or intellectual companionship whatsoever.

Now, many of Nietzsche's letters from this three-year period separating the composition of *The Gay Science*, Books I–IV, and Book V—that is, the period of *Zarathustra's* composition—present a remarkably personal, if not somewhat strident, tone, and they offer a most unusual insight into the nature of *Zarathustra* itself. In a letter to von Gersdorff, for example, Nietzsche writes:

> My *Zarathustra* . . . will be sent to you within a few weeks. . . . Don't be put off by the mythic style of the book: my entire philosophy is behind those homey and unusual words, and I have never been more serious. It is a beginning at self-disclosure—nothing more! I know perfectly well that there is no one alive who could write anything like *Zarathustra*.[6]

Likewise, he writes Peter Gast:

> It is incredibly full of detail which, because it is drawn from what I've seen and suffered, only I can understand. Some pages seem to be almost *bleeding*.[7]

In another note to Gast, he writes:

> At the moment *Zarathustra's* value is entirely personal. . . . For everyone else, it is obscure, mysterious, and ridiculous. Heinrich von Stein (a splendid example of a man, whose company has given me real pleasure) told me candidly that of said *Zarathustra*, he understood "twelve sentences and no more." I found that very comforting.[8]

Initially, these remarks appear completely counterintuitive. Wasn't *Zarathustra* precisely *the* most widely read, admired, and commented upon of all of Nietzsche's works?—in practically every language from Ural-Altaic to Urdu? Yet Nietzsche seems to have held—even to the end—that *Zarathustra* was *entirely personal*, bred from his own experience and suffering, and that it was a beginning at *self-disclosure*. In fact, in *Ecce Homo*, he recounts the story of von Stein's incomprehension, this time claiming that von Stein didn't understand even a single word of *Zarathustra* (*EH*, "Why I Write Such Good Books," § 1). In any case, if one is thus provoked by the veritable eruption of Nietzsche's personal life into the text of *Zarathustra* and one turns to the *Nachlass* from early 1882 to late 1885, one will quickly find a huge amount of personal detail therein. In fact, the whole of the Lou affair is bared through tears, the years of ridicule from Wagner, the final sense of Wagner's pitiable transformation into a fawning, repentant Catholic in *Parsifal*, the devious deceptions and slights by Wagner and Rée—it's all rehearsed in the *Nachlass* and finds its expression in the text of *Zarathustra*—usually encoded symbolically, figuratively. But more strikingly, what is really at work in the *Nachlass* of the period is Nietzsche's work of self-therapy, his *working-through—by writing-it-out*—of his desperate sense of rejection, humiliation, and shame, the *memories* of his earlier successes, which now burden him down, as well as the memories of his lonely isolation, despair, impotence, and frustration. And this whole process of self-rehabilitation is orchestrated precisely according to the initial statements of Zarathustra's three metamorphoses—the camel, lion, and child.

Just to give one case: in the *Nachlass* to *Zarathustra*, Nietzsche symbolically works through his own despair, pitting a female protagonist—named Pana—against the broken-hearted Zarathustra. Pana is the symbolic Lou Salomé who had herself created the broken-hearted Nietzsche; so, through several drafts, Nietzsche has Pana *kill* her own now-baleful creation, precisely the despairing, broken-hearted Zarathustra, and in the last of several versions, Pana collapses in death because she could not grasp the eternal return—which states that everything depends on one's own happiness, and that one must simply accept what happens, together with the blessings this brings. Unable to grasp this "secret" of the eternal return, Pana dies, broken by this simple truth, in despair and revenge. She takes her posthumous revenge on the broken-hearted Zarathustra, however, when *he dies* of laughter at *her* pitiful, suffering condition (*SW* 10: 443).

There is an awful lot of dredging-up of painful personal material here, and he recounts a remarkably detailed series of personal and interpersonal dynamics.

But it seems as if Nietzsche himself didn't reach a satisfactory resolution in the text of *Zarathustra*. Zarathustra's self-overcoming is *incomplete* in that he never attains the state of innocence, the third metamorphosis of the child. Rather, he stands accused of, and indeed acknowledges, his final *sin*, namely, that of "pity for the higher man" and wanders off once again with the lion—ever courageous, but not yet innocent, at the very close of Part Four (Z IV. 20). Even if Nietzsche worked through his intense personal suffering and really came to deal with it effectively, what ultimately forecloses resolution in *Zarathustra* is that he can't overcome the *memory content* of his previous states of elation and despair—both kinds of memories are instruments of torture to him—and he simply cannot forget them; that is, he *cannot forget* the "it was," the acceptance of which the eternal return was meant to accomplish. "The *child* is innocence and forgetting": *not* the Nietzsche of *Zarathustra*.

II. Autocritique of Morality in the 1886 Prefaces and *The Gay Science*, V

We know that Nietzsche contemplated writing another, final part to *Zarathustra*. But he didn't, probably for a variety of well-considered reasons. What he did do was to resolve the third metamorphosis of Zarathustra in his immediately suc-ceeding works of 1886: Book Five of *The Gay Science* and his series of new prefaces to his earlier works, for a second, collected edition by his new publisher, Fritzsch.[9] In these works of 1886, Nietzsche comes to realize that—as an individual—he was himself constituted precisely by the elaborate system of cultural encoding that he had so insightfully described and criticized in his earlier work. He real-izes that he, too, was subject, as was everyone else, to the ethics of sympathy and pity, to the elaborate moral and affective determination of his cultural milieu, governed by 2,000 years of Christian-priestly-ascetic values—not the very least of which was the belief that love itself is redemptive, salvific. And, of course, this value tradition is the very source of moral authority, the entire inherited series of "thou shalts" that Zarathustra so labored to destroy.

Nietzsche's turn, his *Kehre*, as it were, lies in his recognition that he must perform an *autocritique* of the values, customs, traditionally sanctioned and sanctified emotions, and affects that *constituted his very being*. In short, that cri-tique had to be supplemented by a rigorous autocritique, and he states this ne-cessity frequently in the new Book Five of *The Gay Science*. Section (§) 380, "The wanderer speaks," is perhaps the most clearly expressed articulation of the real problem: the necessity of being able to critique the very social symbolic order that governs one's identity in the first place. In doing so, he borrows an analogy from Machiavelli's preface to *The Prince*:

> If one would like to see our European morality for once as it looks from a distance, and if one would like to measure it against other moralities, past and future, then one has to proceed like a wanderer who wants to know

how high the towers in a town are: he *leaves* the town. "Thoughts concerning moral prejudices," if they are not meant to be prejudices about prejudices, presuppose a position *outside* morality, some point beyond good and evil to which one has to rise, climb, or fly—and in the present case, at least, a point beyond *our* good and evil, a freedom from everything "European," by which I mean the sum of the imperious value judgments that have become part of our flesh and blood. That one *wants* to go precisely out there, may be a minor madness . . . the question is whether one really *can* get up there. . . . One must have liberated oneself from many things that oppress, inhibit, hold down, and make heavy precisely us Europeans today. The human being of such a beyond who wants to behold the supreme measures of value of his time must first of all "overcome" this time in himself—this is the test of his strength—and consequently not only his time but also his prior aversion and contradiction *against* this time, his suffering from this time, his un-timeliness, his *romanticism*. (*GS*, § 380)

III. The 1886 Prefaces to *Human, All Too Human*:
Artifice and Autocritique

The cure for Nietzsche's despondency and alienation begins with a *ruse*, a deception, namely, with the creation of an imaginary interlocutor. Much as Descartes devised his "evil demon" to test the limits of his resolute reflection,[10] so does Nietzsche say that he "invented" a series of companions—sometimes called free spirits or shadows or even good Europeans—with whom he could engage in a spirited dialogue. And what motivated this—he says in the new 1886 preface to Part One of *Human, All Too Human*—was precisely his profound sense of isolation and loneliness and his need to be, at least at the outset, *diverted away* from his almost obsessive preoccupation with it:

> I had need of them at that time if I was to keep in good spirits while surrounded by ills (sickness, solitude, unfamiliar places, torpor, inactivity): as brave companions and familiars with whom one can laugh and chatter when one feels like laughing and chattering, and whom one can send to the Devil when they become tedious—as compensation for the friends I lacked. (*HAH* I, Preface, § 2)[11]

The products, or results, of these dialogues are, of course, his works, his books, his notes of the period, whose content derived from his recognition of the causes and origins of his own restrictions, inhibitions, and suffering—precisely what he had been debating with his feigned interlocutor. The alterity—or otherness—of the imaginary companion makes concrete the range of his own imagination: by continually varying a perspective, by contradicting an initial judgment, or by insistently prodding himself into recognizing a secondary or tertiary consequence of a position. This imaginary exchange may take the form of a jest or a question, as well: "Is that what you *really* believe?" "Is there a *deeper* motivation for your saying that?" "Is that what *you* think, or is it what most people maintain?" Effectively, such a seriously maintained self-conscious dialogue serves as a critique of beliefs, values, positions, explanations —and it raises underlying questions of conditionality, legitimacy, verifiability, truth-functionality, agency, efficacity, and so on, all of which are discussed repeatedly in Nietzsche's work of the period, published and unpublished.

What initially results from this discursive questioning in Nietzsche's pursuit of a "cure," or a "self-overcoming," is his discovery of the particular elements that bind or restrict himself—and he finds these elements to be the causal agents, the cohesive factors, that structure the morality of mores and define the individual as such within the traditional system of morality. He terms these defining and determining elements fetters, and he claims that they serve to constitute normalcy itself, one's "home," or one's "being at home"—the regularity and normalcy of convention, of all that is usual, familiar, and day-to-day in social life. He enumerates those fetters that most palpably bond the individual not only to the traditional order, but to his own personally experienced past, thereby preventing his liberation. As he says in the new preface to *Human, All Too Human*:

> What fetters the fastest? What bonds are all but unbreakable? In the case of men of a high and select kind they will be their duties: that reverence proper to youth, that reserve before all that is honored and revered from of old, that gratitude for the soil out of which they have grown, for the hand which led them, for the holy place where they learned to worship—their supreme moments themselves will fetter them the fastest, lay upon them the most enduring obligation. (*HAH* I, Preface, § 3)

It is upon conducting this intense and highly focused experience of analyzing the nature of his fetters, and of being able to critically articulate them—their number, type, and range; their purchase upon himself and upon the culture at large—that something personally dramatic occurs to Nietzsche. He is struck by the *feeling* (literally, an emotional *shock*) that many of these formerly revered duties, values, obligations, and past memories are simply meaningless, nonsensical, absurd, and that they merit little more than his honest contempt for their obtrusive pettiness and small-mindedness. Once this emotionally-charged thought befalls him, he realizes that he has himself changed, and this is the first step in his self-liberation. *He* can no longer hold these fetters in respect and esteem, and by this very fact, *they* no longer bind him. What it was, formerly, to be "at home" is now revealed to him under an entirely new sensibility—and this is felt as a new "drive," or "impulse"—as unworthy of residence; indeed, they are felt to be contemptible:

> "Better to die than to go on living *here*"—thus responds the imperious voice and temptation: and this "here," this "at home" is everything it had hitherto loved. (*HAH* I, Preface, § 3)

Nietzsche described the immediate effects of his new revelation as being twofold: he experienced a practically intolerable feeling of *shame* for the loss brought about by his obsessive inquisitiveness, his going to the utmost limits of his imagination to *understand* his distress, and by doing so, to have lost the veneration and respect for everything that until then constituted belonging, identity, value, and honor—everything worthy of love and worship. But this feeling of loss was tempered, then overwhelmed, by a new feeling for the enormity of what he had accomplished, a feeling of immense *pride* and personal *exultation that* it was *possible at all*, that his contempt could overturn the very norms by whose agency he had previously suffered. Thus, he was tempted, even dangerously, to test other norms, limits, prescriptions, and proscriptions, to question what was formerly forbidden and find it delightful, joyous, the sweetest fruit. From this feeling of exultation and delight there follows a determination to will and esteem, to evaluate, on one's *own* account, in one's *own* name—and one leaves "home," the "at home," seeking to relish and to develop the further capacity of self determination through new, multiply transforming and overturning valuations and estimations. Literally and figuratively, for Nietzsche, this involves the determination to *travel*, to get *beside* himself,[12] to self-consciously seek other, *strange* abodes and customs, other entire systems of valuation, other realms of the human spirit itself: to be an "Argonaut of the ideal" (*GS*, § 382). Thus, *one uses oneself as an experiment*, as an open-ended source of experiences for experiment in the construction of one's developing hierarchy of values—one's own considered construal of what really *is* important, what *is* significant, of worth and merit—what is worthy of admiration, affection, and esteem: again, in one's own name and in one's own service (*HAH* I, § 292).

At the same time, one progressively uncovers the truth of things, of people and of events. By withholding the conventional value-positing perspective, the prevailing mode of esteem or belief that enshrouds something, by "turning it around," one can uncover the distorting biases that contextualize and determine the very significance, the symbolic "truth," of things. And, gradually, they begin to appear to a less biased eye as things yet unseen, marvelous in their complexity of texture, their simplicity of intent, ever adaptable to the disposition of the observer—mutable in their very disclosure. As Nietzsche says in the new preface to *Human, All Too Human*:

> With a wicked laugh he turns round whatever he finds veiled and through some sense of shame or other spared and pampered: he puts to the test what these things look like *when* they are reversed. It is an act of willfulness and pleasure in willfulness, if now he perhaps bestows his favor on that which has hitherto had a bad reputation—if, full of inquisitiveness and the desire to tempt and experiment, he creeps around the things most forbidden. (*HAH* I, Preface, § 3)

Spurred on by the possibility that "*all* values" may be turned around, Nietzsche says that he began to cultivate a curious sort of cynicism, thinking that the very absolutes themselves may well have been little more than platitudes. This acquired cynicism, and a certain irony attendant to it, provokes even further "wandering" and testing of limits—until he is quite far afield, in "the desert" of his tempting experiments. This "experimentalism" produces in him, Nietzsche says, a kind of "solitude," sometimes even a "morbid isolation," but one that has gathered into itself such a breadth of values and penetrating perspectives that he no longer feels constrained at all—least of all by the old fetters:

> One lives no longer in the fetters of love and hatred, without yes, without no, near or far as one wishes . . . also [without] the quantum of stupidity that resides in antitheses of values and the whole intellectual loss which every For, every Against costs us. (HAH I, Preface, §§ 4–6)

Having broken these fetters, one has the feeling of a great elation, namely, "that *mature* freedom of spirit which is equally self-mastery and discipline of the heart, and permits access to many and contradictory modes of thought" (HAH I, Preface, § 4). Freed from "the spirit of gravity" and free to will one's own "scale of values," one is no longer compelled by the old fetters or compelled to suffer from them. This sense of elation, or "weightlessness," one has attained, together with the fact that one has welcomed *so much*—in gratifying one's inner temptation to experiment with a plethora of experiences—means that one *returns* from one's desert transformed. One possesses a generosity of spirit, an "inner spaciousness and indulgence," such that everything appears benign and innocent, drained of ominous portent and freed from malice of intent. One gains the stability of one's own power over one's perspective, and this at once liberates the individual from bitterness and recrimination while it places one above—at a distance, with a feeling of distance from[13]—the pettiness and vindictiveness of others; rather, with a spirit of exuberance and freedom in which "curiosity is united with a tender contempt," he remarks:

> It again grows warmer around him, yellower, as it were; feeling and feeling for others acquire depth, warm breezes of all kinds blow across him. It seems to him as if his eyes are only now open to what is *close at hand*. He is astonished and sits silent: where had he been? These close and closest things: how changed they seem! what bloom and magic have they acquired! He looks back gratefully—grateful to his wandering, to his hardness and self-alienation, to his viewing of far distances and bird-like flights in cold heights. What a good thing he had not always stayed "at home," stayed "under his own roof" like a delicate apathetic loafer! He had been beside himself: no doubt of that. Only now does he see himself—and what surprises he experiences as he does so! (HAH I, Preface, § 5)

Attaining such a state, such an attitude of mind, one is "cured," as of a past illness and a long convalescence, by the "Great Liberation." And everything is welcomed, without addition or loss, even "the *necessary* injustice . . . as inseparable from life, life itself as *conditioned* by the sense of perspective and its in-justice" (*HAH* I, Preface, § 6). Thus, finally having gained possession of his own self-mastery through controlling his sense of perspective, having freed himself from bondage to the imperative of the "thou shalt"—and the personal discontent caused by it—Nietzsche would reflect, "You come to realize how you have given ear to the voice of nature, that nature which rules the whole world through joy" (*HAH* I, 5, § 292). Reviewing the joys that nature itself bestows upon someone so "cured" as himself, Nietzsche ends the discussion of his own "liberation" with a series of light-hearted "injunctions"—the last of which affirms the resolution to Zarathustra's paradoxical departure: smiling, strong as bronze, accompanied by his laughing lion:

> You shall . . . You shall . . . You shall . . . You shall—enough: from now on the free spirit *knows* what "you shall" he has obeyed, and he also knows what he now *can*, what only now he— *may* do . . . (*HAH* I, Preface, § 6)

IV. The "Foundations" of Morality in the Preface to *Daybreak*

Having freed himself from the injunctions of the traditional morality, Nietzsche raises the subsequent issue as to the real conditions of their remarkable perva-siveness, their resistance to philosophical inquiry, their status as cultural givens, indeed, as "truths." Was it sufficient for Nietzsche to feel personally liberated from his own inner experience of the morality of mores—that is, the experi-enced facticity of the old fetters, and his personal rejection of them—or could his autocritique itself be generalized? Could it be generalized beyond the analysis of his own moral feelings, for example, of shame, humiliation, pity, duty, love, reverence, and so on, and to the occasions that provoked them, much less, to the painful memories that sustained them? He addresses these issues in another of his 1886 prefaces, the preface to *Daybreak*, where the autocritique is extended as a metacritique to the very nature of morality itself, understood as "the problem of morality"—effectively serving as a "critique of morality."

If morality had constituted the "foundations" of Western thought since Plato—due to the latter's identification of the transcendent unity of the One, the Good, and the True; the Greek philosophical adequation of virtue and happiness; or the Christian ascetic ideal (all variants of the "old God")—Nietzsche sees it as his task to tunnel into "the foundations." "Digging out an ancient *faith* . . . I com-menced to undermine our *faith in morality*" (*D*, Preface, § 2). Indeed, he likens himself to a "subterranean man," even a "mole," like those spirits who "bore, dig, gnaw, and moisten" to assist in the work of destruction (*GS*, § 358).

The initial "problem" of morality, as Nietzsche states it in the preface to *Daybreak*, is its resistance to criticism. It is the subject "reflected on least ad-equately" because it was far too dangerous to do so. On the one hand, morality has traditionally arrogated to itself a position of transcendent authority, in the face of which "one is not *allowed* to think, far less to express an opinion," due to what is conventionally held to be at stake for the individual: "Conscience, reputation, Hell, sometimes even the police" (*D*, Preface, § 3). But second, what is also "problematic" about morality for Nietzsche is its seductiveness, its agency of persuasion, of commanding thought and action, in function of its received prescriptive power: namely, its symbolic agency to constitute the very motivation of will, desire, and affect in the individual, as well as to provide the very terms of intelligibility for self-understanding. As he says:

> But morality does not merely have at its command every kind of means of frightening off critical hands and torture instruments: its security reposes far more in a certain art of enchantment it has at its disposal—it knows how to "inspire." With this art it succeeds, often with no more than a single glance, in paralyzing the critical will and even in enticing it over to its own side. . . . For morality has from of old been master of every diabolical nuance of the art of persuasion. (*D*, Preface, § 3)

If faith in morality orchestrates the social symbolic itself, or what Nietzsche terms the entire order of "speech and persuasion," in a gesture of authority, power, and valuation—resistant even to self-criticism—then, he asks, "Why is it that from Plato onwards every philosophical architect in Europe has built in vain?" The *correct* answer would be precisely that the philosophers themselves "were building under the seduction of morality"—even though every artifice built upon such a foundation of morality "is threatening to collapse or already lies in ruins" (*D*, Preface, § 3).[14] The *wrong* answer would be the Kantian response, namely, that the critique of reason had not yet been made, and hence, that the traditional foundations of philosophy were still dogmatic and insecure. Under the Kantian account, one could restore the proper range and compass of reason and thus attain a transcendentally grounded and purified philosophical system, rendering it immune to error and falsehood; yet, from the standpoint of reason one could secure room for faith and a universal morality. Nietzsche's response, however, tellingly demonstrates the contrary: namely, that reason itself is *diminished* in range and scope due to Kant's prior moral commitment:

> To create room for his "moral realm" [Kant] saw himself obliged to posit an undemonstrable world, a logical "beyond"—it was precisely for that that he had need of his critique of pure reason! In other words: *he would not have had need of it* if one thing had not been more vital to him than anything else: to render the "moral realm" unassailable, even better, incomprehensible to reason—for he felt that a moral order of things was only too assailable by reason! In the face of nature and history, in the face of the thorough *immorality* of nature and history, Kant was, like every good German of the old stamp, a pessimist; he believed in morality, not because it is demonstrated in nature and history, but in spite of the fact that nature and history continually contradict it. (*D*, Preface, § 3)

Even granting the Kantian position of limiting the capacity of reason to make room for faith,[15] Nietzsche extends his critique of reason to show that the ostensible foundation of reason, our trust in reason, is itself grounded in a moral choice:

> But *logical* evaluations are not the deepest or most fundamental to which our audacious mistrust can descend: faith in reason, with which the validity of these judgments must stand or fall, is, as faith, a *moral* phenomenon. (*D*, Preface, § 4)

That truth, reason, logic, and knowledge derive from social needs and communicative requirements is, of course, one of the most central and ongoing concerns of Nietzsche's entire work. Likewise, that traditional moral values find their origins in the political and religious community's set of self-preservative (i.e., vital) prescriptions and prohibitions and so forth, all this ultimately points to the moral foundations of veracity, validity, and science itself.[16] But in the 1886 prefaces and in Book V of *The Gay Science*—anticipating his analysis in *On The Genealogy of Morals*—what is at issue is not so much the *origins* of morality as its *critique*. And, for Nietzsche himself, after completing the arduous feat of recovering his own "youth," his "innocence of the child," or the "great cure" of self-overcoming—through his performative writing of *Zarathustra*, and his articulation of this experience in the new preface to *Human, All Too Human*—it is increasingly incumbent on him to express his personalized "experience" of self-critique in clearly more analytical and philosophical terms. Nietzsche perhaps most directly addresses this need in the new preface to *Daybreak* and in sections 344 and 345 (Book V) of *The Gay Science* (both texts were completed on the same day, November 13, 1886).

V. Autocritique, Truth, Morality—In One's Person

The magnitude of the problem of morality, its identity with the whole of the social symbolic, and its ability to govern all reasoned judgment, signify that it is extremely difficult to criticize and to effectively evaluate it—which is why Nietzsche terms it the "Circe of the philosophers" (*D*, Preface, § 3). Traditional historical analysis of morality has tended to focus on the origins of particular systems of morality, but additionally, for Nietzsche, quite often historians unwittingly import the value terms of their own culture when attempting to evaluate the moral systems of other cultures. Gently paraphrasing the introduction to Hume's *Treatise*, Nietzsche remarks that

> These historians of morality . . . are still quite unsuspectingly obedient to one particular morality and, without knowing it, serve that as shield-bearers and followers—for example, by sharing that popular superstition of Christian Europe which people keep mouthing so guilelessly to this day. . . . Their usual mistaken premise is that they affirm some consensus

of the nations, at least of tame nations, concerning certain principles of morals, and then they infer from this that these principles must be unconditionally binding also for you and me. (*GS*, § 345)

Alternatively, such historical analysis may just as well conclude "that among different nations moral valuations are *necessarily* different and then infer from this that *no* morality is at all binding" (*GS*, § 345). Nietzsche concludes that both approaches are "equally childish." What such interpretations do have in common is that they mistakenly criticize received public opinion about morality, stemming from such considerations as the "origins" of the particular morality, its purported divine sanction, the "superstition of free will," the "soul" fiction, or other such errors and think they have criticized the morality itself. Ultimately, the "value" of any particular moral injunction is different from and quite independent of such opinions and errors as to its origin.

Interestingly—and problematically—what entitles Nietzsche to critically address "the problem" of morality will turn out to be his own *personality*. That is to say, his own formation within the traditional morality—his "at home"—the whole set of inherited valuations, that he articulated in the prefaces to *Human, All Too Human*. It is precisely those valuations that he rejected, reversed, and contradicted from within, due to the appalling effects he suffered from them in his own person—his so-called sickness—and, in his "travels," their reversal and overcoming, which brought about his newly found "happiness." As he would remark:

> It makes the most telling difference whether a thinker has a personal relationship to his problems and finds in them his destiny, his distress and his greatest happiness, or an "impersonal" one, meaning that he can do no better than to touch them and grasp them with the antennae of cold, curious thought. In the latter case nothing will come of it. (*GS*, § 345)

Rather, Nietzsche says, he

> approached morality in this personal way and . . . knew morality as a problem, and this problem as his own personal distress, torment, voluptuousness, and passion. (*GS*, § 345)

By focusing on his personal criticism of moral values, that is, by stressing his own autocritique, Nietzsche nonetheless raises a whole set of questions in turn. To what extent is the imperative to criticize morality itself a moral imperative? Would such a moral critique thus be a contradiction? To what extent would such a critique be truth functional? If the new valuations were in fact true, could they be extensional, that is, universally binding? In which case could they assume the form of a moral injunction at all, a "thou shalt," as it were? Or, finally, is the very notion of morality itself at stake in the prefaces of 1886 and in Book V of *The Gay Science*. Indeed, it is.[17]

In the remarkable section 344 of *The Gay Science*, titled, "How we, too, are still pious," Nietzsche proposes an itinerary that he will develop formally in the preface to *Daybreak*. In raising the "problem of morality," one necessarily has to confront the issues of moral probity, honesty, and truth—all elements involved in a critique of morality. In the aforementioned section, Nietzsche examines the paradigmatic case of truth itself, which is the stated objective of the modern scientific account. He asks whether such "truth" may merely be the object of conviction, the deeply held conviction that truth is the most important value—and whether this conviction serves largely as a "regulative illusion." He then claims that the presupposition behind this conviction is that "*nothing* is needed *more* than truth, and in relation to it everything has only second-rate value" (*GS*, § 344; see also *BGE*, §§ 1 and 8). Given this hierarchy of valuation, Nietzsche then develops his argument in terms that more easily accord with his personalization of the problem: what, he asks, is this "unconditional will to truth"? Opposing truth to its opposite, falsehood and deceit, he introduces two possible responses: (A) that the will to truth signifies the will not to deceive *oneself*, and (B), that it means the will *not to deceive*. The first response would suggest that truth—and by extension, science—would serve as an instrument of utility, as a "caution," he says, against deceit, harm, and danger. But Nietzsche makes the rejoinder that life itself often enough *demands* "semblance, meaning error, deception, simulation, delusion, self-delusion," and so on, and one's trust is often better served with a bit of deception than with adhering to an unconditional will "to truth at any price." As he remarks, "'At any price': how well we understand these words once we have offered and slaughtered one faith after another on this altar!" (*GS*, § 344). Hence, the will to truth—or, "the faith in science"—stems not from concerns of utility or caution but from the second response, which can be construed to entail the first, namely, the will not to deceive oneself. And with this, he says, "*we stand on moral ground.*"

Nietzsche's autocritique of morality inevitably leads to the question of its truthfulness, and the question of truth in turn raises that of our faith in science, which finally leads us back to the order of faith, conviction, and morality.

> Thus the question "Why science?" leads back to the moral problem: *Why have morality at all* when life, nature, and history are "not moral"? No doubt, those who are truthful in that audacious and ultimate sense that is presupposed by the faith in science *thus affirm another world* than the world of life, nature and history. (*GS*, § 344)

Nietzsche then draws the conclusion as to the wellsprings of this conviction, this "will" to truth and "faith" in science:

> But you will have gathered what I am driving at, namely, that it is still a *metaphysical* faith upon which our faith in science rests—that even we seekers after knowledge today, we godless anti-metaphysicians, still take

our fire, too, from the flame lit by a faith that is thousands of years old, that Christian faith which was also the faith of Plato, that God is the truth, that truth is divine. (*GS*, § 344)

VI. *German, All Too German*: The Self-Sublimation of Morality

Despite the passing of the old, angry God, we nonetheless live under his shadow—as Nietzsche constantly reminds us—namely, within the terms of traditional ontotheology. Indeed, its "diabolical persuasion" extends to the very constitution of one's own personality, and the resolution of *this* contradiction (i.e., between Nietzsche, the individual, and the moral codes that constitute him according to the traditional order) is ultimately what Nietzsche attempts to delineate in the late prefaces, especially in the preface to *Daybreak*. He had already signaled one of the principal reasons why even the modern individual—the godless antimetaphysician—is regulatively governed by the faith that the "truth is divine": precisely by the sublimation of the Christian conscience into the scientific conscience, of faith into atheism. In part, as a consequence of Luther's "peasant revolt" of the spirit, "the most fateful act of two thousand years of discipline for truth in the end forbids itself the *lie* in faith in God." As he explains this in section 357 of *The Gay Science*,

> You see what it was that really triumphed over the Christian god: Christian morality itself, the concept of truthfulness that was understood ever more rigorously, the father confessor's refinement of the Christian conscience, translated and sublimated into a scientific conscience, into intellectual cleanliness at any price. Looking at nature as if it were proof of the goodness and governance of a god; interpreting history in honor of some divine reason, as a continual testimony of a moral world order . . . that is *all over* now, that has man's conscience against it. (*GS,* § 357)

Given the terms and perspectival limitations of the 1886 prefaces, however, this rejection of the moral world order might be better expressed by saying that it had Nietzsche's personal conscience against it.

The maintenance of the contradictions between faith and reason ultimately made room for the admission of moral absurdity itself. Nietzsche invokes two historical figures who, to his mind, typically advanced such views, Kant and Luther. In the case of Kant, one is "content to fill up the gap with an *increase* in trust and belief, with a renunciation of all provability for one's belief, with an incomprehensible and superior 'ideal' (God)."[18] In the case of Luther, Nietzsche quotes his remark that "If we could grasp by reason that the God who shows so much wrath and malice can be just and merciful, what need would we have of faith?" Equating this remark about Luther's somewhat desperate view of theodicy with Tertullian's celebrated credo, "I believe because it is absurd," Nietzsche proudly announces, "It was with this conclusion that German logic first entered the history of Christian dogma" (*D,* Preface § 3).

Indeed, Nietzsche continues, a millennium later, even among his own contemporaries:

> We Germans of today . . . still sense something of truth, of the *possibility* of truth behind the celebrated dialectical principle with which in his day Hegel assisted the German spirit to conquer Europe—"Contradiction moves the world, all things contradict themselves"—: for we are, even in the realm of logic, pessimists. (*D*, Preface, § 3)

But the contradiction between reason and faith, which opens the space of morality, is itself sublated by the recognition that reason's dialectical capacity is in turn predicated upon faith, or as he claimed, "faith in reason," and the moral "will" to truth. In which case, Tertullian's "belief" is set alongside the "absurd," whereby morality itself is simply withdrawn from reason, argument, or reality. To follow out Nietzsche's jocular Hegelianism at this point, one might well object that precisely morality alone remains as the detritus—or as the sublimated synthesis—of a failed contradiction. In this case it must be asked "why should" morality be withdrawn at all? What kind of imperative would be invoked to make such a claim? Nietzsche's conclusion is both ironic and astute: ironic, in that the imperative to overcome morality—"to go beyond faith in morality"—is itself a moral imperative. In this respect, the preface to *Daybreak* exhibits his pessimism toward morality (and any sense of its universal authority, purchase, or truth). It does so, he claims, in function of logical contradiction, which, of course, he has already discredited. *Daybreak* (and in particular, the preface, with its task of giving a critique of morality)

> does in fact exhibit a contradiction and is not afraid of it: in this book faith in morality is withdrawn—but why? *Out of morality!* Or what else should we call that which informs it—and *us*? (*D*, Preface, § 4)

The final, stressed "us" is telling in its astuteness. "Us" is, of course, the "we," or better, the "me" of the author himself. By the same token, the use of the plural indicates Nietzsche's continuity with the tradition—in this case, of a certain German "pessimism" regarding reason and, indeed, skepticism, concerning the rational defensibility of faith and morality, which is why he terms the present work "a German book."

More positively, the distributive "us" designates Nietzsche's Reformationist and Enlightenment credentials in his adhering to the traditional imperative of truth—"translated and sublimated"—from the Christian morality of the confessional conscience into the "morality" of the scientific conscience.[19] To this extent, at least, one could say that Nietzsche seems to be quite content to be "morally informed" by the prevailing *nomos*, the "modern" sense of German philosophical culture. Indeed, he goes on to say, "there is no doubt that a 'thou shalt' still speaks to us too, that we too still obey a stern law set over us . . . and this is the last moral law which can make itself audible even to us, which even we know how to *live*" (*D*, Preface, § 4). But having just "withdrawn morality . . . out of morality," he qualifies "this last moral law" as being one of *taste*: "Or, what else should we call that which informs it—and *us*?" He responds that "our taste is for more modest expressions" (*D*, Preface, § 4).[20] Thus, the impetus for withdrawing morality is that of a personally cultivated artfulness, an "aesthetic aversion," bred from experience and experimentation, always factored by the perspective of one's own judgment—and this impetus emerges as conscience, "intellectual cleanliness," or as he would specify this in *The Gay Science*, an "intellectual conscience. . . . A conscience behind your 'conscience'" (*GS*, § 335). In the preface to *Daybreak* he would say,

> we too are still *men of conscience*: namely, in that we do not want to return to that which we consider outlived and decayed, to anything "unworthy of belief," be it called God, virtue, truth, justice, charity; that we do not permit ourselves any bridges-of-lies to ancient ideals . . . it is only as men of *this* conscience that we still feel ourselves related to the German integrity and piety of millennia, even if as its most questionable and final descendents, we immoralists, we godless men of today. (*D*, Preface, § 4)

Having experienced and explained in his own person the death of God, and the moral foundations subtending the very tradition of Western thought, Nietzsche returns from his "five or six years" of being a "subterranean man," a "solitary mole" who "tunnels and mines and undermines" those foundations, with a sense of joy (*D*, Preface, § 1–2):

> Like a new and scarcely describable kind of light, happiness, relief, exhilaration, encouragement, dawn. . . . Indeed, we philosophers and "free spirits" feel . . . as if a new dawn shone on us; our heart overflows with gratitude, amazement, premonitions, expectation. (*GS*, § 343)

Such an individual is personally capable of contradiction and of sublating contradiction. On the one hand, he can contradict morality "out of morality." And this occurs "in us." Such a will "does not draw back from denying itself because it denies with *joy*." On the other hand, such a will has, in the course of these "five or six years," been itself transformed from that of the moralist to that of the "artist"—informed by "my taste—a malicious taste, perhaps?"—whose "venerable art" of philology, a "goldsmith's art and connoisseurship," yields a conscience "hostile, in short, to the whole of European . . . idealism." He effectively concludes his moral metacritique in the preface to *Daybreak* by claiming, "in us there is accomplished—supposing you want a formula—the self-sublimation of morality" (*D*, Preface, §§ 4, 5). Realistically, such a mock-Hegelian formula of itself is hardly extensional or unconditional in character. Rather, his stated aim in the preface to *Daybreak* is far more modest and personal. As he tells the reader:

> Here in this late preface, which could easily have become a funeral oration . . . I have returned and, believe it or not, returned safe and sound. Do not think for a moment that I intend to invite you to the same hazardous

enterprise! Or even only to the same solitude! For he who proceeds on his own path in this fashion encounters no one: that is inherent in "proceeding on one's path." . . . For his path is *his alone*. (*D*, Preface, § 2)

Ultimately, the authority and power of the traditional moral order of valuation—its effective agency—may well be critiqued and challenged by the individual. In this sense, its significance for the individual is fully mutable, precisely according to the codes of the larger symbolic order.[21] And precisely for this reason, when Nietzsche begins his extended critique of morality in *On the Genealogy of Morals,* his starting point is the question, "What was the real etymological significance of the designations" for certain moral *terms*—good, bad, and so forth—"coined in the various languages?" (*GM* I, § 4). But to say that the "self-sublimation of morality" occurs in his own person is simply to acknowledge that a cultivated aesthetic judgment more appropriately designates or denotes what were previously held to be moral acts or sentiments. If, indeed, there are only "moral interpretations" of the signifying order, one may well, as Luther did, merely withhold assent: "Here I stand, I cannot do otherwise." Or, as Nietzsche himself would remark in one of the concluding sections of *On the Genealogy of Morals,* "I have the taste of two millennia against me: but there it is! 'Here I stand, I cannot do otherwise'" (*GM* III, § 22). A *very* German book. And yet, "his path is *his alone*."

Notes

1. Letter to Malwida von Meysenbug, May 1887, in F. Nietzsche, *Selected Letters of Friedrich Nietzsche*, ed. and Eng. tr., Christopher Middleton (Chicago: University of Chicago Press, 1969), p. 266.
2. Eng. tr., Carol Diethe, in F. Nietzsche, *On the Genealogy of Morality*, ed. Keith Ansell-Pearson (Cambridge: Cambridge University Press, 1994), pp. 176–186.
3. Eng. tr., W. Kaufmann, in Carl Dahlhaus, *Between Romanticism and Modernism: Four Studies in the Music of the Later Nineteenth Century* (Berkeley: University of California Press, 1980), pp. 106–119.
4. Eng. tr., Christa D. Acampora, in F. Nietzsche, *Nietzscheana*, No. 5 (Urbana, Ill.: North American Nietzsche Society, 1996). Cf. also Carol Diethe's translation of "Homers Wettkampf," as "Homer on Competition," in F. Nietzsche, *On the Genealogy of Morality*, op. cit., pp. 187–194.
5. Jacob Burckhardt, *The Greeks and Greek Civilization*, ed., Oswyn Murray, Eng. tr., Sheila Stern (New York: St. Martin's Press, 1998), pp. 160–213.
6. Letter to Carl von Gersdorff, June 28, 1883, in F. Nietzsche, *Selected Letters of Friedrich Nietzsche*, p. 213.
7. Letter to Peter Gast, August 1883, in ibid., p. 218. Cf. also *Z* I, "On Reading and Writing": "Of all that is written I love only what a man has written with his blood. Write with blood, and you will experience that blood is spirit. It is not easily possible to understand the blood of another."
8. Letter to Gast, Sept. 4, 1884, in *Selected Letters*, p. 230.
9. For a remarkably clear and detailed account of the events leading up to the appear-

ance of the second edition of Nietzsche's writings, see William H. Schaberg's *The Nietzsche Canon: A Publication History and Bibliography* (Chicago: The University Press of Chicago, 1995), pp. 126–140.

10. René Descartes, *Meditations on First Philosophy*, in *The Philosophical Writings of Descartes*, Eng. tr., John Cottingham, Robert Stoothoff, Dugald Murdoch (Cambridge: Cambridge University Press, 1989), Vol. II, Med. I, p. 15.

11. In the 1886 preface to Part Two of *HAH*, he reformulates this "invention" of an other "free spirit" and, less dramatically, says that "As a solitary I spoke without witnesses," thus internalizing the discussion as an "inner" dialogue (*HAH* II, Preface, § 5). Cf. also, *Kritische Studienausgabe* (*KSA*) 12: 146, a working note to the new preface of *HAH*, I, where he says that "solitude constrains him to create beings who resemble him."

12. Even if this involves an initial period of studied affectation or pretense, such that by repetition, one could induce oneself to acquire in person those attitudes one initially feigns: "It was then I learned the art of *appearing* cheerful, objective, inquisitive, above all healthy and malicious . . . here a sufferer and self-denier speaks as though he were *not* a sufferer and self-denier. Here there is a *determination* to preserve an equilibrium and composure in the face of life and even a sense of gratitude towards it, here there rules a vigorous, proud, constantly watchful and sensitive will that has set itself the task of defending life against pain and of striking down all those inferences that pain, disappointment, ill-humor, solitude, and other swampgrounds usually cause to flourish like poisonous fungi" (*HAH* II, Preface, § 5).

13. Nietzsche would call this "the pathos of distance" in *Beyond Good and Evil,* § 257. Cf. also *BGE*, §§ 43–44 and *EH*, "The Untimely Ones," § 3.

14. This parallels Nietzsche's extended discussion of the "death of God" and its enormous consequences in, for example, *GS*, §§ 345, 357, and 358, following his claim that the "belief" in the Christian God has become "unbelievable."

15. Which, of course, is exactly what Nietzsche denies: ". . . come to think of it, was it not somewhat peculiar to demand of an instrument that it should criticize its own usefulness and suitability? That the intellect itself should 'know' its own value, its own capacity, its own limitations? Was it not even a little absurd?" (*D,* Preface, § 3). Likewise, in a note for the same preface, he remarks, "In the end: is it likely that an instrument *can* criticize its own effectiveness?—What I focused on was rather the fact no skepticism or dogmatism . . . could be brought forth without ulterior motives or mental reservations—by the fact that they have a second order value as soon as one considers *what*, basically, *compels* one to take that position: even the will to certainty, if not only the will, 'first of all, I want to live'—this is a fundamental idea: for Kant, just as well for Hegel and Schopenhauer—even the skeptic's position of maintaining the epoché, the historicist's, and the pessimist's positions are all *moral* in origin" (*KSA* 12: 143–44).

16. One of the earliest statements to this effect is from his work of 1872, "The Philosopher": "What does the truth matter to man? The highest and purest life is possible with the belief that one possesses truth. Man requires *belief in truth*. Truth makes its appearance as a social necessity. Afterwards, by means of metastasis, it is applied to everything, where it is not required. All virtues arise from pressing needs.

The necessity for truthfulness begins with society. Otherwise man dwells within eternal concealments. The establishment of states promotes truthfulness. The drive towards knowledge has a *moral* origin" ("The Philosopher," in F. Nietzsche, *Philosophy and Truth*, ed. and Eng. tr., D. Breazeale [Atlantic Highlands, N.J.: Humanities Press, 1979], pp. 34–35). For an extensive analysis of Nietzsche's complex attitudes toward, and understanding of, science, see B. Babich, *Nietzsche's Philosophy of Science: Reflecting Science on the Ground of Art and Life* (Albany: State University of New York Press, 1994); cf. also, B. Babich and R. Cohen, eds., *Nietzsche and the Sciences*, 2 vols. (Dordrecht: Kluwer Academic Publishers, 1999). In his 1886 preface to *BT*, Nietzsche claims in retrospect that *BT* first raised the "problem of science" already in his discussion of the Socratic demise of the tragic: "And science itself, our science—indeed, what is the significance of all science, viewed as a symptom of life? . . . for the problem of science cannot be recognized in the context of science." He goes on to say: "The task which this audacious book dared to tackle for the first time: to look at science in the perspective of the artist, but at art in that of life" (*BT*, Preface, §§ 2, 3).

17   In Section 5 of the new preface to *On the Birth of Tragedy*, his veritable attack against traditional Christian morality is particularly strident, engaging what he terms his own *"antimoral* propensity" (*BT*, "Attempt at Self-Criticism," § 5).

18.   Note "For the Preface to 'Daybreak,'" in F. Nietzsche, *Writings from the Late Notebooks*, ed. Rüdiger Bittner, Eng. tr., Kate Sturge (Cambridge: Cambridge University Press, 2003), Notebook 2 [165], Autumn 1885–Autumn 1886, p. 92.

19.   "A world we can revere, that accords with our drive to worship—that continually *proves* itself, by guiding the individual and the universal: this is the Christian view from which we are all descended. A more and more precise, mistrustful, scientific attitude (and a more ambitious instinct for sincerity, thus again under Christian influence) has increasingly *disallowed* us that interpretation" (note "For the Preface to 'Daybreak,'" op. cit., p. 92).

20.   He clarifies this in a note from the period of the new prefaces, where he describes his earlier writings as being "distinguished by a clear will to open up horizons, a certain artful prudence in dealing with convictions, a distrust towards the traps set forth by [the traditional sense of] conscience, and for those magic towers that every strong faith evokes; one can see in them, on the one hand, the circumspection of the child who has been burned, and on the other, the disappointed idealist—but more essential, it seems to me, is the Epicurean instinct of the lover of enigmas who doesn't want to be rid of the enigmatic character of things in advance, and finally, more essential than all, the aesthetic aversion towards the grand words of virtue and the absolute; this taste that rebels against all those too blunt oppositions, wants a good part of uncertainty in things and suppresses oppositions, as a friend of the half-tone, shadows, afternoon light, and infinite seas" (*KSA* 12: 144). The note also anticipates *GS*, V, § 375.

21.   See, especially, *GS*, § 354, "On the 'genius of the species.'"

Chapter Two

Forgetting the Subject

Christa Davis Acampora

> It is possible to live almost without memory, and to live
> happily moreover, as the animal demonstrates; but it is al-
> together impossible to *live* at all without forgetting.
> —*On The Uses and Disadvantages of History for Life*

> Why must the preying lion still become a child? The child
> is innocence and forgetting, a new beginning, a game, a
> self-propelled wheel, a first movement, a sacred "Yes."
> —*Thus Spoke Zarathustra* I: On the Three Metamorphoses

> Remembering is possible only on the basis of forgetting,
> and not the other way around.
> —Heidegger, *Being and Time*

The subject of *forgetting*, generally, is intentionally marginalized in the history of Western philosophy. As paradigmatically the "science of knowledge" or, more broadly, the "love of wisdom," philosophy characteristically strives to grasp and preserve, to have and to hold forever, its objects of investigation and the fruits of its labor. Forgetting threatens such an enterprise. It indicates weakness, decay, and deficiency. From the perspective of moral philosophy, forgetting is not only an indication of cognitive inferiority; it is a potentially sinister and reckless trait. Forgetting is the nemesis of what advances philosophy's aims, namely *remembering*. Thus, there should be little surprise that the history of philosophy does not elaborately treat forgetting, remaining focused on memorializing truth, goodness, and the fundamental nature of reality. But does forgetting play a role in garnering these very same goods that it appears to jeopardize? Nietzsche argues that it does. This is most clearly reflected in his account of the development of the individual and its significance in the growth and course of moral psychology. In forgetting the subject, Nietzsche endeavors to supply a new way of conceiving the subject that he thinks is more suitable to a metaphysics that would relinquish permanence, and he does this in such a way as to emphasize the significance and value of *forgetting* itself, which at the same time calls into question how we think about knowledge. Thus, Nietzsche's forgetting of the subject bears on the most central concerns in philosophy despite the marginal status of forgetting in its history and the marginal attention forgetting has received in the secondary literature on Nietzsche.

To develop these points, this essay is divided into five sections. In the first, I selectively consider some prominent ideas about forgetting in the history of philosophy. This section is useful for appreciating some of the ideas that Nietzsche explicitly addresses in his own work. The account also highlights certain ideas about philosophy itself, learning, and truth that continue to be embraced today. I briefly consider also how forgetting has been treated by several thinkers following Nietzsche in order to supply the basis for a later section that will treat how the significance of forgetting in Nietzsche's philosophy has yet to be fully appreciated. In the second part, I elaborate the role of forgetting in Nietzsche's account of the formation of the self. It draws on one of the more potent discussions of forgetting in his works, and it is crucial to his account of the development of human moral psychology. I argue that mistaking the role of forgetting in Nietzsche's account greatly affects whether one appreciates the end of the story he tells in the *Genealogy* and the possible future he envisions for humanity, namely how Zarathustra is supposed to facilitate the "overcoming" of humanity. How this process is tied to the history of moralization is more elaborately addressed in the third section, which considers how Nietzsche connects the battle against forgetting with cruelty. Nietzsche specifically ties the torturous practices of mnemonics to the development of reason. I discuss the passages in Nietzsche's *Genealogy* where these ideas are introduced and then more fully develop those ideas in the broader context of Nietzsche's philosophy generally. In the fourth section, I claim that the idea of forgetting the subject provides a reflective basis for the development of an ecstatic logic that is compatible with Nietzsche's critique of Platonic metaphysics and the epistemological views it supports. By way of conclusion, I recap and emphasize what is lost in the continued marginalization of forgetting not only in Nietzsche's works but also in philosophy generally. Finally, I suggest some paths for further pursuit.

I. Forgetting History

Of course, Nietzsche is not alone in the history of philosophy in reflecting on forgetting, although his interest joins him to a rather sparsely populated community of philosophers. Plato certainly stands out as concerned about forgetting, but the apparent views of his character Socrates have had a lasting influence on how forgetting has been pushed to the margins of concern in philosophy ever since. The so-called theory of recollection is perhaps the best-known example of philosophical discussion that bears on the matter of forgetting. Recollection is supposed to account for how learning is possible at all. According to this view, learning is not a matter of being filled up with new things (a process that proves difficult to imagine and which has the consequence of presenting knowing as a passive process) but rather is a matter of recollecting what it is that one already has as contents of knowledge. The *Meno*'s uneducated slave, who proves himself competent in geometry when appropriately prompted, is supposed to illustrate a case in point. We know, but don't always know that we know, many things, and education is aimed at educing such knowledge from us. We are constituted knowing, but have somehow forgotten. The task then of education and philosophy more generally is to overcome this forgetfulness.

One explanation of how we managed to forget what we already know, such that it needs to be brought out of us, is suggested in the *Republic*'s Myth of Er (another is found in the *Phaedrus*). At the end of the long journey during which the transmigration of souls from one life to another is accomplished, the participants must cross the hot, dry plain of *Lēthē* (literally "forgetfulness"), where they are given the opportunity to drink from a river. "All of them had to drink a certain measure of this water," we are told, "but those who weren't saved [*sōizomenous*] by reason drank more than that, and as each of them drank, he forgot everything and went to sleep" (*Republic* 621a.[1] Compare this line with 621b in which Socrates tells Glaucon in explaining how Er returned to his body to tell the story, "And so, Glaucon, this is a story that was saved and not lost," in which the word *esōthē* appears. Both words translated as "saved" have the root *sōzō*, meaning to save, preserve, and remember. These multiple meanings are later exploited by Heidegger.) Presumably, variety in depth of intellection and ease of recollection can be explained, then, according to how much or what measure of water one drank from the river at Lēthē. Those whose souls were not conditioned to ascertain the measure that was appropriate (i.e., those without a sense of justice, those with less refined rational powers) drank too much and thus set for themselves a difficult course in their next lives. They will have already forgotten so much that recollecting will be difficult, and they will not be able to choose well the things that are worth pursuing in their new lives. Forgetting will make them morally degenerate and less happy. The goal of philosophy, of the exercise and enhancement of the rational powers, the myth instructs us, is to *avoid forgetting* so that one may choose and fare well (*eu prattōmen*).[2]

Two points are worth underscoring at this juncture. The first is that this story reminds us of the etymology of the common Greek word for truth— *alētheia*—literally, non-forgetting, an idea to which I shall return shortly below. And the second is that there is at least another way of interpreting the upshot of the myth as it relates to the significance of forgetting—drinking the water at Lēthē was *necessary*; the fact of drinking was not itself the indication of weakness or degeneration. The problem, for those who fared poorly, was not that they drank at all but rather that they exceeded their reasonable measure. Thus, forgetting might yet play an important role in the formation of the basis of the lives that become ours (although this is not explained). If so, then the task of philosophy is to *temper forgetting*—not eliminate it—to keep it from exceeding its bounds. But this sense of forgetting from Plato's myth was not saved.[3]

Forgetting does appear much later in the history of philosophy, in the philosophy of Schopenhauer, as playing an important role in shaping the basis of our lives and sense of ourselves. Forgetting oneself is important for Schopenhauer, since that self that we think we are (on account of the *principium individuationis*) is merely a representation of will and not the effect of an independent will that we in essence truly are. "Forgetting [of] oneself as individual" is an important insight for Schopenhauer and serves as the basis for being in a position to momentarily still the will whose cravings are the source of our suffering and dissatisfaction (Schopenhauer, 1966, I:199; see also Parkes, 1994, pp. 60–89, esp. 68ff for discussion of how this relates to Nietzsche's conception of subjectivity and forgetting, particularly in light of *The Birth of Tragedy* and the conception of Dionysian ecstasy [*Rausch*]. I more fully develop similar ideas in my section four below). For Schopenhauer, it is crucial to forget what was the most transparent and self-evident phenomenon for Descartes, the basis for all possible knowledge, namely the "I," or the self. Such forgetting is necessary not only for any possible happiness, for Schopenhauer, but also for our understanding of the truth of the way the world really is.

As noted above, a dependency of truth on forgetting is saved in the Greek word *alētheia*. Truth conceived as nonforgetting at first glance appears to set up the two terms as polar opposites, as though they might be mutually exclusive or perhaps essentially contradictory. Indeed, this is how much of the history of philosophy has regarded the relation between truth (or what is known) and what is forgotten (what is not known), but some modern philosophers have suggested that such a view was not shared by certain ancient Greek philosophers themselves, at least not the predecessors of Socrates. Heidegger, of course, makes much of this idea. In his effort to revive a sense of truth that he alleges has been forgotten since Plato, Heidegger emphasizes the significance of forgetting as a fundamental feature of human ontology and the understanding of some of the most basic philosophical questions.

Quite unlike many of his predecessors, Heidegger gives prominence to forgetting when he writes that "remembering is possible only on the basis of forgetting and not the other way around" (Heidegger, 1996, II:4, §68). With this, Heidegger reiterates a predominant theme in his writings: human beings have *forgotten* Being. This *resembles* the Platonic idea of having knowledge, or the truth, without realizing it until it is drawn out of us. (And given the way Heidegger emphasizes truth as a kind of relationship or communion with Being and the way in which he conceives of the emergence of this relationship as an event, especially in his later writings, it might also be the case that Heidegger, like Plato, has his own mythos to go along with his conception of the relation between forgetting and remembering, too.) For Heidegger, we quite clearly have some understanding of Being—we do, after all, make claims about the existence of things and their character, and we convey such understanding not only in our use of language, but also in our use of things, in the way in which we interact with them in the world and the way in which they can become for us objects of care. Moreover, the very fact that we can even ask the question "What is Being?" suggests that we at least have some sense of what it is that we are seeking. But we fail to "save" (or remember) what we gather from the standpoint of interacting with beings in relations characterized by care.

Part of the explanation for this forgetting is that such relations, which are themselves interpretations (for Heidegger, ways of taking something *as* something), do not yet rise to the level of a theoretical or conceptual understanding. It is clear that this is not a case of forgetting in the usual use of the term, although it could be a case of forgetting in the sense of not "saving" what we have been shown, which echoes somewhat the Platonic association of saving and remembering.[4] Heidegger's conception of phenomenology, as introduced in §7 of *Being and Time*, and his characterization of what he calls the "circle of understanding" (esp. §§ 31–34) provide a basis for more fully elaborating this relation. Another explanation for forgetting, as Heidegger considers it, is that what is disclosed to us in our relations to things in the world gets forgotten or obscured (for Heidegger, "covered up") through the application of ready-made interpretations supplied by the history of metaphysics and the variety of ways in which it conceives of being as itself an entity or thing and the commonplace adaptations of such metaphysical concepts that have made their way into everyday language. This influences not only how we relate to other entities in the world, including other human beings, but also how we relate to ourselves (our conceptions of self and what is meant by "I") and to the most basic philosophical questions that we can ask. The tasks of philosophy as they relate to forgetting, then, for Heidegger include: 1) developing an understanding of human beings as *fundamentally in a condition of forgetfulness* (i.e., of not saving all that is potentially apparent to us), and 2) *overcoming the forgetfulness* that the history of philosophy has facilitated.

I have given priority here to the ideas of Heidegger because it seems to me that virtually no one after Nietzsche gives greater prominence to the idea of forgetting than he, and Heidegger draws upon a number of the ideas that I have emphasized in the history of philosophy while at the same time developing his own views on the matter.[5] There are a number of people after Nietzsche, who make mention of Nietzsche's emphasis on forgetting. Among them are Deleuze, Derrida, and Kofman. I make mention of each of these in various sections below and do not include them in this survey section because their comments on forgetting are generally brief or are made almost entirely in relation to making observations about Nietzsche's philosophy. Thus, I treat them as I reach the relevant point in my discussion of Nietzsche's view, to which I now direct my focus.

II. Forgetting the Self

It is already widely recognized that Nietzsche describes forgetting not as an absence or lack of memory but rather as an *active force* in its own right (*GM* II, § 1). This feature of Nietzsche's philosophy has been briefly noted by numerous commentators and is emphasized indirectly in the work of Deleuze, who writes extensively about the significance of active forces in relation to reactive ones in Nietzsche's work (Deleuze, 1983, pp. 39–72).[6] But how Nietzsche casts the nature of this activity and its vitality with regard to forgetting continues to be mischaracterized and misunderstood. Alan Schrift, writing of Deleuze's contributions to understanding Nietzsche's philosophy in terms of "becoming," ties active forgetting to "the sovereign individual" (Schrift, 1995, p. 74), and this figure has played a prominent role in numerous other interpretations of Nietzsche's vision for the future of humanity.

The figure of the sovereign individual makes its lone appearance in Nietzsche's corpus in the section of the *Genealogy* that immediately follows the one identifying forgetting as an active force. Schrift links forgetfulness, as it is ascribed by Nietzsche to "a form of *robust* health" in *GM* II, § 1, with the power and freedom allegedly claimed and enjoyed by the sovereign individual as described in *GM* II, § 2. According to this view, the first two sections appear thematically continuous: the entity described in the first section is the same as that described in the second. But the proximity of the passages is deceptive. In those few paragraphs, Nietzsche provides a sweeping overview of a story of the moralization of humankind—of the production of "humanity," what Nietzsche also describes as the "animal with the right to make promises." He covers considerable ground between his reference to the active force of forgetting and the so-called fruit that is the sovereign individual. It is crucial that one appreciate that great distance if one is to understand the vision Nietzsche reaches toward at the end of the very same essay, in which he speculates about the future development of humanity, or what he at times designates as "overhumanity." In other words, to understand how Nietzsche envisions the possibilities of overhumanity, one must understand the importance given to forgetting and how it stands in relation to what is said about the sovereign individual.

The moral ideal that Nietzsche finds in the history of philosophy from Plato to Schopenhauer is one that increasingly prizes *willing*, and in so doing, ties it to responsibility, autonomy, and freedom: the greater one's exercise of will, the more complete one becomes, the more one realizes the real potential of humanity, the more *being*, or actuality, one achieves. Acquiring the relevant form of willing to reach this ideal requires the development of memory, specifically "*memory of will*" (*GM* II, § 1). Such memory is crucial for the establishment of what Nietzsche describes as a "long chain of will" in which the original "I will" (or the promise of some action or deed) and "the actual discharge of the will," that is, the action or actions one actually undertakes, remain essentially *bound* despite changes of circumstance and the emergence of other desires and acts of will. Taking this on as a goal, human beings have cultivated powers of memory that significantly outstrip those of forgetting, and the service of this end has had dramatic secondary effects, including how one regards the past, present, and future, and the expectations one has of others and oneself. In particular, what we might call the "memory project" requires certain dispositions toward the past and future and the necessity of securing, determining, and effecting it in such a way as to be in the position to maintain the "chain of will" mentioned above; all of this is needed to secure the conditions that make it possible to fulfill the promise made in the past and to make human affairs as regular and predictable as possible in the future in order to ward off circumstances that would interfere with the execution of the relevant actions dictated by the economy of prom-ise-keeping. Nietzsche thus sees the *telos* of this kind of willing as inextricably bound with: 1) the development of reason, 2) a very peculiar sense of history and temporality, and 3) a philosophical anthropology in which "Man himself must first of all have become *calculable, regular, necessary,* even in his own image of himself, if he is to be able to stand security for *his own future,* which is what one who promises does!" (*GM* II, § 1).

The human being who stands security for his or her own future, though, is quite different from the creature with which *GM* II begins. That creature is de-scribed in terms of being an animal, and although human beings certainly retain their animality for Nietzsche, they are nonetheless cultivated to such an extent that they are not merely animals or, at least, are animals that have been bred to distance themselves from those of other species. In Nietzsche's *Genealogy,* it is the development of conscience more than reason that distinguishes human beings, and the second essay in particular examines how such a conscience is produced and how it played a role in effecting the kind of animals modern human beings are. At the *end* of this process stands the ideal of "the sovereign individual":

> If we place ourselves at the end of this tremendous process, where the tree at last brings forth fruit, where society and the morality of custom at last reveal *what* they have simply been the means to: then we discover that the ripest fruit is the *sovereign individual,* like only to himself, liberated again from morality of custom, autonomous and supramoral (for "autonomous" and "moral" are mutually exclusive), in short, the man who has his own independent, protracted will and the *capacity to make promises* [*der ver-sprechen darf*]—and in him a proud consciousness, quivering in every muscle, of *what* has at length been achieved and become flesh in him, a consciousness of his own power and freedom, a sensation of mankind come to completion. (*GM* II, § 2; Kaufmann and Hollingdale's transla-tion emended)

The ideal of the sovereign individual is the goal or the ultimate fruit sought by the process of moralization and refinement of conscience. It is a serious mistake to read it as Nietzsche's ideal, for when one does so, one remains blind to the fact that the sovereign individual is the very ideal that Nietzsche seeks to replace and whose possible overcoming Zarathustra heralds.

Emphasis in the critical literature on the centrality of the sovereign individual obscures Nietzsche's emphasis on forgetting and its importance in human moral psychology in the second essay of *GM*. This is especially so because those who are wont to emphasize sovereign individuality as Nietzsche's central counterimage and ideal in the *Genealogy* also celebrate *promising* as the signature feature of this ideal. But it is the demands of the economy of promise-making that have necessitated the development of memory (and secondarily reason) and the diminution of forgetting that Nietzsche thinks is responsible for the degenerate state of the "sick animals" we have become. Thus, some further scrutiny of the sovereign individual and how it stands in relation to forgetting is warranted.

I have discussed problematic readings of the sovereign individual at greater length elsewhere (Acampora, 2004), so I shall only recap the most salient points of those arguments. For Nietzsche, pursuit of the ideal of the sovereign individual has produced creatures—that is, the animals we call human—who are in many respects dystrophic and dysfunctional. By emphasizing the activity of forgetting and its diminution in the process of enhancing the will, the second essay of the *Genealogy* commences an account of a struggle between two opposing forces: remembering and forgetting. Their relation can be thought of in terms similar to the agonistic dynamic of the artistic forces of the Apollinian and Dionysian in *The Birth of Tragedy*. (I shall highlight one aspect of this similarity in later sections insofar as forgetting is linked with Dionysian self-forgetting and the disruption of the boundaries that remembrance establishes.) Just as our physical health depends upon the accomplishment of nutrition through an active process of consumption and digestion so does the formation of our psychic life occur through "inpsychation" (*Einverseelung*), which is achieved in the interactive processes of taking in experience and excreting what is unnecessary or undesirable to absorb. A disruption of this catalytic dynamic of opposing forces risks *dyspepsia*. We can, Nietzsche claims, suffer from a kind of mental *agita* when our ability to "be done with" our experiences is compromised. Forgetting is important for this reason and numerous others that Nietzsche stresses elsewhere in his writings. The task of the second essay is to describe how this is the current human condition and to envision a way of restoring the health that has been compromised. The news is not all bad for Nietzsche: the "breeding of the animal given the capacity to make promises" (*GM* II, § 1) that required the special strengthening of memory produced creatures that possess a peculiar capacity for willing. That capacity has tremendously creative possibilities, which is what makes humankind so interesting (*GM* I, § 6). By the end of *GM* II, Nietzsche essentially asks *What now?* . . . How can we recover from the psychic dyspepsia of our moralization in the deployment of the special capacity for willing we acquired along the way? But we do not hear that question, and thus cannot pursue it along with or without Nietzsche's Zarathustra, if we remain fixated on the very activity that instigated our decadence, namely the atrophy of memory and the valorization of remembering that promising required.

The value of forgetting also points toward a conception of the subject that is difficult to conceive and frequently ignored, namely one that is not a specific entity or essence but rather a composite of interacting forces. Nietzsche writes in *GM* II, § 1, that forgetting is valuable and necessary because it allows for an evacuation of consciousness that frees it for other pursuits and preoccupations. This regulatory functioning is important because "our organism is oligarchically arranged." In describing the subject in this way, Nietzsche gestures back toward ideas that he develops more elaborately in *BGE,* §§ 16–20, in which he challenges the metaphysics of subjectivity, the ways in which we conceive of selves and individuals, and how he described the mistaken ideas we have about subjectivity based on our projection of a "doer behind the deed" in *GM* I, § 13:

> A quantum of force is equivalent to a quantum of drive, will, effect—more, it is nothing other than precisely this very driving, willing, effecting, and only owing to the seduction of language (and of the fundamental errors of reason that are petrified in it) which conceives and misconceives all effects as conditioned by something that causes effect, by a "subject," can it appear otherwise. [. . .] there is no such substratum; there is no "being" behind doing, effecting, becoming; "the doer" is merely a fiction added to the deed [. . .] Scientists do no better when they say "force moves," "forces cause," and the like— [. . .] our entire science still lies under the misleading influence of language.

More will be said about the role of language below. For now it is important to notice that the idea of a free and sovereign individual of the likes described in the ideal identified at *GM* II, § 2, is simply at odds with much else that Nietzsche conceives about individuality and how he conceives the subject. This lack of consistency between the radically free sovereign individual and what Nietzsche writes elsewhere about the subject is reason enough to be suspicious about taking it as Nietzsche's ideal. Combine that with the facts that the sovereign individual appears in no other place in Nietzsche's writings, that its signature characteristic of promise-making is not touted as a laudable or distinguishing feature of nobility either in the *Genealogy* or in any of Nietzsche's other writings (indeed, one finds barely any references to making a promise at all in Nietzsche's other texts), and one has very little reason to believe (and certainly little ground to argue) that the sovereign individual is an important idea that Nietzsche wants to retain at all.

So, what is the brief account of the sovereign individual describing if not a goal that Nietzsche seeks to pursue? Virtually every commentary on the passage in question emphasizes the apparent strength of will of the sovereign, which accounts for its freedom and is somehow realized in exercising its right to make promises (for my criticism of the translation of *der versprechen darf*, see Acampora, 2004). But I find the conclusion of the passage more interesting and relevant. What is it that makes the life of the sovereign individual desirable? How does it attract those inspired to pursue it? The *real* promise of the sovereign individual is a particularly powerful sensation: "a proud consciousness, quivering in every muscle, of *what* has at length been achieved and become flesh in him, a consciousness of his own power and freedom, a sensation of mankind come to completion" (*GM* II, § 2). There is an aesthesis of power that courses throughout the entire economy of promise-making—making promises, breaking them, and punishing others who are unable or unwilling to keep promises, and it is so great that humans have even instigated their own further deformity in the form of diminishing their powers of forgetting in order to pursue that feeling. The "sovereign individual" is a peculiar conceptual accretion formed by the gravitational pull of the sensation of power that accumulates through the processes of cultivating memory and will to the degree that promising becomes not only desirable but also possible. It is a conceptual ideal that has oriented the process of moralization, finally culminating in modern rationalistic accounts of human subjectivity. Modern individuals, for Nietzsche, have become something of monstrous creatures; the hypertrophy of reason is advanced by an undercurrent of the dystrophy of forgetting.

Thus far, I have focused my discussion of Nietzsche's conception of the relation between subjectivity and forgetting on the idea that what we call the subject is formed through forces (*Kraften*) of remembering and forgetting and on how the formative influence of forgetting has been diminished. Elsewhere in Nietzsche's writings, he emphasizes the significance of forgetting in the process of conceptualization more generally: not only is our concept of the subject formed through an activity of forgetting, all concepts are, and this bears on how we regard the relation between our ideas and what they are supposed to identify and describe.

Sarah Kofman emphasizes the role of forgetting in the activity of conceptualization. In *Nietzsche and Metaphor*, she elaborately describes how Nietzsche considers the formation of concepts as a metaphorical activity, an artistic and inventive process (hence not simply mirroring objects). Casting things in terms of concepts is a specialized form of metaphorical thinking. A distinctive feature of this kind of thought, however, is that we have *forgotten* its metaphorical nature. Moreover, in tying the conceptual to the true and the real, that which is acknowledged as metaphor, in contrast, has been cast aside as less desirable, less pure, derivative, and ultimately less powerful, a pale imitation or image of what truly is.

Kofman makes much of Nietzsche's claim that the specialized language and conceptualization that philosophy utilizes is metaphorical, which we have forgotten is metaphorical:

Because of this fetishization of value, the fact that value is the product of evaluation gets forgotten, and the latter is now measured against the former; the fact that the concept results from a metaphorical activity gets forgotten, and it is taken for a transcendent model, with all specific things and actions being simply degraded copies or simulacra of it. The phantasmatic construction of a transcendent world means that the genesis of the measuring standard gets forgotten. (Kofman, 1993, p. 44)

The concept is based on metaphor, a metaphor of a metaphor, but it is judged as the standard and, thereby, as superior in relation to the metaphoric process from which it is derived, as itself *proper*. It forgets and denigrates its origin. The concept is based upon forgetting in another respect, too, insofar as its insistence on sameness, regularity, and identity amounts to an *active forgetting of differences* (Kofman, chapter 3, "The Forgetting of Metaphor," *passim*). Thus, the process of conceptualization is itself a *secondary* metaphoric process that is itself derived from the original metaphoric grasping that characterizes human understanding and description of its experience. And this derivative, or secondary, metaphoric transformation works in such a way that it *forgets*—in the sense of extracting or refusing to recognize as significant—many differences, distinctions, and other possible features that might be further investigated or otherwise emphasized. Therefore, what we generally take to be the legitimate scrutiny of the world is actually a willful blindness to and intentional forgetting of many different aspects of our experience.

Kofman emphasizes that Nietzsche replaces the traditional conception of humankind as rational animals with the idea of the human as the metaphorical animal (Kofman, pp. 25ff). The shift does not signal that Nietzsche is tossing rationality to the wind or denying that it is a useful function of human cognitive activity. Instead, he is claiming that what we identify as *reason* is but one—and a very specialized and, at times, narrow—kind of metaphorical activity, one that is not based solely on remembering, recollecting, or purely reasoning but in which much forgetting plays an active role. It is the capacity to engage in metaphorical thinking generally and to direct our actions in light of such that is characteristic of human being for Nietzsche. But humankind—committed as it is to its conception of humanity, the good as such, and the relentless reduction of all existence to conformity of what it calls reason—is currently experiencing a kind of stasis (e.g., Z, Preface, § 3). What must we do in order to create something beyond ourselves, and what would it mean to "overcome man," as Zarathustra puts it and as Nietzsche anticipates it in *On the Genealogy of Morals* II, § 24 and throughout the third essay?

The conception of the subject that drives the ideal of the sovereign individual supplies a fundamental sense of boundary and containment. It serves as a primary metaphor that is extended and applied to our understanding generally; it supplies the formal structure for extension of our other metaphorical activities and serves as a rule or guide for the assertion of limits and boundaries utilized in cognition more broadly. It grounds a feature of reason that might very well be undermined if we developed a different conception of self. If we supplant the idea of the subject as responsible (remembering) agent, we might very well require and develop a different kind of logic. (I shall return to this point in the fourth section below, where I discuss the role of forgetting in developing an ecstatic logic.)

The overcoming of humanity involves overcoming, by reconsidering and reconceiving, our *concept* of humanity. This occurs not simply by redescribing or renaming the human. And it involves even more than revaluing humanity in the sense of asserting different ways of conceiving of the value of human life and the possibilities for human community. What the story of the sovereign individual from *GM* II, § 2, helps us to appreciate (once the roles of promising and remembering are better understood in their context) is the significance of the organization of desire in the specification of choice-worthy ends or ideals. Following the first two sections of the second essay of the *Genealogy* that have been the main focus of this part of the paper, Nietzsche suggests a rather sinister motivation for the process of moralization that is guided by the ideal of the subject as a responsible agent, and he ties this to a history of the development of reason. It is to this genealogy that I turn as prelude to discussions of the ways in which the reactivation and renewed cultivation of forgetting might facilitate the replacement of the concept of humanity that Nietzsche associates with such destructive ends and motives.

III. Memory's Cruelty and the Development of Reason

If further evidence is needed for Nietzsche's emphasis on the significance of forgetting and the disaster that the emphasis on remembering has wrought, one need only consider the remainder of the second essay of the *Genealogy*. The rest of the essay is devoted to the history of the moralization of humanity, specifically the production of *conscience* and *bad conscience*. Conscience, Nietzsche claims, became possible through torturous processes of mnemonics that aimed to instill a sense of duty and obligation that required the extirpation of forgetting. What do we need in order to have a conscience? Nietzsche claims it fundamentally rests upon the cultivation of special powers of memory. "'How can one create a memory for the human animal? How can one impress something upon this incarnate forgetfulness, attuned only to the passing moment, in such a way that it will stay there?'" (*GM* II, § 3, translation emended).

Nietzsche offers graphic examples of how "mnemotechnics" have been employed in the form of human sacrifice and mutilation: "all this has its origin in the instinct that realized that pain is the most powerful aid to mnemonics" (*GM* II, § 3). It is clear that Nietzsche conceives quashing forgetfulness as the way in which ascetic practices achieved the fixity of their standards and norms. Memory was quite literally emblazoned in the psyche, initially by means of torture of the body, to render the ideals of asceticism "inextinguishable, ever-present, unforgettable" and also to free "these ideas from the competition of all other ideas, so as to make them 'unforgettable'" in the sense that there is no possible alternative to eclipse them or win out as desirable in comparison or contrast with them. Nietzsche writes, "the severity of the penal code provides an especially significant measure of the degree of effort needed to overcome forgetfulness and to impose a few primitive demands of social existence as *present realities* upon these slaves of momentary affect and desire" (*GM* II, § 3). So, a goal of ascetic mnemnotechnics was the permanent fixation of desire such that no other possible goal could even emerge on the horizon as one worthy of pursuit, much less as a potential rival. Again, Nietzsche's description of the techniques employed to acquire such direction of desire is quite graphic: the penal codes and sagas detail punishments involving flaying or boiling alive, trampling by horses, ripping the criminal body to shreds, piercing the body and cutting out the vital organs while the criminal is alive, stoning, crushing the skull on the wheel, and so on—and all of this in full public view. These practices have the purpose of producing a memory that contains "five or six 'I will not's'' in regard to which one had given one's *promise* so as to participate in the advantages of society" (*GM* II, § 3). This is the brutal basis of promising that Nietzsche highlights, and he thinks it also serves as the primal basis of reasoning: "it was indeed with the aid of this kind of memory that one at last came 'to reason'!" (*GM* II, § 3).

Nietzsche's anticipated overcoming of humanity, which I have suggested might include reassignment of the boundaries of the self and its attendant conception of reason, might also be seen as an overcoming of the torture and cruelty that lie at reason's fundamental basis. In this sense, crossing the boundaries that were erected in forging the ideal of the sovereign subject signals not only a kind of liberation but also, at least potentially, a new kind of compassion or, at least, relief from prospective torture that the further "advancement" of reason might require. Forgetting the subject could entail foregoing the brutality of the practices that served modern processes of subjectification.

IV. The Freedom of Forgetting: Ecstatic Logic and History

Near the end of Derrida's 1968 lecture "The Ends of Man," he identifies the spirit of a disruptive form of critique of the concept of humanism in Nietzsche's idea of active forgetting, linking it to the laughter of the lion in *Thus Spoke Zarathustra* (although Nietzsche himself associates forgetting with the figure of the child). The lion does not violently destroy but, rather, radically forgoes by ferociously laughing at its opposition. Derrida writes: "His laughter then will burst out, directed toward a return which no longer will have the form of the metaphysical repetition of humanism. . . . He will dance, outside the house [of Being, as Heidegger describes it], the *aktive Vergesslichkeit*, the 'active forgetting' and the cruel (*grausam*) feast of which the *Genealogy of Morals* speaks" (Derrida, 1982, p. 136).[7] It is worthwhile to consider this link between *active* forgetting and the kind of ecstasies it provides, the way in which it effects its *outside* once the scope of consideration is expanded beyond the *Genealogy*. Nietzsche's emphasis on the Dionysian and his earlier reflections on history indicate important connections between *forgetting* and the kind of freedom it can provide.

In *The Birth of Tragedy*, Nietzsche associates the Dionysian with the dissolution of boundaries, a forgetting of the self, and the basis for an alternative way of symbolically interpreting what it means to be a human being, to have a human body, and to live a human life. It is interesting to observe how the idea of forgetting the subject is described and elaborated—*das Subjective zu völliger Selbstvergessenheit hinschwindet* (*BT*, § 1). The Dionysian is not simply a breaking of boundaries, an absence of self, or a sheer loss of measure. As Nietzsche identifies the features of subjectivity that are dissolved in Dionysian self-forgetting, he also draws attention to a joining, or union, with something else, to the realization of some other possibility that is not a part of ordinary human subjective experience. Two exemplary passages will have to suffice In the first, Nietzsche indicates that the Dionysian is emblematic of the possibility of forgetting definitive human characteristics, such as walking upright and the use of verbal language: "In song and dance man expresses himself as a member of a higher community; he has forgotten [*verlernt*] how to walk and speak and is on the way toward flying into the air, dancing" (*BT*, § 1). This prospectively connects one to a more-than-human community of other living beings, grounding other ways of meaningfully interacting with them as one shares in their expressive and locomotive possibilities. A second passage suggests a different relation to the human community that we ordinarily take as our own: "The dithyramb is thus essentially different from all other choral odes. The virgins who proceed solemnly to the temple of Apollo, laurel branches in their hands, singing a processional hymn, remain what they are and retain their civic names: the dithyrambic choric is a chorus of the transformed [*Verwandelten*] whose civic past and social status have been totally forgotten" (*BT*, § 8, translation emended). This characterization of Dionysian possibilities envisions forgetting (or forgoing) two further defining characteristics of human community: civic identity and social standing. The Apollinian standpoint strives to *remain* and *retain*; the Dionysian conjures a different set of possible relations among human beings, ones that are not principally organized along Apollinian lines. Thus *forgetting* is not simply a loss. In *The Birth of Tragedy* and in the numerous other discussions of the Dionysian elsewhere in Nietzsche's writings, forgetting is liberating not only because *it frees one from* certain claims and ties but also because *it frees one to* form new associations and different affiliations, to have, gain, or save what would not be had otherwise.

There are two further points about forgetting that I wish to briefly mention, both warranting more elaboration than such a brief paper allows: 1) the relevance of forgetting in the formation of basic concepts that also inform how we conceive of the character and place of logic (anticipating what others have described as "ecstatic logic") and how this supplies important critical tools, and 2) the way in which Nietzsche ties forgetting to the *definition* and *formation* of the subject (i.e., that he does not simply valorize formlessness or meaninglessness). Introduction of these themes provides a basis for the concluding discussions of how Nietzsche considers forgetting as a condition for the possibility of happiness and goodwill toward others and of how forgetting might bear on other issues in moral and social philosophy even if one would rather leave Nietzsche behind.

An ecstatic logic is one that investigates and interrogates or challenges the terms upon which logic unfolds and proceeds. (It is one of the two kinds of critique at issue in Derrida's discussion at the conclusion of "The Ends of Man" [e.g., p. 135]). It questions, or contests, the foundations of logic and the basic concepts upon which it rests. An ecstatic logic does not simply "stand out" of logic in a flight into the irrational or illogical; rather, it is one in which the terms of development, conflict, incorporation are potentially themselves transgressed, reoriented, *in play* (and accounts for Nietzsche's association of forgetting with the child rather than the lion in Z). One "stands out," achieves *ekstasis*, not simply through a rejection of logic but through an interrogation of the foundations of logic (the reflective ground that logic itself might not provide). Overcoming such challenges might result in a redefinition of the very terms upon which logic progresses. This appears to be, at least in part, what Nietzsche has in mind in his conception of the relation of the Apollinian and Dionysian with regard to the dynamic of erecting boundaries and distinctions and then erasing, annihilating, or transgressing them in the course of the Apollinian-Dionysian *agon*.

I have emphasized the connection between the Dionysian and the forgetting of measure in *The Birth of Tragedy*, claiming that it is more than a sheer celebration of liberation from claims of reason, more than just the absence of any boundaries. This point requires further elaboration, which I can only begin here. (For an excellent account of the place of measure in Nietzsche, see Van Tongeren, 2002. One also finds a stunning and sweeping account of the significance of the measureless [*das Masslose*] and ecstatic logic in Sallis, 1991, although I think the relation between *das Masslose* and restraint needs yet more explanation and emphasis.) The selfless Dionysian *appears* to be fully liberated: free from the limitations associated with confinement within boundaries of the modern conception of subjectivity, free of the values and standards that issue from that determination. I write "appears" because this kind of freedom, which I take the early Nietzsche to find rather provocative but fundamentally unsatisfying, seems to be nearly exclusively negative. I think even the early Nietzsche takes it to be also meaningless. To make "the crossing into the abyss" toward which the Dionysian draws us is to completely lose ourselves insofar as we lack any relative relation in light of which the transgression of the boundary has any significance. Without such context it *disables* or *disengages* the norms it breaks, but Nietzsche envisions such crossing as also *enabling* and *engaging* possibilities for reformation and re-creation. Meaningful freedom for Nietzsche has both the negative and this positive aspect.

The formative role of forgetting in the shaping of the subject and its possibilities for happiness and concern for others are described in relation to our desire to remember and memorialize in Nietzsche's *On the Uses and Disadvantages of History for Life* (hereafter *HL*). For now, I wish to focus on the formative process, deferring the rest for discussion below. Although Nietzsche describes the forgetting of the Dionysian in *The Birth of Tragedy* as in opposition to the plastic powers of the Apollinian, in *HL* he describes *forgetting* as intimately tied to the exercise of plastic powers, which he defines as "the capacity to develop out of oneself in one's own way, to transform and incorporate into oneself what is past and foreign, to heal wounds, to replace what has been lost, to recreate broken moulds" (*HL*, p. 62). Too much remembering can become meaningless and stultifying:

> Imagine the extremest possible example of a man who did not possess the power of forgetting at all and who was thus condemned to see everywhere a state of becoming: such a man would no longer believe in his own being, would no longer believe in himself, would see everything flowing asunder in moving points and would lose himself in this stream of becoming. . . . Or, to express my theme even more simply: *there is a degree of sleeplessness, of rumination, of the historical sense, which is harmful and ultimately fatal to the living thing, whether this living thing be a man or a people or a culture.* (*HL*, p. 62)[8]

Forgetting, it seems, is an important condition for experience—important for giving the shape, form, rhythm, texture, and depth that make the seemingly endless stream of possible objects of concern and attention *an* experience, to recall Dewey's famous distinction. This occurs not simply by piling up experiences but also by taking some away, by encouraging some to fade, recede, fall away. Forgetting in this sense *grants* rather than evacuates or eliminates; too much remembering leaves us with experience without pause and strips from us possibilities for action.

What determines the limit, the degree to which forgetting is necessary, the point at which remembering becomes poisonous? After all, too much forgetting is also dangerous. Strength and health are characterized by the capacity to efficiently and creatively incorporate experience; "that which such a nature cannot subdue it knows how to forget" (*HL*, p. 63). This conception of the relation between forgetting and the formation of the subject resonates with Nietzsche's account of "inpsychation" in the dynamic of forgetting and remembering in *GM* II, § 1, which he also compares with processes of nutrition. In *HL* he puts it thus: "a living thing can be healthy, strong and fruitful only when bounded by a horizon; if it is incapable of drawing a horizon around itself, and at the same time too self-centred to enclose its own view within that of another, it will pine away slowly or hasten to its timely end" (*HL*, p. 63). The human needs to be "just as able to forget at the right time as to remember at the right time" (*HL*, p. 63). Nietzsche continues the theme later in the essay when he writes, "Sometimes, however, this same life that requires forgetting demands a temporary suspension of this forgetfulness; it wants to be clear as to how unjust the existence of anything—a privilege, a caste, a dynasty, for example—is, and how greatly this thing deserves to perish. Then its past is regarded critically, then one takes the knife to its roots, then one cruelly tramples over every kind of piety" (HL, p. 76). Critical history is an example of *remembering* at the right time.

Forgetting is important for monumental history, for creating the possibility for some things to stand out as exceptional by letting other things fall away, but it is also important that monumental history not rule or dominate the other modes (antiquarian and critical). It is not simply a willful fictionalizing of all history, for when that happens "the past itself suffers *harm*: whole segments of it are forgotten, despised, and flow away in an uninterrupted colourless flood" (HL, p. 71). What Nietzsche advocates instead is the cultivation of a sense for the "unhistorical." He explains:

> With the word "the unhistorical" I designate the art and power of *forgetting* and of enclosing oneself within a bounded *horizon*; I call "suprahistorical" the powers which lead the eye away from becoming towards that which bestows upon existence the character of the eternal and stable, towards *art* and *religion*. *Science* . . . hates forgetting, which is the death of knowledge, and seeks to abolish all limitations of horizon and launch mankind upon an infinite and unbounded sea of light whose light is knowledge of all becoming. (HL, p. 120)

Thus Nietzsche reaches conclusions about the relation between forgetting and remembering, having limits and being free, and being and becoming that are at odds with much of the tradition and even certain strands of his other thinking. Nietzsche's readers would expect him to praise a perspective that appreciates *becoming* and prioritizes it over *being*, but in *HL* Nietzsche describes how such genuine appreciation is actually thwarted and suggests that our apprehension of being, made possible when we can "pause" experience by letting some of it drop out from its stream, is a condition for the direction of our actions and our assessments of our possibilities. *Too much remembering actually makes us less able to know* or to hold on to experiences such that they can stand out as meaningful. But too much forgetting is also detrimental, particularly in light of our possibilities for freedom. Although forgetting superficially promises freedom, Nietzsche argues that the conditions of meaningful freedom are realized in an interactive dynamic in which remembering and forgetting each play a role in constituting the subject, enable it to incorporate its experience, and reconstitute it in light of what it has been and might possibly become.

I previously noted that in *HL*, Nietzsche further claims that forgetting is important both for our happiness and our ability to attend to the well-being of others. His *On the Uses and Disadvantages of History for Life* opens with a meditation on this theme. Nietzsche writes, "In the case of the smallest or of the greatest happiness, however, it is always the same thing that makes happiness happiness:

the ability to forget. . . . He who cannot sink down on the threshold of the moment and forget all the past . . . will never know what happiness is—*worse, he will never do anything to make others happy*" (*HL*, p. 62; my emphasis). I take Nietzsche to mean that our happiness is not achieved simply by balancing out pleasures and pains. The sheer joy we take in the affiliation with loved ones, for example, is not founded upon balancing or canceling out the hardships we have also shared with them. Our joy in companionship does not simply bubble up occasionally out of a context in which we equalize and then exceed the despair we have also shared. Joy rushes out from a moment when suffering is *forgotten*, and in that moment it is as though our pains never existed at all. Our pleasures and pains differ not only quantitatively, or in degrees of intensity, but also qualitatively, with differences in kind. Some pains that we suffer simply cannot be canceled or balanced by past or future pleasures—the death of a child, the witnessing of torture and humiliation of others, the long slow pain of debilitating illness. Were it not for *forgetting*, joy following such experiences would be simply impossible. Forgetting is significant for our attention to the happiness of others, too, Nietzsche claims, and it is this relevance to the possibility of community that I want to briefly highlight as one of the ways in which Nietzsche's meditations on forgetting might be relevant to other concerns in moral and social philosophy.

V. Forgetting Ourselves and Saving Community

Insofar as *forgetting the subject* potentially supplies us with different possibilities for conceptualizing human subjectivity and individuality, as argued above, it may be relevant to resolving certain tensions in moral and social philosophy that pit the interests of the self and its autonomy against the interests of others and their claims on us for assistance and nurturance. It might very well be that different possibilities for conceiving and resolving these tensions open when seen in light of a different conceptual basis of subjectivity. We find similar relations between alternative conceptions of selves and different social and moral possibilities, for example, in care ethics and its conception of the relational self, and the compassionate basis of Buddhist ethics and its "no-self" model. What different possible ethics might we be able to conceive in saving the forgetting of subjectivity?

Forgetting the self in the ways I have suggested above might soften the rigid boundaries of the dominant view of the self and provide more porous access to a shared basis of human subjectivity and recognition of fragility. For a possible connection between such a subject and an ethics of generosity, see Cixous and Clément (1986; see also Schrift, 1995, pp. 82–101). Although I cannot engage this literature in this paper, I do think that the nature of forgetting that happens in the alternative logic of the economy of the gift, as it is described, needs further exploration. The character of such forgetting is not fully developed in the work of Cixous and Clément, and it is toward such a project that I think Nietzsche's work might make useful contributions.

In his book on the phenomenology of remembering, Casey (1987) argues that an emphasis on the overcoming of forgetfulness in the modern tradition results in an even greater forgetfulness (or marginalization) of remembering than does forgetting itself. But perhaps the diminution of forgetting is tied to the problem of failures of recognition and granting (and hence to coping and understanding) of the fragility of human existence. Lest we think we have passed through the age of cruelty (in the formation of mnemonics), we might give further consideration to the idea that the marginalization of forgetting in the conceptualization of the significance of remembering is also tied to how we conceive the objects of our concern (human and otherwise) in terms of control, domination, power, which Heidegger and many others explore. Our conceptions of forgetting bear on these discussions, which have further implications and applications in our moral and social philosophies.

Casey also emphasizes the significance of remembering for building community and notices that the disappearance of remembering demotes the role of elders (Casey, 1987, p. 7). Drawing on the ideas elaborated here, we might also say that the marginalization of forgetting also demotes the value of the elderly in our society. They are forgotten, in part, because it is believed they have nothing valuable to contribute (inferior as "storage" devices to books, movies, CDs, etc.), and because they are feared as the emblems of forgetting. In a social context in which a characteristic of human existence is defined in terms of being an efficient *manager* of memory storage, the sluggishness or inability of the elderly to engage in memory retrieval results in a perceived *loss of humanity*. If forgetting is replaced at the center of our conception of humanity, its appearance in our everyday lives and in the macrorhythms of human life more generally might appear less monstrous and afford different possibilities for how we relate to persons who appear to have a *surplus* of forgetting.

Nietzsche's praise of forgetting should by no means be taken as a dismissal or denigration of remembering (notice the point about critical history and the formation of boundaries and horizons that the *dynamic* of remembering and forgetting makes possible). As I have argued, forgetting the subject is not simply a celebration of mindlessness or oblivion. Nietzsche's emphasis on the activity of forgetting and its implied interactive context (as a formative force shaping the individual, analogous to the formative forces of the Apollinian and Dionysian in *BT*) suggests that the forgetfulness of forgetting, the marginalization of forgetting bodes ill for remembering, too. Delving a bit further into the analogy indicated in the Apollinian and Dionysian in *BT* is a worthy point of departure. Just as forgetting the Dionysian resulted, for Nietzsche, in the deformity of the Apollinian, so too does the forgetting of forgetting result in the transmogrification of remembering. Our conceptualization of these two possibilities is intimately related, and these conceptual formations give shape to and organize our practices in the world, thereby giving structure to how we relate to each other and other objects of concern.

Works Cited

Acampora, C. D. 2004. "On Sovereignty and Overhumanity: What It Matters How We Read *Genealogy* II:2." *International Studies in Philosophy* 36/3: 127–145.

Casey, E. S. 1987. *Remembering: A Phenomenological Study*. Bloomington: Indiana University Press.

Cixous, H., and C. Clément. 1986. *The Newly Born Woman*. Translated by Betsy Wing. Minneapolis: University of Minnesota Press.

Deleuze, G. 1983. *Nietzsche and Philosophy*. Translated by Hugh Tomlinson. New York: Columbia University Press.

———, and F. Guattari. 1983. *Anti-Oedipus: Capitalism and Schizophrenia*. Translated by R. Hurley, M. Seem, and H. Lane. Minneapolis: University of Minnesota Press.

Derrida, J. 1982. *Margins of Philosophy*. Translated by Alan Bass. Chicago: University of Chicago Press.

Heidegger, M. 1996. *Being and Time*. Translated by Joan Stambaugh. Albany: State University of New York Press.

Kofman, S. 1993. *Nietzsche and Metaphor*. Translated by Duncan Large. Stanford, California: Stanford University Press.

Nietzsche, F. 1872, 1876. *The Birth of Tragedy Out of the Spirit of Music*. In *The Birth of Tragedy* and *The Case of Wagner*. Translated by Walter Kaufmann. New York: Vintage Books.

———. 1969. *On the Genealogy of Morals* (1887). In *On the Genealogy of Morals* and *Ecce Homo*. Translated by Walter Kaufmann and R. J. Hollingdale. New York: Vintage Books.

———. 1983. *On the Uses and Disadvantages of History for Life* (1874). Translated by R. J. Hollingdale. Cambridge: Cambridge University Press.

———. 1883–1885. *Thus Spoke Zarathustra*. In *The Portable Nietzsche*. Edited and translated by Walter Kaufmann. New York: Viking Press.

Parkes, G. 1994. *Composing the Soul*. Chicago: University of Chicago Press.

Plato. 1969. *Republic*. Translated by P. Shorey. *Plato in Twelve Volumes*, vols. 5 and 6. Cambridge, MA: Harvard University Press.

Sallis, J. 1991. *Crossings: Nietzsche and the Space of Tragedy*. Chicago: University of Chicago Press.

Schopenhauer, A. 1966. *World as Will and Representation*. Translated by E. F. J. Payne. Mineola, NY: Dover Publications, Inc.

Schrift, Alan D. 1995. *Nietzsche's French Legacy: A Genealogy of Poststructuralism*. London and New York: Routledge.

Seidel, G. J. 1966. *The Crisis of Creativity*. South Bend, IN: University of Notre Dame Press.

Van Tongeren, P. 2002. "Nietzsche's Greek Measure." *Journal of Nietzsche Studies* 24: 5–24.

Notes

1. For translations of Nietzsche's texts, I use Hollingdale's *HL*, Kaufmann's *BT* and *Z*, and Kaufmann and Hollingdale's *GM*, unless otherwise indicated.

2. The famous ending of the *Republic* is worth recalling: "And so, Glaucon, the tale was saved, as the saying is, and was not lost. And it will save us if we believe it,

and we shall safely cross the River of Lethe, and keep our soul unspotted from the world. But if we are guided by me we shall believe that the soul is immortal and capable of enduring all extremes of good and evil, and so we shall hold ever to the upward way and pursue righteousness with wisdom always and ever, that we may be dear to ourselves and to the gods both during our sojourn here and when we receive our reward, as the victors in the games go about to gather in theirs. And thus both here and in that journey of a thousand years, whereof I have told you, we shall fare well [*eu prattōmen*]." In his discussion of nobility as it relates to its essential activity (in contrast to the *reactivity* of slave morality) in *GM* I, § 10, Nietzsche writes, "they likewise knew, as rounded men replete with energy and therefore *necessarily* active, that happiness should not be sundered from action—being active was with them necessarily a part of happiness (whence *eu prattein* takes its origin)—all very much the opposite of 'happiness' at the level of the impotent, the oppressed, and those in whom poisonous and inimical feelings are festering, with whom it appears as essentially narcotic, drug, rest, peace, 'sabbath,' slackening of tension and relaxing of limbs, in short *passively*." The association in Nietzsche of forgetting with a kind of activity (*GM* II, § 1), one crucial for happiness (e.g., *HL*, p. 4 and *GS*, "Jokes," § 4) echoes in this passage.

3. Forgetting is not the only process that has been rendered passive. Edward Casey (1987) explores how the contemporary conceptualization of memory as instrumental and as part of an essentially passive process has its roots in the philosophies of Plato (where remembering becomes instrumentalized) and Aristotle (where it becomes construed as something passive). Nietzsche's point seems to be that both forces, remembering and forgetting, are active and involved in an interactive dynamic that facilitates or grounds our distinguishing, valuing, or coming to know things.

4. Ultimately, Heidegger's view represents quite a departure from the Platonic sketch offered above. Insofar as Heidegger thinks that truth is a relationship and an activity of disclosure, remembering what has been forgotten is a way of relating to things in the world rather than the retrieval of lost knowledge.

5. Those interested in reviewing a collection of the few occasional remarks about forgetting that are made by modern philosophers in particular might find Seidel 1966, pp. 81–98, of some use. Seidel's work on the nature of mind and consciousness is now rather dated, but his general thesis about the relation between forgetting as providing a reservoir of resources for creativity and his historical observations might be helpful to those pursuing relevant topics. There is also some brief discussion of forgetting in the history of philosophy in the context of a more elaborate account of the history of remembering in Casey 1987. I make only a few references to this work below, but it certainly would repay further study for those interested in the themes of this paper.

6. Deleuze (1983) argues that Nietzsche distinguishes forces only in relation to quantity and that active and reactive forces differ with regard to whether they obey or command in relation to each other (e.g., pp. 39–40). Consciousness is the work of reactive force: "Consciousness merely expresses the relation of certain reactive forces to the active forces which dominate them. Consciousness is essentially reactive; this is why we do not know what a body can do, or what activity it is capable

of (*GS*, § 354). And what is said of consciousness must also be said of memory and habit" (p. 41). In contrast, "The body's active forces make it a self and define the self as superior and astonishing: 'A most powerful being, an unknown sage—he is called the Self. He inhabits your body, he is your body' (*Z* I, 'Of the Despisers of the Body,' p. 62)" (Deleuze, p. 42). If we map these to Nietzsche's discussion of the role of memory in the creation of consciousness, *remembering* is cast as a *reactive* force while *forgetting* is the *active* force that is responsible for the creation of the subject more generally. In *Anti-Oedipus*, Deleuze and Guattari offer some further elaboration of this idea of the active forces forming the self, particularly in relation to forgetting when they attribute to Nietzsche the idea that (in relation to the creation of the body as specified and articulated in terms of its parts, organs, and functions, and therefore accountable in a system of desire and exchange) "it is a matter of creating a memory for man; and man, who was constituted by means of an active faculty of forgetting (*oubli*), by means of a repression of biological memory, must create an *other* memory, one that is collective, a memory of words (*paroles*) and no longer a memory of things, a memory of signs and no longer of effects. This organization, which traces its signs directly on the body, constitutes a system of cruelty, a terrible alphabet" (Deleuze and Guattari 1983, pp. 144–145). What I take this to mean is that our sense of ourselves as human beings, as having specifically human bodies and being specific human individuals, stems from actively forgetting many facets and aspects of our bodies that we share with other nonhuman animals. There is a process of carving up the body into parts that is necessary for fitting them into a system of significances and meanings of what constitutes our humanity and to what we would do well to aspire (Deleuze and Guattari, p. 143).

7. Derrida's lecture begins with a call for a more attentive history of the development of concepts, and he considers in greater detail the development of the idea of "the human" (or, the concept "man") in phenomenology, particularly in Heidegger's works. He distinguishes two ways to critically evaluate and challenge philosophical frameworks that supply the basis for conceptual economies (concepts that are basic for others and are crucially interrelated). One critical approach works from "within," attempting to open and expand the existing framework, and the other approach works from "without" by seeking to abandon the rejected framework and to effect a complete and total dissociation from it. Both risk failure insofar as the first may well remain blind to what lies outside of itself and which could nevertheless be useful for the expansion and change it hopes to bring about. The second critical approach risks failure insofar as it insists upon its absolute distinction to such an extent that it might not recognize essential similarities that it holds and adopts rather naively and might not subject those features to a thorough-going critique (Derrida 1982, p. 135). Derrida associates Heidegger's work with the first kind of strategy and his own contemporary French thinkers with the second. He appears to include Nietzsche in the second group as well, and it is at this point that he briefly mentions Nietzsche's idea of active forgetting as described above.

8. Some commentators and persons who asked questions when I gave earlier versions of this paper at conference meetings objected that Nietzsche does not really praise forgetting, recalling that as Nietzsche writes in *HL*, *even* animals forget;

what distinguishes us as humans is that we remember. I shall not address whether this is literally true since it is not relevant to the present discussion or the broader question of whether it is good *for us* to remember so much as we do, or to prize memory of a certain sort as highly as we do and for the reasons that we do. It is clear from this passage in *HL* that Nietzsche thinks that forgetting is essential to vitality. Others further object that if Nietzsche has in mind a renewal of forgetting it must be a kind that is different from that of animals. This also strikes me as unsupported. While many readers might be keen to distinguish human beings as essentially different from all "other animals," Nietzsche is not. I am not making a wholly reductive claim here—I am not saying that for Nietzsche we are *just like all the other animals*. Such a claim cannot be true if one thinks that "all the other animals" as a contrast term with "human beings" has no meaningful reference. All animals, Nietzsche seems to claim, need to forget in order to live: they need to do this in order to function biologically (processes of digestion conceived as forgetting) and in order to have any possible conscious psychic life (processes of "inpsychation" mentioned above). Many specific animals may not have psychic lives, and it might be that no other animals have cultivated the powers of memory that human beings wrought in the processes of moralization. These speculations and qualifications, however, do not imply that human forgetting is qualitatively different from the kind of forgetting vital to all animal life.

Part Two

Laughing at the Margins
Nietzsche's Tragic/Comic Sense of Life

Chapter Three

Suffering in Nietzsche's Philosophy

Kathleen Marie Higgins

Nietzsche is a puzzle. Anyone who sustains an interest in Nietzsche's thought has found inconsistencies in his statements. Famously, Karl Jaspers insists that an interpreter of Nietzsche must begin by finding the contradiction to each assertion he appears to make. To make sense of Nietzsche's philosophy as a whole, an interpreter must construct some conception of his central concerns as a basis for determining what he really thought about any particular issue. Many philosophical commentators develop this touchstone by attempting to ascertain which propositions were most central to Nietzsche and giving weight to his various remarks in accordance with the degree of support they give to these central claims. While this strategy enables one to draw conclusions about Nietzsche's views, it does not necessarily go to the heart of his thought. Analyzing Nietzsche in terms of some philosophical motivation or other is not really an interpretation of Nietzsche's thought unless it resonates with his own philosophical motivations. And these motivations are not purely abstract. Nietzsche's philosophical motivations are of a piece with his psychological motivations.

Nietzsche's psychological motivations, however, are not straightforward. This is so whether one seeks them in his biography or restricts oneself to evidence from his published writings. Biographically, one can observe that this bombastic author, renowned for such bon mots as "God is dead" and "life is will to power," was mild-mannered and exceedingly polite. Meta von Salis claims that he was "shy about offending others" (Janz 2, p. 530), and Krell and Bates observe that "Nietzsche's letters to friends and family, urging many of them *not* to read his books, were not disingenuous" (Krell and Bates, p. 196). Mrs. Emily Fynn, an acquaintance he knew to be a devout Catholic, reports that he had tears in his eyes when he asked that she not read his books since they were bound to hurt her feelings (Gilman, p. 195). Nietzsche's writings present a parallel inconsistency. He urges that what is falling, one should push (Z III:12, § 20), and yet he has scruples about laughing at Don Quixote (GM III, § 6).

Nietzsche has a reputation for being insensitive to human suffering. I will argue that this view is misguided and that sensitivity to suffering is the presupposition of Nietzsche's work throughout his career. He is reputed to be insensitive because he does not object to pain, at times seeming to encourage it, and because he seems to reject sympathetic responses to suffering. But Nietzsche thinks that pain cannot be eliminated from the human condition and that some of the strategies humanity has developed for dealing with suffering, such as pity, actually intensify it. His own approach to the theme of suffering is to accept it as playing an indispensable role within the economy of human life. He believes that the mode of acceptance that he recommends is healthier than that advocated by traditional Western morality. His strategy for accepting suffering is to encompass it toward an attitude of joy within life, as opposed to the otherworldly approach that treats suffering as the price of happiness in the hereafter.

I. The Quest for a Theodicy

Nietzsche's many harsh statements notwithstanding, his philosophical trajectory revolves around his efforts to come to grips with the reality of suffering. He was already concerned with the problem of evil while a schoolboy, as his reminiscences in On the Genealogy of Morals reveal.

> In fact, the problem of the origin of evil pursued me even as a boy of thirteen: at an age in which you have "Half childish trifles, half God in your heart," I devoted to it my first childish literary trifle, my first philosophical effort—and as for the "solution" of the problem I posed at that time, well, I gave the honor to God, as was only fair, and made him the father of evil. (GM, Preface, § 3)

Fanciful as this resolution of the problem of evil may be, it foreshadows the kind of theodicy that the adult Nietzsche attempted, from his first book-length publication to the writing of his final sane year. Nietzsche rejected theodicies that attempted to eliminate the problem of evil by definition. One example of this is St. Augustine's argument that evil is only the absence of good, and hence not one of God's creations. Another, from Nietzsche's view, is the argument that suffering in this world is of little concern by comparison with the more important life that begins after death. By contrast, Nietzsche sought to come to terms with what seems objectionable in life not by defining it away but by embracing it as an essential element within the whole.

I will describe this strategy as Nietzsche's aesthetic approach to theodicy. It is aesthetic because it involves interpreting suffering as an element in a larger whole, much as the artistic element is interpreted as an element essential to the larger organism of the artwork. It is also aesthetic because it depends on a par-ticular way of perceiving. The significance of suffering, on Nietzsche's approach, is vastly different depending on whether one perceives it as a blemish that is alien to the sufferer's life or as an element that is essential to the structure and devel-opment of that life as a whole.

Nietzsche's first book, *The Birth of Tragedy*, presents exactly this kind of analysis. In examining why the Athenians developed the artistic institution of tragedy, Nietzsche argues that they were attempting to respond to the judgment of the Greek demigod Silenus that for human beings, "What is best of all is ut-terly beyond your reach: not to be born, not to *be*, to be *nothing*. But the second best for you is—to die soon" (*BT*, § 3). The tragic plays of the ancient Athenians consistently raised the issue of the value of life in the face of human vulnerability to suffering. The solution these tragedies offered their audiences was to remind them that they already valued being part of the powerful flux of life so much that they took it to be worth the price of admission.

Artistically, this effect was achieved by music, the Dionysian element in tragedy. Caught up in the musical atmosphere, the audience felt a sense of one-ness with each other and the entire world. Audience members recognized their participation in a thrilling dynamism that transcended their individual persons. The audience ideally already experienced this Dionysian state before encounter-ing the Apollonian aspect of the play, the enacted story of hideous suffering. In the sway of the Dionysian vision, one came to recognize that one's sufferings as an individual do not matter because one's true nature—one's being a part of the vibrant whole—transcends one's individuality. Nietzsche concludes that a transformation of one's vision of oneself and of suffering is the only successful theodicy: "It is only as an *aesthetic phenomenon* that existence and the world are eternally *justified*" (*BT*, § 5).

Although Nietzsche later finds fault with his first book, he did not aban-don the general form of theodicy employed in *The Birth of Tragedy*, redemption of suffering by interpreting it as integral to the flux of life as a whole. This is the type of theodicy provided by his later "doctrine" of eternal recurrence, which interprets time as cyclical and repeating.

Nietzsche's first published formulation of his idea of eternal recurrence, in *The Gay Science*, makes explicit his concern with the suffering involved in life.

> What if some day or night a demon were to steal after you into your lone-liest loneliness and say to you: "This life as you now live it and have lived it, you will have to live once more and innumerable times more; and there will be nothing new in it, but every pain and every joy and every thought and sigh and everything unutterably small or great in your life will have to return to you, all in the same succession and sequence. . . ."
>
> Would you not throw yourself down and gnash your teeth and curse the demon who spoke thus? Or have you once experienced a tremendous moment when you would have answered him, "You are a god and never

have I heard anything more divine." If this thought gained possession of you, it would change you as you are or perhaps crush you. The question in each and every thing, "Do you desire this once more and innumerable times more?" would lie upon your actions as the greatest weight. Or how well disposed would you have to become to yourself and to life *to crave nothing more fervently* than this ultimate confirmation and seal? (*GS*, § 341)

Significantly, Nietzsche does not imply here that accepting suffering is easy. Rhetorically, he indicates his expectation that most people's initial reaction to the recurrence of life would be horror, presumably because the repetition of one's suffering would be entailed. But he goes on to suggest the possibility of an attitude that valued life's joys so thoroughly that suffering would be accepted along with it. From this perspective suffering is no longer the focus, but instead, the delight of being alive, which by the way necessarily includes suffering.

Nietzsche claims that the idea of eternal recurrence is "the fundamental conception" of *Thus Spoke Zarathustra* (*EH* III: Z, § 1). His protagonist, Zarathustra describes the implications of this vision for an understanding of suffering in "The Drunken Song," the book's penultimate section.

Have you ever said Yes to a single joy? O my friends, then you said Yes too to *all* woe. All things are entangled, ensnared, enamored; if ever you wanted one thing twice, if ever you said, "You please me, happiness! Abide, moment!" then you wanted *all* back. All anew, all eternally, all entangled, ensnared, enamored—oh, then you *loved* the world. Eternal ones, love it eternally and evermore; and to woe too, you say: go, but return! *For all joy wants—eternity.* (Z IV, § 19)

Even in the final creative year of his life, 1888, Nietzsche continues to assert the importance of eternal recurrence (*TI* XI, § 4). In *Ecce Homo*, his autobiography, he explicitly links eternal recurrence to his understanding of the Dionysian. The psychological problem of Zarathustra, according to Nietzsche, is

. . . how he that has the hardest, most terrible insight into reality, that has thought "the most abysmal idea," nevertheless does not consider it an objection to existence, not even to its eternal recurrence—but rather one reason more for being himself the eternal Yes to all things, "the tremendous, unbounded saying Yes and Amen.". . . *But this is the concept of Dionysus once again.* (*EH* III: Z, § 4)

Similarly, Nietzsche reaffirms the connection of eternal recurrence with the Greek tragic vision in *Twilight of the Idols*, another work of 1888. After referring to the Dionysian mysteries, Nietzsche asks,

What was it that the Hellene guaranteed himself by means of these mysteries? *Eternal* life, the eternal return of life; the future promised and hallowed in the past; the triumphant Yes to life beyond all death and change; *true* life as the over-all continuation of life through procreation, through the mysteries of sexuality. For the Greeks the *sexual* symbol was therefore the venerable symbol par excellence. . . .

This symbol, Nietzsche continues, addresses the problem of suffering and transfigures it.

In the doctrine of the mysteries, *pain* is pronounced holy: the pangs of the woman giving birth hallow all pain; all becoming and growing—all that guarantees a future—involves pain. That there may be the eternal joy of creating, that the will to life may eternally affirm itself, the agony of the woman giving birth *must* also be there eternally. (*TI* XI, § 4)

Nietzsche explicitly connects eternal recurrence and the transfiguration so frequently that suffering must surely be among his primary concerns. One reason this is seldom acknowledged may be that he focuses mainly on individual, personal suffering, not that of humanity more generally. Except when he is discussing the Greeks, and then of necessity speaking of something outside his immediate experience, Nietzsche's published formulations of eternal recurrence are rather introverted. As the parable of the demon indicates, his idea of eternal recurrence raises a personal question (though one relevant to any particular reader): "Do you love your life enough to will its eternal recurrence?"

Psychological suffering appears to be paradigmatic for Nietzsche. In fact, he even suggests that "real" suffering is an antidote to the fantasized mental misery so common in his time.

Perhaps there is nothing that separates men or ages more profoundly than a difference in their knowledge of misery: misery of the soul as well as the body. Regarding the latter we moderns may well be, all of us, in spite of our frailties and infirmities, tyros who rely on fantasies, for lack of any ample firsthand experience—compared to the age of fear, the longest of all ages, in which individuals had to protect themselves. In those days, one received ample training in bodily torments and deprivations and one understood even a certain cruelty against oneself and a voluntary habituation to pain as a necessary means of self-preservation. . . .

There is a recipe against pessimistic philosophers and the excessive sensitivity that seems to me the real "misery of the present age"—but this recipe may sound too cruel and might itself be counted among the signs that lead people to judge that "existence is something evil." Well, the recipe against this "misery" is: *misery*. (*GS*, § 48)

Real afflictions of the body strike Nietzsche as a welcome alternative to agitations of the high-strung mind.

The inward focus of Nietzsche's account of suffering may partially explain why many consider him unfeeling. Such readers perhaps expect a treatment of suffering to deal with the problems of humanity as a whole. Nietzsche's rejection of pity toward the multitudes reinforces the idea that he does not concern himself much with humanity's pain. Nietzsche's interpretation of pity is one aspect of his infamous attack on his Christian moral upbringing. His denunciation of Christian moral platitudes such as "love thy neighbor" do not undercut the impression that his reflections on suffering tend to be formulated from the first person point of view, but his analysis once again reveals his distress over psychological suffering and the dismissal of earthly suffering as unimportant in light of one's eternal destination.

The preface to the second edition of *The Birth of Tragedy* summarizes some of the grounds for Nietzsche's opposition to Christian morality on these and other matters. Nietzsche describes Christianity as "the most prodigal elaboration of the moral theme to which humanity has ever been subjected."

> Christianity was from the beginning, essentially and fundamentally, life's nausea and disgust with life, merely concealed behind, masked by, dressed up as, faith in "another" or "better" life. . . . For, confronted with morality (especially Christian, or unconditional, morality), life *must* continually and inevitably be in the wrong, because life is something essentially amoral—and eventually, crushed by the weight of contempt and the eternal No, life *must* then be felt to be unworthy of desire and altogether worthless. (*BT*, Preface, § 5)

Nietzsche claims here that Christianity, and any similarly unconditional morality, must inevitably fail to provide a theodicy justifying the entire texture of life. Such moralities inevitably find fault with life because suffering does not bear any direct relationships to desert. The theodicy offered by Christianity appeals to an afterlife as a *deus ex machina*—the afterlife is brought in to resolve a problem left unsolved without such an intervention. This, according to Nietzsche, is to abandon the quest to find meaning in life in the face of suffering, since meaning is deferred to existence outside this world.

In *On the Genealogy of Morals* Nietzsche analyzes Christian morality as characterized by *ressentiment*, a desire on the part of those who are suffering to blame and to inflict suffering in recompense. Christian morality attempts to rationalize suffering by seeking someone to blame—evildoers, who deserve damnation, which they will receive if unrepentant, in contrast to the innocent, who will be rewarded in a future life. More insidiously, Christianity encourages its followers to find the evildoer in themselves, thus inducing them to wallow in guilt and fear of retribution unless they throw themselves on the mercy of God (or more accurately, the clergy).

Christianity's approach to suffering is barbaric, according to Nietzsche. It inspires terrifying emotions in its adherents, which they will act desperately to expiate. Moreover, God himself is the inventor of hell, a site of eternal torture, which is interpreted as the ultimate destination of those who remain insubordinate to him. Worst of all, the Christian doctrine that the crucifixion occurred as atonement for sin suggests that God enjoys cruel spectacle, so much that he accepts the broken, bleeding body and life of Jesus as repayment for humanity's faults. God is a ruthless accountant, adamantly insisting on what is owed him and willing to accept a payment of blood.

Nietzsche's opposition to Christian morality again shows him to be concerned with suffering, in this case to resist the suffering he claims Christianity brings into the world, again primarily inward suffering. *On the Genealogy of Morals* analyzes the mechanisms that Christian morality exploits, all of which increase suffering: its exploitation of its adherents' self-doubts and its encouragement of harsh judgments against others as a means to self-esteem; its incitement of bad conscience in those who are already suffering; and its "explanation" of personal suffering in terms of guilt, and the ascetic practices it encourages. Nietzsche also stresses the sufferer's interpretive perspective on his or her own life, a perspective that Christianity manipulates so as to heighten the person's suffering.

Even when Nietzsche does consider how one should respond toward others who are suffering, he similarly focuses on inner life and interpretive orientation. In accounting for pity, for example, he asks what pity does to the parties involved—the one who pities and the one who is pitied. His conclusion is that pity does not ameliorate suffering but instead increases the amount of suffering in the world (see *AC*, § 7). Nietzsche recommends that one adopt not pity but his own brand of justice, which itself involves taking a particular interpretive view. In what follows, I will consider his views on pity and justice further, for they reveal his strongly aesthetic orientation toward the suffering of others, as well as oneself, and a more sympathetic outlook than that with which he is usually associated.

II. Perspectivism, Vengeance, and Justice

Nietzsche's analysis of morality, pity, and justice depend on perspectivism. Nietzsche's perspectivism has often been considered an epistemological or a metaphysical theory, but rarely has its aesthetic character been emphasized. It is, however, a thoroughly aesthetic theory, insofar as aesthetics is concerned with what and how one perceives. The optic through which one views something, the stance one takes toward it, one's relative position— these features of perception all figure in what one can come to know or understand about it, according to Nietzsche. One cannot remove oneself from all perspectives, nor can one observe from all perspectives at once. One can, at most, travel through a variety of perspectives, refining one's judgments in light of one's diverse experiences.

Nietzsche's perspectivism figures in his account of justice, which he often associates with revenge, and his account utilizes a notion of stance that is akin to the model of aesthetic distance. If the aesthetic character of Nietzsche's outlook has not been recognized, I think that a large part of the reason is that Nietzsche's analyses of justice and mercy are complex, if not outright contradictory. He rails against the conception of punishment, and yet he complains that the modern tendency toward mercifulness is a sign of cultural decadence. He denounces social movements bent on justice for all, and yet he himself advocates "a new justice." His Zarathustra contends that "a little revenge is more human than no revenge" (Z I, § 19) but simultaneously "That man be delivered from revenge—that is for me the bridge to the highest hope, and a rainbow after long storms" (Z II, § 7). At times Nietzsche suggests that the motive behind those who demand justice is revenge, but his Zarathustra asks, "Where is that justice that is love with open eyes?" (Z I, § 19).

We can begin to sort through Nietzsche's notions of justice and vengeance by noting that he frequently distinguishes between what passes for justice in the traditional morality or modern political world and justice of a different, more legitimate, sort. We might call this the distinction between "justice" and Nietzschean justice. When Zarathustra itemizes the range of prevailing views on justice, he is elaborating on theories of "justice."

Fundamental to "justice," in Nietzsche's view, is the motivation of revenge. Revenge, as Nietzsche sees it, is a symptom of spiritual poisoning, as well as an incitement to further decay. His focus is concern to eliminate the grip of revenge as a motive. Its vindictive motivation is a central reason for Nietzsche's attack on "justice" and those who promote it, and an important ground for his opposition to traditional morality. In a passage titled "The Revenge against the Spirit and Other Ulterior Motives of Morality," he remarks,

> There is a human being who has turned out badly, who does not have enough spirit to be able to enjoy it but just enough education to realize this. . . . Such a person who is fundamentally ashamed of his existence . . . eventually ends up in a state of habitual revenge, will to revenge.
>
>   What do you suppose he finds necessary, absolutely necessary, to give himself in his own eyes the appearance of superiority over more spiritual people and to attain the pleasure of an *accomplished revenge* at least in his imagination? Always morality; you can bet on that. Always big moral words. Always the rub-a-dub of justice, wisdom, holiness, virtue. . . . (*GS*, § 359)

Nietzsche considers morality to be a mode of imaginary revenge. The moralist gets revenge on someone who might otherwise be envied by calling that person's gratifying actions "sins" and that person "immoral." These characterizations are imposed by imagination. Pronouncement of moral judgment, even without external sanction, is a gratifying act of revenge.

Significantly, "justice" and morality accomplish revenge by means of a decision regarding how one views another. The decision, in both cases, is motivated by a desire to avenge oneself, and the vision of the other is, accordingly, uglified, denigrated. "Justice," so motivated, is inherently unjust, for it adopts an interpretive mode that is always at the expense of the person observed.

By contrast, Zarathustra's "justice that is love with open eyes" interprets differently.

> Those who are evil or unhappy and the exceptional human being—all these should also have their philosophy, their good right, their sunshine! What is needful is not pity for them. We must learn to abandon this arrogant fancy, however long humanity has hitherto spent learning and practicing it. What these people need is not confession, conjuring of souls, and forgiveness of sins; what is needful is a new justice! . . . The antipodes, too, have the right to exist. There is yet another world to be discovered—and more than one. Embark, philosophers! (*GS*, § 289)

Nietzschean justice, too, involves a particular optic. It depends on adopting a nonmoralistic perspective on a person and that person's behavior. Justice, in effect, involves seeing without being judgmental in a moral sense, that is, without rendering the verdict that the person is "good" or "evil."

So understood, Nietzschean justice involves an orientation that resembles the stance of the traditional aesthetic viewpoint. The traditional aesthetic viewpoint is contrasted with a practical one in which one's projects and purposes direct one's interpretation of what one observes. In the "disinterested" aesthetic viewpoint, one contemplates without attending to the potential for one's personal gain. In Nietzschean justice, similarly, one observes the other person's behavior without the interference of one's ulterior motives, in particular, one's motives toward revenge. The standpoint of Nietzschean justice differs from the Kantian aesthetic orientation, however, in that Nietzsche explicitly builds emotional engagement into his concept. Love, in some sense, still shapes one's interpretation.

What kind of love does Nietzsche have in mind? María Lugónes' notion of loving perception might assist us here (Lugónes, p. 4). Lugónes contrasts her view of loving perception with Marilyn Frye's characterization of arrogant perception, which Frye sees as the typical orientation of those who feel superior to others, particularly on the basis of group membership (Frye, p. 73). For example, someone who dismisses the views of a member of a minority group just because of that membership perceives that person arrogantly. Lugónes considers her attitude toward her own mother, and she concludes that she has been guilty of arrogant perception. She has tended to take her mother's concerns less seriously than her own, dismissing her mother's viewpoint as old-fashioned, rather ignorant, and stuck in the values of the old country.

Lugónes goes on to characterize an alternative mode of perceiving, which she describes as "loving perception." Loving perception involves imaginatively embracing another's worldview and attempting to make sense of that person's viewpoint, in effect, from the inside out. By imagining her mother's viewpoint with sympathy, Lugónes becomes a "fellow-traveler" with her mother. This does not, according to Lugónes, amount to abandoning her own orientation in favor of her mother's. But it does involve extending the boundaries of her orientation to allow for the possibility of "visiting" her mother's world to some degree. Loving perception, according to Lugónes, undercuts a sense of absolute distinction between one's own outlook and that of another. If vindictiveness requires such a distinction, then presumably the "world-traveling" involved in loving perception should help to undercut it.

In light of Nietzsche's bombastic authorial personality, it may seem surprising to suggest that his conception of justice resembles the loving perception that Lugónes recommends. And yet I think this is precisely what Nietzsche attempts in much of his work. What is he calling for if not world-traveling in the passage cited above when he pronounces, "Embark, philosophers!"?

Certainly, world-traveling is the aim of many of Nietzsche's philosophical projects. *The Birth of Tragedy* attempts to enter imaginatively the world of the ancient Athenians in order to see why tragedy mattered to them. In *The Gay Science,* along with discussions of art and the artistry of world-making, we see Nietzsche attempting to make sense of the outlook of the women in his society, suggesting to his largely male audience that these women's perspectives are often in striking contrast to what they suppose (see Higgins, pp. 73–89). The selection of the Persian prophet Zarathustra as his spokesperson, I submit, similarly involves Nietzsche's effort to imagine his way into the worldview of this early proponent of morality (see Higgins, pp. 151–166). What Nietzsche rejects, consistently, is the notion that one can be so disinterested as to have no personal investment at all, and he contends that we should be suspicious of anyone who claims to have such a viewpoint. But he considers it possible to traverse many states of mind and thus to transcend a narrow sense of the limits of oneself in favor of some degree of identification with others (See *BT,* §§ 7–10 and *GS,* Preface, § 3).

The perspectival orientation that Nietzsche contrasts with his own brand of justice, pity, can be seen as a matter of arrogant perception on Nietzsche's analysis (see *GS,* § 278). He explicitly opposes pity because it is inherently arrogant despite its pretense of a more loving motivation. "Pity is essentially . . . an agreeable impulse of the instinct for appropriation at the sight of what is weaker" (*GS,* § 118).

> Our "benefactors" are, more than our enemies, people who make our worth and will smaller. When people try to benefit someone in distress, the intellectual frivolity with which those moved by pity assume the role of fate is for the most part outrageous; one simply knows nothing of the whole inner sequence and intricacies that are distress for *me* or for *you*. The whole economy of my soul and the balance effected by "distress," the way new springs and needs break open, the way in which old wounds are healing, the way whole periods of the past are shed—all such things that may be involved in distress are of no concern to our dear pitying friends. (*GS,* § 338)

In this passage, Nietzsche indicates his view of suffering as playing a complex role in the life of the person who suffers. An experience of suffering is not an isolated event in a person's life. It comes about as a consequence of what has gone before. Moreover, suffering is not altogether negative. It creates the pressure through which new energies and priorities become apparent; it reveals one's level of strength; it brings one's real values into focus, enabling one to move on to a new phase of life. To ignore the many functions that suffering may serve in a person's life is to judge it insensitively. And yet that is precisely what those who encourage a morality of pity do.

Pity in this view involves a truncated aesthetic outlook. Strikingly, Nietzsche considers pity as a deficient mode of aesthetic response in *The Birth of Tragedy*. Contrary to Aristotle, who contended that the essential purpose of tragedy was to arouse pity and fear and to accomplish a catharsis of these emotions, Nietzsche treats pity as a limited mode of response. Nietzsche objects to the theory that pity is central to tragedy on the ground that this is a moral reaction, not an aesthetic one

> ... I know full well that many of these images also produce at times a moral delight, for example, under the form of pity or moral triumph. But those who would derive the effect of the tragic solely from these moral sources—which, to be sure, has been the custom in aesthetics all too long—should least of all believe that they have thus accomplished something for art, which above all must demand purity in its sphere. If you would explain the tragic myth, the first requirement is to seek the pleasure that is peculiar to it in the purely aesthetic sphere, without transgressing into the region of pity, fear, or the morally sublime. (*BT*, § 24)

The moral viewpoint is an obstruction to actually entering into the drama. From Nietzsche's point of view, it overdistances the spectator while granting a sense of security in the process. Moral judgment absolutizes the significance of another's behavior, and it encourages a sense that everyone—oneself as well as others—stands in a definite, stable position. One sees one's own position, when one pities, as secure; one assumes the stance of being "less vulnerable than thou." According to Nietzsche, this prevents the transformation of self that is central to tragedy, in which one's understanding of oneself as a particular individual gives way to a sense of oneself as part of the tumultuous current of life. Pity, in particular, preserves the spectator observer in the Apollonian state of the rapt spectator and thus prevents the ultimate Dionysian effect, the breakdown of one's sense of individuation, which is the true aim of tragedy. But this is precisely what the stance of pity prevents. "However powerfully pity affects us, it nevertheless saves us in a way from the primordial suffering of the world. . . ." (*BT*, § 21)

Ultimately, for Nietzsche, the artistic impact of tragedy depends on a transformation of one's conception of self. He does not disagree with Aristotle on the importance of identifying with the tragic hero. But if one's identification remains too distanced, if one's sense of identity is not challenged or altered in the process, one has blocked oneself from real identification. And this is what happens when one engages in pity. One believes oneself to stand in a protected position, one that justifies arrogance. As a consequence, one is unable to "travel" to the "world" of the tragic hero and, beyond, to the Dionysian insight that each of our individuated existences is a transient manifestation of a more fundamental underlying reality.

Nietzschean justice involves open-eyed love not only with respect to others but also with respect to oneself. Nietzsche calls for an abandonment of the moralistic map as a means of locating one's own and others' positions.

> *Whom do you call bad?*—Those who always want to put to shame.
> *What do you consider most humane?*—To spare someone shame.
> *What is the seal of liberation?*—No longer being ashamed in front of oneself. (*GS*, §§ 273–275)

One way of reading Nietzsche's theory of eternal recurrence, one suggested by Nietzsche's Zarathustra, is to see it as an antidote to revenge. According to this theory, the entirety of time recurs. If this is so, then the need to "will backwards" in response to "the will's ill-will against time and its 'it was'" becomes moot. One's current action is so bound up with everything that precedes it that it makes no sense to try to undo or retaliate against any part of it. One's activity in the present has impact on the entirety of time anyway, even disagreeable moments in the past. One's activity in each moment reweighs the entire causal nexus in which one exists.

Living well—in Nietzsche's view, actively, without the attitude of vindictiveness—*is*, in fact, the best revenge. It is the best revenge because it is not revenge (in which one is merely a reactive pawn of the past), but it is also best because it does actually impact the past in the sense of reinterpreting the entire past's significance. Revenge wants the last word on some event, and reinterpreting each moment accomplishes this—for the moment. If one fully internalizes this vision, Nietzsche suggests, one can divert the motive of vindictiveness into action without encumbrances. In effect, one eliminates vindictiveness much as one changes a slide in a slide-projector—one simply moves on. One says with Zarathustra, "Well, then—that has had its time."

III. Conclusion

I have argued that Nietzsche's philosophy is motivated in large part by concern with suffering. Nietzsche's emphasis on the first-person point of view in suffering plays a role in his being considered hard-hearted, as does his attack on pity as a virtue. Yet the details of that very attack, as well as his approach to justice, themselves suggest a sympathetic outlook toward other human beings.

My analysis does not explain the full range of Nietzsche's attitude toward suffering. He seems to have valued "hardness" in the face of pitiable sights, and his rhetoric at times seems to celebrate indifference, if not outright sadism. I am inclined to think that such comments reflect a strategy of overcompensation for a personal trait. Nietzsche seems to have regarded himself as particularly vulnerable to sympathy. To his friend Franz Overbeck he wrote,

> I think you know what Zarathustra's warning, "Be hard!" means in my own case. My idea that justice should be done to every particular person, and that I should in the last analysis treat precisely what is most hostile to me with the greatest gentleness, is disproportionately developed and involves danger upon danger, not only for me but also for my task: it is *here* that the hardening is necessary and, with a view to educating others, an occasional cruelty. (Middleton, p. 224; *Sämtliche Briefe* 6, p. 498)

Nietzsche seems to think that taking a deliberately blind eye to suffering is sometimes preferable to sympathy. What cases he had in mind is unclear. Would letting Mrs Fynn read his books be a case of the "occasional cruelty" he mentions? How literally are we to take his "I welcome all signs that a more virile, warlike age is about to begin" (*GS*, § 283) and "I am a bringer of glad tidings like no one before me; . . . there will be wars the like of which have never yet been seen on earth" (*EH* IV, § 1)? One senses an intentional blindness in some of his rhetoric. In his later works, moreover, when he has formulated his theory of rank, one sometimes suspects that he has narrowed his focus of real concern to those of the "higher" ranks, giving little attention to the suffering (actual or prospective) of those he judges as lower. The psychological possibility of restricting one's sense of humanity to one's own favored subset has been all too often instantiated, and it is not clear that Nietzsche entirely avoids this option. This, too, would be consistent with the strategy of overcompensating for an overly sympathetic nature.

And yet Nietzsche does not disregard suffering, even in *Beyond Good and Evil*, where he most clearly calls for a reorganization of society in accordance with rank. There he addresses those who would reorganize it with the goal of eliminating suffering. This, he claims, is impossible. Suffering has always been a means to human transformation and essential to human development, including spiritual development.

> The discipline of suffering, of *great* suffering—do you not know that only *this* discipline has created all enhancements of man so far? That tension of the soul in unhappiness which cultivates its strength, its shudders face to face with great ruin, its inventiveness and courage in enduring, persevering, interpreting, and exploiting suffering, and whatever has been granted to it of profundity, secret, mask, spirit, cunning, greatness—was it not granted to it through suffering, through the discipline of great suffering? In man *creature* and *creator* are united: in man there is material, fragment, excess, clay, direct, nonsense, chaos; but in man there is also creator, form-giver, hammer hardness, spectator divinity, and seventh day: do you understand this contrast? And that *your* pity is for the "creature in man," for what must be formed, broken, forged, torn, burnt, made incandescent, and purified—

that which *necessarily* must and *should* suffer? And *our* pity—do you not comprehend for whom our *converse* pity is when it resists your pity as the worst of all pamperings and weaknesses?

Thus it is pity *versus* pity. (*BGE*, § 225)

Even in the context of some of his "hardest" statements, Nietzsche feels compelled to attempt a justification of the presence of suffering in human life. Significantly, he concludes, his rejection of pity is itself motivated by pity. This defense of the rightness of suffering is particularly poignant in that it is written by a man who suffered greatly, both physically and emotionally, as his letters in particular testify. Perhaps he was trying to convince himself as well as his readers when he concludes in *On the Genealogy of Morals*, "Man, the bravest of animals and the one most accustomed to suffering, does *not* repudiate suffering as such: he *desires* it, he even seeks it out, provided he is shown a *meaning* for it, a *purpose* of suffering" (*GM* III, § 28).

Certainly, Nietzsche himself sought a meaning for suffering over the span of his philosophical development. The tone of hardness he adopts at certain points in his writings has blinded many of his readers to the centrality of the theme of suffering in his philosophy as a whole. Nietzsche feared being misunderstood, and the intensity and scope of his concern for suffering is a feature of his work that has been unappreciated. Yet he addresses suffering throughout his work. Suffering remains his focus even at the conclusion of his autobiography, *Ecce Homo*, completed just before his breakdown. In the final lines of this book, whose title compares Nietzsche himself to the suffering Jesus, Nietzsche summarizes his message by evoking the alternative deifications of suffering in the Greek and Christian traditions: "Have I been understood?—*Dionysus versus the Crucified*" (*EH* IV, § 9).

Works Cited

Frye, Marilyn. 1983. *The Politics of Reality: Essays in Feminist Theory.* Trumansburg, NY: Crossing Press.

Gilman, Sander. 1987. *Conversations with Nietzsche: A Life in the Words of His Contemporaries.* Oxford: Oxford University Press.

Higgins, Kathleen Marie. 2000. *Comic Relief: Nietzsche's Gay Science.* New York: Oxford University Press.

Janz, Carl Paul. 1981. *Friedrich Nietzsche Biographie.* 3 vols. Munich: Deutscher Taschenbuch Verlag.

Krell, David Farrel, and Donald L. Bates. 1997. *The Good European: Nietzsche's Work Sites in Word and Image.* Chicago: University of Chicago Press.

Lugónes, María. 1987. "Playfulness, 'World'-Traveling, and Loving Perception." *Hypatia* 2, 2 (Summer): 3–19.

Middleton, Christopher, trans. and ed. 1969. *Selected Letters of Friedrich Nietzsche.* Chicago: University of Chicago Press.

Nietzsche, Friedrich. 1975–1984. *Sämtliche Briefe: Kritische Studienausgabe.* Berlin/New York: de Gruyter.

Chapter Four

To Laugh Out of the Whole Truth

Nietzsche as Tragicomic Satyr

Lawrence J. Hatab

In the history of philosophy, perhaps the most marginal phenomenon has been laughter. Philosophers have written about laughter as a subject of study but simply as one among other human capacities calling for explanation or analysis. Moreover, the affective force and disruptive effects of laughter have generally earned it low esteem in the "serious business" of philosophy's pursuit of truth. In comparison, a distinctive feature of Nietzsche's thought is a demarginalization of laughter unmatched in the history of philosophy: Nietzsche elevates laughter to a level of importance so pronounced that it becomes joined with truth.

> To laugh at oneself as one would have to laugh in order to laugh *out of the whole truth*—to do that even the best so far lacked sufficient sense for the truth, and the most gifted had too little genius for that. Even laughter may yet have a future. (*GS*, § 1)

What can it mean that laughter is expressive of truth? In this essay I want to sketch an answer by focusing on two elements in Nietzsche's philosophy: 1) his negative sense of truth that dismisses foundationalism and objectivism; and 2) his retrieval of the central role of tragic and comic drama in early Greek culture. (Some of what follows is drawn from Hatab, 1988, and Hatab, 2004.)

I. The Truth of Becoming

Truth, for Nietzsche, must always be a matter of existential meaning in a finite world of becoming. Knowledge cannot be based in a fixed, objective foundation because the variegated, fluid field of experience can never admit stable conditions of being but only perspectives within forces of becoming (GM III, § 12). And perspectives are always expressions of existential interests, so that "disinterested objectivity" is a fiction (BGE, § 207; GM III, §§ 12, 26; WP, § 588). Since Nietzsche rules out a baseline being, the only "ultimate" truth is a negative "truth of becoming," a primal, destructive flux that renders all positive forms and structures in the end groundless (TI, "Reason in Philosophy," §§ 2, 6; EH P, § 3; WP, § 708). As an existential matter, the truth of becoming is not simply a function of cognition; it is experienced as something dark, fearsome, and difficult (GS, § 110; BGE, § 39; GM I, § 1).

Given Nietzsche's commitment to the truth of becoming, it is no surprise that he expressed a lifelong interest in tragic drama, beginning with his first published work, The Birth of Tragedy. Tragedy gives voice to the lived significance of finite limits in human life, of the terrible inevitability of loss, ruin, and death. In The Birth of Tragedy, Nietzsche does not give much attention to the "other side" of drama, namely comedy, but in subsequent writings, the comic becomes a major motif in his texts, to the point where laughter is given a status at least equal to the tragic.

The tragic and the comic involve two fundamental existential dispositions: the tragic is a response to the inevitable dissolution of human life and meaning; the comic is an exuberant expression of laughter in a host of sociocultural situations where a joyous vocal discharge erupts and disables the normal function of serious regard. Usually the tragic and the comic are thought to denote a contrary pair of negative and positive dispositions. But Nietzsche's approach to these phenomena indicates a deep ambiguity in this purported oppositional relation: both the tragic and the comic express an affirmative posture toward life, and they both exhibit a disruption of "being." I argue that tragic pathos and comic laughter present a primal existential bivalence in the human experience of negative limits and that for Nietzsche both phenomena depict an *affirmative negation* that avoids both a pessimistic denial of life and an optimistic fantasy that negative limits can be overcome or resolved in some way. Nietzsche often deploys motifs of tragedy and comedy to name the general character of life, and such motifs do not contradict each other. In fact, Nietzsche comes to emphasize comic laughter as an especially positive response to the tragic, a response that does not overcome or cancel tragic negativity. In short, comedy represents a special way in which the tragic need not involve a negative disposition. To understand the ambiguity in Nietzsche's outlook, we need to consider the way in which tragedy and comedy functioned in early Greek culture.

II. Greek Tragedy and Comedy

Tragedy and comedy in ancient Greece were distinct phenomena, yet both shared a common origin in the worship of the god Dionysus (see Riu, 1999; Winkler and Zeitlin, 1990). And if we can grant that Greek religious belief was a serious engagement with the sacred (rather than mere fanciful stories or conventional props), then tragedy and comedy were more than merely "artistic" works; they portrayed deep cultural meanings with world-disclosive significance.

Tragic drama had its origins in the dithyramb and satyr play (see Aristotle's *Poetics*, 4), both of which were associated with Dionysian religion. The mythos of Dionysus told of the death and rebirth of a god who suffers a violent dismemberment followed by restoration, a narrative that gave voice to the dynamic cycles of life and death in nature. Dionysian rituals (originally a feminine cult) generated ecstatic, self-eclipsing communion with the surging energies of creation and destruction, which gave sacred meaning to the shattering of boundaries between the self and exuberant nature (see Kerenyi, 1976).

In *The Birth of Tragedy*, Nietzsche stresses the religious dimension of tragedy by reading the fatal destruction of the individual hero as the affirmation of a primal Dionysian power. Nietzsche recognizes that mature tragedy was not purely Dionysian because Homeric myths and finely structured forms were in the foreground of dramatic performances. He selects another Greek deity, Apollo, to capture the cultivated beauty of tragic dramas, which countered Dionysian dissolution with a display of individuated forms *confronting* fatal dissolution. The conjunction of Dionysian and Apollonian forces in tragedy produced a two-fold posture of affirmation in early Greek culture: 1) a reverence for the primal power of becoming that renders all forms fragile and impermanent; and 2) the beautification of this negative truth by way of creative appearances of form that delight and educate the viewer, which prevents a pessimistic abnegation of the will to live (*BT*, § 21).

The affirmative character of Greek drama that attracted Nietzsche can be further explored by detailing the Dionysian connection between tragedy and comedy. Dionysian rites generally assumed two forms: 1) joyous erotic feasts and the eclipse of the self in unrestrained passion; and 2) somber destructive rites in which frenzied worshippers reenacted the mythos of Dionysus by dismembering and devouring animal victims. Both ritual forms were said to bring peace and sacred communion with the god. Violent rites were only one side of Dionysian religion. As the god of cyclic natural forces, Dionysus was the divine source of life as well as death. The god of life prompted erotic passion, the fuel of regeneration. Eroticism, however, can be seen to generate an analogous "dismemberment" of conventional order and propriety. Dionysian religion, therefore, fostered destructive and passional subversions of individuated form and everyday social norms.

The Dionysian roots of comedy display comparable settings of de-formation that indicate overlapping relations with tragic manifestations of Dionysian religion (see Pickard-Cambridge, 1962). Our discussion can be advanced by considering two cultural forms that can be traced to Dionysus: the *komos* and the satyr.

III. The Komos and Comedy

The *komos* named a swarming band of drunken men who engaged in dancing, laughter, obscenity, and mocking language, and who generally dispensed with social conventions and inhibitions (Kerenyi, 1976, pp. 330–348). The *komos* represented a more accessible and less severe form of Dionysian self-abandonment (compared with the feminine cult) and a more public "dismemberment" of human norms and hierarchies. The *komodoi*, or "singers in the *komos*," can be called a forerunner of comic drama, not simply on etymological grounds but in terms of the religious sanctioning of a "reversed world" that came to characterize comedy's public space for the mocking subversion of social, political, and divine authorities (Sourvinou-Inwood, 2003, pp. 172–177).

The two-dimensional character of Dionysian religion prepared a common background for the development of dramatic genres of tragedy and comedy. The somber ecstasy of the violent rites involved participation in actual forces of destruction, which tragedy portrayed in the fatal ruination of a noble hero. The frolicking ecstasy of the *komos* and erotic feasts involved revels of disinhibition and the comparatively harmless (and temporary) "destruction" of conventional propriety and cultural roles, which comedy portrayed in its celebration of obscenity, mockery, and debunking tactics. Both dimensions displayed in their way a singular Dionysian insight: formed conditions (whether natural or cultural) are not fixed or permanent, and a sacred meaning can emerge through the annihilating power of Dionysian ecstasy, which dissolves a fixation on form and opens the self to the self-exceeding truth of natural life energies.

The element of negation in tragedy is clear with respect to how the fate of human life is presented. Yet the Dionysian connection allows us to understand how a de-forming function also operates in comedy. While tragic negation is more cosmic in dimension and complete in depicting a ruinous downfall, comedic negation is more a social matter and depicts the disabling of roles, conventions, and authoritative postures *without* complete destruction—a "safe zone" that simply unmasks, surprises, or mocks in the context of laughable, rather than pitiable, losses. Aristotle confirms this when he claims that comedy portrays human deficiencies but without pain or injury (*Poetics*, 1449a34ff.). The "harmless negation" of comedy can be located in various philosophical theories of laughter (see Monro, 1967, pp. 90–93): superiority theories (e.g., Hobbes), where mockery tears down a social posture and elevates those who laugh; incongruity theories (e.g., Kant), where absurdity or the contradiction of an expected order or norm evokes laughter; relief theories (e.g., Freud), where laughter is discharged in moments of release from social, especially sexual, restraints.

Although tragedy and comedy became separate art forms in Greek theater, earlier stages of drama showed a close, even intrinsic relationship between comic and tragic cultural forms. Tragedy evolved from the satyr play, and even mature dramatic performances for a time took the form of tetralogies, a set of three tragic works followed by a satyr play. A discussion of the Greek satyr figure will give our analysis some depth and focus in articulating the following points: 1) the comic-tragic correlation in early Greek culture; 2) Nietzsche's declared interest in satyr motifs; and 3) the satyr construed as a vivid and telling cultural expression of *marginal* forces, in particular of crossing the limits between humanity and animality, between culture and nature.

IV. Nietzsche and the Satyr

> I am a disciple of the philosopher Dionysus; I should prefer to be even a satyr to being a saint. (*EH*, P, § 2)

> I estimate the value of men, of races, according to the necessity by which they cannot conceive the god apart from the satyr. (*EH*, "Why I Am So Clever," § 4)

With these references to the satyr in his last published work, Nietzsche retrieved an image that had figured significantly in his first published work, *The Birth of Tragedy*. The satyr was an ancient Greek mythical being that displayed a combination of animal and human features and that can be taken to represent an ambiguous confluence of nature and culture. This ambiguity characteristic of early Greek culture inspired Nietzsche, and it can be seen to mark a fundamental task of his work: how to think human culture and the forces of animal nature as an indivisible blend, which departs from the Western conception of carnal nature as something to be transcended, mastered, or reformed. Nietzsche advocates the notion of *homo natura* (*BGE*, § 230), a return of humanity and philosophy to the primal forces of nature (*GS*, §§ 109, 294), which exhibit indigenous energies of striving, domination, and destruction (captured in Nietzsche's concept of will to power). Yet Nietzsche's naturalism is not a denial or subordination of culture. Forms of culture simply emerge as modifications of natural drives that never fully surpass their base (see *Homer's Contest*, in *SW* 1, pp. 162ff.). Even consciousness and philosophy, for Nietzsche, are not the opposite of natural instincts but, rather, the refined and redirected expressions of instinct (*GS*, § 354; *BGE*, § 3). Nietzsche's cultural naturalism can serve as a backdrop for considering the significance of the satyr figure.

In *The Birth of Tragedy*, the satyr is an important image in Nietzsche's project of demonstrating the Dionysian sources of Greek tragedy. Nietzsche takes the satyr as a synthesis of god and goat (the goat being associated with Dionysus) and as a symbol of Dionysian enthusiasm, a "primal humanity" that experiences the healthy ecstasies of divine madness (*BT*, "Attempt at Self-Criticism," § 4). The satyr is an expression of the Greek "longing for what is original and natural," an *Urbild* of nature unmediated by knowledge and reflection, of an ecstatic release into the sexual omnipotence of nature driven by the force of the god (*BT*, § 8). The satyr represents a more dark and wild phenomenon than the modern "idyllic shepherd," and it exposes the delusion of culture taken as the only reality (*BT*, § 8). The satyr-Dionysus connection, however, is in Nietzsche's estimation a more cultivated dynamic than the "barbaric" expressions of the Dionysian given over to more brutish and licentious forces (*BT*, § 2).

The satyr chorus and dithyramb in honor of Dionysus are seen by Nietzsche as forerunners of tragic drama. The phenomenon of "drama" (literally an action) and dramatic impersonation are born in the mimetic enchantment of Dionysian enthusiasts who identify with the satyr celebrants of the god who have identified with Dionysus through ecstatic transformation (*BT*, § 8). So for Nietzsche, tragedy begins with the satyr, representing a Dionysian experience of exuberant life forces beneath the Apollonian veil of civilization (*BT*, § 7). And the Dionysian life force behind passing manifestations evokes the positive, celebratory mood that Nietzsche insists be recognized in any account of the Greek phenomenon of tragedy.

What can classical scholarship tell us about Nietzsche's account of the satyr? Nietzsche has been quite influential in opening up concealed or underdeveloped elements in early Greek culture and tragic drama. Nietzsche was roughly right about tragedy's deriving from the satyr chorus and Dionysian worship, and he was prescient in overcoming more prudish scholarship by stressing connections between tragedy, Dionysian passion, and the sexual energy of the satyr (Silk and Stern, 1981, pp. 142ff.). What do we know about the satyr? Satyrs were a race of their own, a hybrid of animal and human traits, depicted as a human form with a horse's tail and ears, sometimes with hooves. Satyrs were usually associated with negative moral traits such as laziness and licentiousness. The relationship between satyrs and other animals was not one of hunting or domesticating but of play, dancing, erotics, and role exchanges. The anatomy, dress, and behavior of the satyr suggest an ambiguous human-animality and an oscillation between barbarian and civilized traits (see Lissarraque, 1993, pp. 208ff.).

The association between the satyr and Dionysus may not be primeval, but there are clear connections in the sixth century. Dionysus's entourage did not include males but rather women, nymphs, and satyrs (Lissarraque, 1993, p. 207). The behavior of satyrs as companions of Dionysus included drinking, flute playing, dancing, acrobatics, and erotic gestures directed toward maenads and nymphs, all usually presented with comic effects (Ganz, 1993, p. 137). The leaping and gamboling of the satyrs expressed the joyful delirium of those who follow Dionysus, who call into question established norms, who undo divisions between social roles, sexes, age groups, animals and humans, humans and gods (Vernant and Vidal-Naquet, 1988, p. 204).

Satyrs were on the margins of the human world but not isolated from it. As servants of Dionysus, who appeared among humans, satyrs performed roles such as artisans, sculptors, and cooks. Yet they were also depicted as wanton drunkards, thieves, and gluttons, beings who could not control or still their desires. At the same time they were shown as "inventing," or better, *discovering* many elements of human culture, usually exhibiting expressions of amazement, astonishment, or an eager gaze. One can surmise that the wildness and marginality of the satyr were given to represent a primal uncovering or renewal of the human world. The "negative" posture, burlesque, and fringe realm of the satyrs can be said to have functioned as an inversion/deforming of human norms that brought both a comic and an exploratory effect. The satyr, then, was an experimentation with alterity that evoked a heightened attention to human culture by exceeding its normalcy and familiarity (Lissarraque, 1993, pp. 214ff.).

Visual representations of satyrs usually depicted human mimetic performances of these sacred mythical beings in religious rituals and protodramas, typically dancing and cavorting around the god Dionysus (Vernant and Vidal-Naquet, 1988, p. 183). They were shown as masked figures with attached animal ears, tail, and phallus. Such a mimetic, masking mode was typical of *thiasoi*, or cult associations where humans achieved identification through imitation of sacred prototypes. In the case of the satyrs, the mimetic identification was with Dionysian ecstasy and latent animality (Burkert, 1985, pp. 104, 173).

Such mimetic performances set the stage for dramatic arts, especially the role of satyr plays in tragic drama (for the following, see Easterling, 1997, pp. 37–44). The dithyramb was a mode of poetry sung and danced in honor of Dionysus by choruses of fifty men or boys. Such practices were continued in the satyr play, a short fourth play following a trilogy of tragic dramas. The Dionysian connection was clear to the audience, and they knew during tragic performances that a satyr play was meant to conclude the presentation. In addition, the same performers acted the parts in all four plays. Accordingly, the satyr play was intrinsic to tragedy's cultural function, and the audience's *anticipation* of the satyr play should be kept in mind when trying to understand the effect of tragic drama (for Nietzsche on the satyr play, see *SW* 7, pp. 42–43).

The satyr play involved a chorus of singers and dancers, part human, part animal, engaged in playful, violent, sensual burlesque, very dissimilar in style and tone from the tragic chorus. Here the heroes and sacred figures of the tragedies were presented in a different, far from somber register, and yet the link with tragedy was evident, since the same performers were involved and the vocabulary and metrics of the characters were carried over.

What can we make of the satyr effect in tragedy? The satyr was an antitype (especially compared with male citizens) found on the fringes of the human world. Satyr plays presented exotic locales with fantastic characterizations, often with themes of discovery/invention of something in the human world (wine, music, fire, metallurgy, the first woman). Satyrs, then, represented an inversion/distancing effect creating a scene of surprise and rediscovery of familiar cultural meanings, but always in the setting of a human-animal-nature convergence. With the tragedies portraying somber confrontations with fate, death, the gods, and limits, the satyr effect "played" with culture by way of a disorientation-reorientation structure.

If we recall the Dionysian phenomenon as both a negative and productive force given over to both ecstatic abandonment and erotic energies symbolizing the cycle of death and regeneration in nature, the tragic trilogies and satyr play can be understood as a confrontation with limit situations in two registers, one a "serious" expression of loss, the other a "playful" expression of comic juxtapositions, celebration, rediscovery, and reorientation. The intrinsic function of the satyr play in tragic performance lends much credence to Nietzsche's insistence that Greek tragedy was at bottom a life-affirming cultural force understood by way of the dual nature of Dionysian worship. The function of the satyr was to give presence to the ambiguous commixture in life of animal and human, nature and culture, and to celebrate this ambiguity with a playful modulation of tragic alterity. And Nietzsche would stress the cultural juxtaposition of satyric and tragic drama in distinct performances as an ongoing exchange and as an implicit Greek recognition of the productive tension between the two forms, which would be weakened if the two forms were somehow blended together and lost if one form were to overcome or replace the other.

The duality of Dionysian experience can also apply to the historical links between tragedy and comedy and thus to a correlation between pathos and laughter. The buffoonery displayed in satyr plays signals an intermediate genre between tragedy and comedy, with closer affinities to comedy (Vernant and Vidal-Naquet, 1988, p. 152). Clearly the satyr figure stands as a gathering point for the multiform boundary-crossing dynamic of Dionysian religion—with an edge given to restorative comic forces—that so impressed Nietzsche and that in many ways marked his thought and manner of writing.

Nietzsche often refers to the relation between philosophy, comedy, and tragedy, including references to the satyr figure. In an 1888 letter to Ferdinand Avenarius, he says the following:

> . . . this year, where a monstrous task, the reevaluation of all values, lies upon me and I literally have to bear the fate of humanity, it belongs to my proof of strength to be something of a buffoon, a satyr, or if you prefer, a "Feuilletonist.". . . That the deepest spirit must also be the most frivolous, this is almost the formula for my philosophy: it could be that I, above all other "greats," have indeed become cheerful in an unlikely manner. (*KGB* III 5, pp. 516–517)

In *Beyond Good and Evil*, Nietzsche warns against the solemnity of truth and a moral indignation that can ruin one's "philosophical sense of humor." To be a martyr for the truth is a degenerative excess. In fact, philosophy is called a kind of tragedy, but the "fall" of the philosopher is better taken in the spirit of a satyr play, an "epilogue farce" that is the true *end* of any tragedy (*BGE*, § 25). And a great tragedian shows greatness most in the satyr play, "when he knows how to *laugh* at himself" (*GM* III, § 3). Indeed, a good case can be made that the notorious fourth part of *Thus Spoke Zarathustra*—where the figures and import of the first three parts seem to degenerate into lampoonery—can be read as a satyr play concluding the tragic trilogy of the preceding parts (see Shapiro, 1989; Loeb, 2000). This helps us make sense out of Nietzsche's reference to *Zarathustra* as both a tragedy and a parody (see *GS*, § 342 and the first section of the preface).

To conclude, the human animality of the satyr can stand as a symbol for Nietzsche's exuberant naturalism, his affirmation of a finite, carnal existence. For Nietzsche, human culture is not a transcendence of animal nature but a "sublimation" of natural energies that modulates but never surpasses its base. Indeed, Nietzsche refers to another hybrid figure in defining the "genius of culture," calling it a "centaur, half beast, half man" (*HAH* I, § 241). The satyr embodies this ambiguous animal-human hybrid who lives on the fringes of the human world and who exhibits astonishment at the unfolding of that world, and whose transgressions and crossings are experienced as comical—which is to say *not* repulsive but pleasurable, interesting, revelatory, and rejuvenating.

V. Tragicomic Truth

The key to Nietzsche's interest in tragedy and comedy is their overlapping expression of a de-formation of being. If tragedy and comedy each present an affirmative response to negative limits, it would not be puzzling that a boundary line between them is often hard to draw. We have noticed a distinction between "harmful" and "harmless" negation, each evoking respectively pathos and laughter. But humans can also laugh when suffering from terrible conditions. Though rare, "tragic laughter" would be analogous to comic laughter in being a visceral affirmative response to a destructive limit. This special form of laughter was one of Nietzsche's preoccupations, as indicated in the shepherd scene in *Thus Spoke Zarathustra*. The shepherd appears after the tragic doctrine of eternal recurrence is recounted. He is writhing in pain and nausea because a black snake has lodged in his throat. But then he bites off the head of the snake.

> No longer shepherd, no longer human—one changed, radiant, *laughing*! Never yet has a human being laughed as he laughed! O my brothers, I heard a laughter that was no human laughter; and now a thirst gnaws at me, a longing that never grows still. My longing for this laughter gnaws at me. (Z III, "On the Vision and the Riddle," § 2)

For Nietzsche, laughter can be, among other things, a most positive, vibrant form of tragic affirmation, a healthy incorporation of the negative limits of being. In this respect, Nietzsche saw himself inheriting the "cheerful fatalism" of the Greeks:

> . . . the short tragedy always gave way again and returned to the eternal comedy of existence; and "the waves of uncontrollable laughter"—to cite Aeschylus—must in the end overwhelm even the greatest of these tragedians. (*GS*, § 1)

At another level, laughter can be called a virtue when it is self-directed. The ability to laugh at oneself can manifest an enjoyment of one's own limits in social life, as opposed to the posture of overly "serious" people, who seem defensively fixated on their roles, beliefs, or causes. The virtue of self-directed laughter exhibits the freedom to sacrifice form-ality, to enjoy a lapse of identity, and to embody a nondogmatic disposition about oneself and one's convictions.

It may be difficult to construct a theoretical explanation of the nature of laughter and why we laugh (which would have to be serious, of course), but a phenomenology of laughter may suffice. *When* we laugh, something special about the human condition is revealed: the peculiar human capacity to appropriate limits in a positive manner; in the laugh, something deep and instinctive in us recognizes and *enjoys* the disruption of structure and being. It is no wonder, then, that Nietzsche, the champion of becoming, would find laughter so important: "Laughter at something is the first sign of a higher psychic life" (Kaufmann, 1968, p. 422). It may be clearer now why Nietzsche associates laughter with a "sufficient sense for the truth." The "truth" expressed in a laugh is the visceral deconstruction of a fixed truth. Nietzsche's celebration of laughter goes beyond psychological questions to include his critique of foundational truth. The "seriousness" of Western philosophy and religion has manifested a struggle for, and fixation on, truth and certainty in an unstable world. Truth and salvation have been no laughing matter; frivolity has been scolded because in the end there is "something at which it is absolutely forbidden henceforth to laugh" (*GS*, § 1). Nietzschean laughter abandons certainty and embraces limits in knowledge and life—and *enjoys* such delimitation (see Higgins, 2000). Moreover, when it comes to confronting instances of philosophical seriousness, laughter and humor could be an appropriate form of "critique." As Zarathustra put it, the spirit of gravity is killed "not by wrath . . . but by laughter" (*Z* I, "On Reading and Writing"). Indeed, the ascetic ideal—at bottom a belief in foundational truth of any sort, even in science (*GM* III, § 24)—is susceptible to only *one* enemy capable of harming it: "comedians of this ideal" (*GM* III, § 27).

The substantive role of laughter as a Dionysian supplement to the tragic subversion of truth can help illuminate a prominent motif in *Thus Spoke Zarathustra*. In Part I of the text, "The Three Metamorphoses" offers images of spiritual development in the figures of the camel, the lion, and the child. The camel is the beast of burden symbolizing obedience and cultural conformity. The lion is a powerful force of no-saying, the denial of stable conditions, which lets loose the freedom that makes possible the creation of new values. But the creation of new values only comes with the yes-saying innocence of the child. Later in the text, the free lion and the creative child are joined with the spirit of laughter. When Zarathustra anticipates the replacement of old tablets with new writings, he says he is waiting for a "laughing lion" (*Z* I, "On Old and New Tablets," § 1). Near the end of the text, Zarathustra again anticipates the arrival of laughing lions, and he calls them his "children" (*Z* IV, "The Welcome"). In the last section of the text, the children are near, signaled by a laughing lion (Z IV, "The Sign"). In this way, creative innocence is connected with leonine negativity by way of laughter, a "disabling" force that does not destroy but rather *enables* creative activity. Moreover, a poetic interlude joins laughter and poetry counterposed to truth; indeed, an echo of Dionysian dismemberment, a "tearing to pieces," is modified by a comic supplement to tragic disintegration—a joyful *"laughing while tearing"* (Z IV, "The Song of Melancholy," § 3).

VI. Nietzsche's Satyrical Style

The exuberant joy of laughter delimits without destroying, and Nietzsche seems to be following the Greeks in recognizing the reciprocal relation of tragedy and comedy, especially the restorative value of comic laughter, given the potential for pessimism looming in the dark truth of tragedy. Nietzsche even highlights this reciprocal relation with regard to his own writing. After having "slain all gods," he asks: "From where am I to take the tragic solution?—Should I begin to think about a comic solution?" (GS, § 153).

The question of Nietzsche's style is quite relevant here. In addition to using techniques not typical of philosophical writing—aphorism, literary narrative, metaphor, ad hominem invective, hyperbole—Nietzsche may have deployed many of his most radical inversions (e.g., immoralism) in the manner of "black comedy," a satirical negation not bent on elimination. Indeed, for Nietzsche, "attack is in my case a proof of good will, sometimes even of gratitude" (EH, "Why I Am So Wise," § 7). In addition, this disabling-while-preserving structure of comic negation is also self-directed in Nietzsche's writings. Zarathustra's "ape" on the surface sounds very much like Nietzsche's supposed fearsome persona, yet he is repudiated in part for being overly serious and vengeful (Z III, "On Passing By"). Nietzsche hints that *Zarathustra* itself is a parody (GS P, § 1; EH, "Why I Write Such Good Books," Z). It is clearly a parody of religious narratives and prophetic revelation. Yet, as we have noted, Part IV may be a self-parody in the manner of a satyr play, meant as a warning about the contingent character of Zarathustra's message and against taking the message too seriously and doing wrong with it—or constructing a new "doctrine" to replace old ideologies.

> I *want* no "believers"; I am much too malicious to believe in myself. . . . I have a terrible fear that one day I will be pronounced *holy*. . . . I do not want to be a holy man; sooner even a buffoon.—Perhaps I am a buffoon.—Yet in spite of that—or rather *not* in spite of it, because so far no one has been more mendacious than holy men.—But my truth is *terrible*. (EH, "Why I Am a Destiny," § 1)

Once again, here Nietzsche associates comedy with a terrible truth. It is evident that a tragicomic intersection should be a guidepost for reading Nietzsche from the standpoints of both style and substance. Laughter can no longer be located on the margins of philosophy: "You higher men, . . . *learn* to laugh away over yourselves! . . . Laughter have I pronounced holy" (*Z* IV, "On the Higher Man," § 20). Of course, Nietzsche was a serious thinker dealing with the most serious issues. But the way in which Nietzsche expressed these issues distinguishes him significantly from other philosophers, and his manner of writing is not separable from the content of his thought. The deployment of comic laughter is Nietzsche's retrieval of Dionysian *wisdom* about life, which "cannot conceive the god apart from the satyr" (*EH*, "Why I Am So Clever," § 4). Laughter, then, is an essential part of wisdom. Rather than being contrary to serious, indeed tragic, matters, comic laughter can be seen as an overture to, and then a consummation of, deeply serious matters. Nietzsche gives us

> the ideal of a human-overhuman (*menschlich-übermenschlich*) well-being and benevolence that will often appear *inhuman*—for example, when it confronts all earthly seriousness . . . as if it were [its] most incarnate and involuntary parody—and in spite of all this, it is perhaps only with this that *great seriousness* really begins, the real question mark is posed for the first time, that the destiny of the soul changes, the hand moves forward, the tragedy *begins*. (*EH*, "Why I Write Such Good Books," Z, § 2)

> For cheerfulness—or in my own language *gay science*—is a reward: the reward of a long, brave, industrious, and subterranean seriousness, of which, to be sure, not everyone is capable. But on the day we say with all our hearts, "Onwards! Our old morality too is part *of the comedy*!" we shall have discovered a new complication and possibility for the Dionysian drama of "The Destiny of the Soul"—and one can wager that the grand old eternal comic poet of our existence will be quick to make use of it! (*GM*, Preface, § 7)

In dramatic fashion, Nietzsche repositions laughter in an unprecedented way, when compared to other philosophers. Through the voice of Zarathustra, Nietzsche tells us that "we should call every truth false that [is] not accompanied by at least one laugh" (*Z* III, "On Old and New Tablets," § 23).

It is plausible, I think, that much of Nietzsche's work, especially its transgressive style and unsettling attacks upon cherished cultural norms by way of startling antipodes, can be seen in the light of a satyr play, in the manner of a comic-noire experiment with inversions and crossovers on the fringe, meant not so much to destroy as to renew human culture by evoking astonishment before its emergence out of animality and by mocking the gravitas that has marked the West's conception of culture as an overcoming of nature. What kind of laughter might we look for in Nietzsche's menacing iconoclasm?

Works Cited
Burkert, Walter. 1985. *Greek Religion*. Trans. John Raffan. Cambridge, MA: Harvard University Press.

Easterling, P. E. 1997. "A Show for Dionysus." In *The Cambridge Companion to Greek Tragedy*, ed. P. E. Easterling. Cambridge: Cambridge University Press.

Ganz, Timothy. 1993. *Early Greek Myth*. Baltimore, MD: Johns Hopkins University Press.

Hatab, Lawrence. 1988. "Laughter in Nietzsche's Thought: A Philosophical Tragicomedy." *International Studies in Philosophy* 20/2: 67–79.

Hatab, Lawrence. 2004. "The Satyr: Human-Animality in Nietzsche." In *A Nietzschean Bestiary: Becoming Animal Beyond Docile and Brutal*, ed. Christa Davis Acampora and Ralph R. Acampora. Lanham, MD: Rowman & Littlefield.

Higgins, Kathleen Marie. 2000. *Comic Relief: Nietzsche's Gay Science*. New York: Oxford University Press.

Kaufmann, Walter, ed. 1968. *The Basic Writings of Nietzsche*. New York: Modern Library.

Kerenyi, Carl. 1976. *Dionysos*. Trans. Ralph Manheim. Princeton, NJ: Princeton University Press.

Lissarraque, François. 1993. "On the Wildness of the Satyrs." In *Masks of Dionysus*, ed. Thomas H. Carpenter and Christopher A. Faraone. Ithaca, NY: Cornell University Press.

Loeb, Paul S. 2000. "The Conclusion of Nietzsche's *Zarathustra*." *International Studies in Philosophy* 32/3: 137–152.

Monro, D. H. 1967. "Humor." In *The Encyclopedia of Philosophy*, vol. 4. Ed. Paul Edwards. New York: Macmillan.

Nietzsche, Friedrich. 1975. *Kritische Gesamtausgabe: Briefwechsel*. Ed. G. Colli and M. Montinari. Berlin: De Gruyter. Abbreviated as *KGB*.

Pickard-Cambridge, A. W. 1962. *Dithyramb Tragedy and Comedy*, 2nd ed. Revised by T. B. L. Webster. Oxford: Oxford University Press.

Riu, Xavier. 1999. *Dionysism and Comedy*. Lanham, MD: Rowman & Littlefield.

Shapiro, Gary. 1989. *Nietzschean Narratives*. Bloomington: Indiana University Press.

Silk, M. S., and J. P. Stern. 1981. *Nietzsche on Tragedy*. Cambridge: Cambridge University Press.

Sourvinou-Inwood, Christiane. 2003. *Tragedy and Athenian Religion*. Lanham, MD: Lexington Books.

Vernant, Jean-Pierre, and Pierre Vidal-Naquet. 1988. *Myth and Tragedy in Ancient Greece*. Trans. Janet Lloyd. New York: Zone Books.

Winkler, John J., and Froma I. Zeitlin, eds. 1990. *Nothing to Do with Dionysos? Athenian Drama in Its Social Context*. Princeton, NJ: Princeton University Press.

Chapter Five

Awaiting Love

Nietzsche's (Com)Passion

Tyler Roberts

> The essence of being human is that . . . one is prepared
> in the end to be defeated and broken up by life, which
> is the inevitable price of fastening one's love upon
> other human individuals.
> —George Orwell

In his notebooks, from the period of *Ecce Homo*, Nietzsche compares "Dionysus and the 'Crucified'":

> Dionysus versus the "Crucified": there you have the antithesis. It is not a
> difference in regard to their martyrdom—it is a difference in the meaning
> of it. Life itself, its eternal fruitfulness and recurrence, creates torment,
> destruction, the will to annihilation. In the other case, suffering—the
> "Crucified as the innocent one"—counts as an objection to this life, as a
> formula for its condemnation. (*SW* 13, pp. 265–7)

Both are martyrs because both expose themselves to life in a practice of radical
vulnerability, compelled beyond instincts of self-preservation. But Nietzsche
believes that Dionysus is compelled by love for life—by a sense of the holiness of
life—and that the martyrdom of the Crucified symbolizes a hatred for life and
a wish to be free of it. For Nietzsche these contrasting passions decisively mark
the difference between his own philosophy and Christianity.

This way of putting the difference has had a profound impact on the philosophical and theological thought of the past century. Even those who argue that Nietzsche gets Christianity wrong now find it necessary to explain how Christian self-sacrifice and "dying to this-world" in fact affirms *this* life, assists us, as Rowan Williams puts it, "in being mortal" (Williams, 1988, p. 36). So, in a recent article Norman Wirzba argues that "Christianity's 'no' to the natural life is in the name of a better, richer *this-worldly* life" and that Nietzsche failed to see this because he misunderstood Christian love (Wirzba, 1997, p. 397). Indeed, Wirzba goes on to argue that Christianity is in fact *more* affirming of life than Nietzsche, that while both Nietzsche and Christianity practice a radical kind of vulnerability, Christianity, precisely in a love that moves to alleviate the suffering and pain of the neighbor, immerses itself in reality to a degree that Nietzsche, with his critique of "neighbor-love," cannot. Similarly, Giles Fraser, developing ideas of Charles Taylor and Stanley Cavell, argues that we find in Nietzsche an expression of *ressentiment* against the "ordinary life" that Christian love, in its acceptance and trust of the neighbor, affirms (Fraser, 2002, p. 145). Hence, for both Wirzba and Fraser, the martyrdom of the Crucified is more life-affirming than that of Dionysus.

These arguments, I think, have much to recommend them. Nietzsche's criticisms of Christianity, no matter how perceptive and applicable to particular manifestations of Christian life, do not exhaust the conceptual and practical resources the tradition has for envisioning and cultivating affirmative life (Roberts, 1998, pp. 164–201). Yet, even as we acknowledge that Nietzsche simplified Christianity, we should not do the same to Nietzsche. Wirzba argues that Nietzsche did not understand Christian love—*agape*. Perhaps. But what, what *exactly*, does he not understand or reject? It has been too easy to view Nietzsche's rejection of "neighbor love" and his valorization of the power of the self as putting him at a radical distance from Christian *agape*. But I think this distance is not as great as it often seems. Consequently, my purpose here is to delineate this difference as precisely as possible. Without arguing for a final convergence, I contend that Nietzsche's love—or at least Zarathustra's—is more affirmative of ordinary life and of his fellow human beings than Wirzba and Fraser allow and that we are able to see this aspect of Nietzsche's love only when we also consider Nietzsche's faith.

Part I: "Great Love" and Untimely Faith:
Book V of The Gay Science

A Confession

With the voice of a madman, Nietzsche first announced the death of God in Book III of *The Gay Science*, published in 1882. Four years later, after writing *Zarathustra*, Nietzsche appended a fifth book to *The Gay Science*. He opens this book with an echo of the madman: "The greatest recent event—that 'God is dead,' that the belief in the Christian god has become unbelievable—is already beginning to cast its shadows over Europe" (*GS*, § 343). Nietzsche goes on to warn that this event is still too distant, that even those, like him, who are "born guessers of riddles"—untimely ones "posted between today and tomorrow"—are not in a position to understand it (*GS*, § 343). But this lack of understanding does not prevent Nietzsche from feeling as if "a new dawn" were shining. It is as if the prospect of grappling with the riddle of the death of God, even knowing that the answer may be centuries away, is enough to make him "cheerful."

Book V is one of Nietzsche's first efforts to solve this riddle—and one of his most provocative and important writings. But in the course of these pages, the riddle takes an unexpected turn: beginning with the death of God, Nietzsche ends with a confession of faith. In a section titled "We Who Are Homeless," which marks, I think, the beginning of the end of Book V, he writes:

> We have also outgrown Christianity and are averse to it—precisely because we have grown out of it, because our ancestors were Christians who in their Christianity were uncompromisingly upright: for their faith they willingly sacrificed possessions and position, blood and fatherland. We—do the same. For what? For our unbelief? For every kind of unbelief? No, you know better than that, friends! The hidden Yes in you is stronger than all Nos and Maybes that afflict you and your age like a disease; and when you have to embark on the sea, you emigrants, you, too, are compelled to this by—a faith! (*GS*, § 377)

What kind of "confession" might this be? Nietzsche certainly remained, to the last, a vehement and vocal enemy of one sort of faith. This is the faith he calls Christian and that in writings ranging from *The Gay Science* to *The Antichrist* he condemns on at least two counts: first, as certainty, such faith serves as a crutch for those who seek security above all and, second, as a transcendentalizing grounding of value in an illusory otherworldly realm, this faith subverts active, affirmative human valuing by rendering it "immoral." Here Nietzsche certainly looks beyond the life-denial of Christian or Platonic *ressentiment*. But he does so with an embrace of faith, a faith that says "Yes" and that is grounded in "great love." Yet Book V also makes it clear that the difference between this affirmative faith and the death-dealing faith Nietzsche despised is not a simple one. For even as he works to separate himself from past convictions, he finds himself confronted with the "problem" of the will to truth and of the "faith" in the divinity of truth that propelled this will. Nietzsche is thus forced to wonder whether his own untimely efforts to understand the meaning of the death of God and to envision a new future are not already infected, in David Krell's sense, by the *ressentiment* of the past (Krell, 1996). It is therefore only in considering carefully how Nietzsche grappled with this problem that it is possible to make distinctions between Nietzsche's criticisms of faith and his own faithful "Yes."

"Our Problem"

Early in Book V, in a section titled "Believers and Their Need to Believe" (*GS*, § 347), Nietzsche contrasts the weakness of the faith that seeks certainty and security to a "sovereign" strength of will that is able to command, that can act and value without relying on belief in God's will or in an ultimate order of the cosmos. Imagining such a will leads Nietzsche to contrast the "believer" with the "free spirit":

> [O]ne could conceive of such a pleasure and power of self-determination, such a *freedom* of the will that the spirit would take leave of all faith, every wish for certainty, being practiced in maintaining himself on insubstantial ropes and possibilities and dancing even near abysses. Such a spirit would be the *free spirit* par excellence. (*GS*, § 347; I have altered Walter Kaufman's translation. He includes an "and" between "faith" and "every wish for certainty" that is not warranted by the German text.)

The free spirit has no need of faith—at least faith understood as certainty. But is it the case, even for Nietzsche, that taking leave of "every wish for certainty" is equivalent to taking leave of "all faith"? Might we view this passage as trading on a distinction between faith as certainty and faith as the "insubstantial ropes and possibilities" that the free spirit apparently does require?

From the beginning of Book V Nietzsche questions the very possibility of freedom from faith. Only a few sections before invoking the free spirit, he examines the "will to truth" (*GS*, § 344, "How We Too Are Still Pious," hereafter referred to as "Pious"). On the one hand, he understands that the search for truth is at the heart of the free-spirited attempt to break away from morality. But, on the other hand, he claims that this search itself implicates him and other free spirits in a certain faith:

> ... it is still a metaphysical faith upon which our faith in science rests—that even we seekers after knowledge today, we godless anti-metaphysicians still take our fire, too, from the flame lit by a faith that is thousands of years old, that Christian faith which was also the faith of Plato, that God is the truth, that truth is divine. (*GS*, § 344)

With this, Nietzsche identifies what in both Book V and at the end of the *Genealogy* he calls "our problem" (*GM* III, § 27). The problem of the will to truth, which Nietzsche later will link with the will to nothingness, or nihilism, is a problem of faith and a problem of morality, for the truth that promises to free us from God ends up leading us back to the faith in truth, to one of the shadows of God that Nietzsche suggests continues to darken our lives. "Our problem," then, poses many questions for Nietzsche. What is the value of truth? Is it possible to seek truth without being committed to faith in its value? Are we who embrace the death of God, who question the will to truth, still thinking out of faith in the absolute value of truth? And, if so, who exactly are we "godless" ones: are we something new, pregnant with a future, or simply a new incarnation of an old, death-dealing faith? Such questions, Nietzsche claims, can be engaged only by someone who experiences them as "his own personal distress, torment, voluptuousness, and passion" (*GS*, § 345). Consequently, though it appears that Nietzsche would like to be able to claim that truth is *not* absolutely valuable, his primary problem here is not so much a question of truth but a question about himself—about his will and about his supposedly "godless" reasons for truth-seeking.

Although this problem was at the center of Nietzsche's writing during 1886 and 1887—in the preface to *Daybreak*, Book V of *The Gay Science*, and Book III of the *Genealogy*—nowhere does he offer a clear way out of it. Rather, he immerses himself in it, he passionately embraces it as a problem, and he seems to be telling us that we, too, need to remain immersed in the problem. But does this mean that Nietzsche's later confession of faith in "Homeless" is simply a recognition of his continued implication in the will to truth? Is the faith to which Nietzsche confesses the same faith that he attacks? Does he suspect that despite his efforts to free himself from metaphysics and the ascetic ideal, the means by which he attempts to do this draws him right back in? In short, is Nietzsche's "confession" penitential?

We should say, rather, that it is affirmative and faithful: "The hidden Yes in you is stronger than all No's and Maybes that afflict you and your age like a disease; and when you have to embark on the sea, you emigrants, you, too, are compelled to this by—a faith!" (*GS*, § 377). This is confirmed, I think, by the trajectory of Book V. In the first section, Nietzsche stresses that we still lack a full understanding of the death of God. He then moves immediately to "Pious," and claims that even "we godless anti-metaphysicians" still have faith in truth and he resolves to examine this will. He begins with the initial formulation: "Nothing is needed more than truth, and in relation to it everything else has only second-rate value." From here, he argues that the "need" in this passage is not utilitarian but moral, for the real meaning of the unconditional will to truth is, "I will not deceive, not even myself." Pursuing this line of thought further, he offers two ways of interpreting this resolve. We need, I think, to consider the whole of Book V from the perspective of these two options for understanding the will to truth. First, Nietzsche notes that there is a "charitable" interpretation: the will to truth is a "quixotism, a minor slightly mad enthusiasm" ("*eine Don-Quixoterie, ein kleiner schwärmerischer Aberwitz*"). The second interpretation is far less generous: the will to truth is "hostile to life and destructive," a "concealed will to death" (*GS*, § 344).

The early sections of Book V, I contend, pursue this latter interpretation, developed especially in the three sections immediately following "Pious" and in great depth in Book III of the *Genealogy*. However, with the series of sections initiated by "Homeless" (*GS*, § 377) and continuing to the end of Book V, Nietzsche returns to the first, generous interpretation, and charts a different course. Speaking as the Wanderer, he once again addresses the desire to push knowledge forward, even to a place "beyond good and evil." In language clearly invoking his earlier "charitable interpretation" of the will to truth as "quixotism" and "minor slightly mad enthusiasm," Nietzsche now suggests that this desire to go beyond morality "may be a minor madness, a peculiar and unreasonable 'you must'" (*eine kleine Tollheit, ein absonderliches unvernünftiges 'du musst'*"; GS, § 380). He admits that he is not sure that it is possible to leave morality behind but asserts that something is commanding him to make the attempt. And, we should gather, unless this is to be another dead end and he is to fall back into nihilism, this attempt cannot be based on or motivated by the "No" or by the need for security that is ultimately a will to death, but rather by a "Yes" to a life of uncertainty.

Something other than belief in the absolute moral value of truth must be compelling the Wanderer—something that from the perspective of morality and truth will appear mad. In the penultimate section of Book V, Nietzsche writes of a new ideal for "an as yet unproven future," an ideal of "great health," of a "spirit who plays naively—that is, not deliberately but from overflowing power and abundance" (GS, § 382). This ideal helps specify the sense in which Nietzsche invokes his "minor madness." He envisions a spirit playful and spontaneous, overflowing with active, creative energy and thus moved not by an inner lack needing to be filled—and so calculating how best to fill it—nor by externally imposed reasons, imperatives, or absolutes. This overflowing spirit thus embodies what Nietzsche refers to earlier in the book as "Dionysian pessimism": a philosophical pathos attracted to the forbidden and ugly and grounded in "overfulness" of life and "excess" of energy (GS, § 370). This is a spirit *attracted* to problems such as truth, nihilism, and the death of God, thrilled by their messiness and intractability and fascinated by their abyssal nature—in other words, a spirit who dances with the problem rather than seeking its solution as quickly as possible. Thinking back to "Homeless," then, we see that although Nietzsche certainly has reasons for leaving home to wander on the seas—God, metaphysics, and morality have become unbelievable—he denies that they ultimately motivate the journey. He does not wander far from home because he no longer believes in it ("For every kind of unbelief? No, you know better than that, friends"). Rather, he is compelled by a "hidden Yes," by a "faith." This faith is not faith as conviction or as the desire for conviction but a passion that risks all security and conviction. It is also a way of taking a stance in the present that wills and hopes but only as it grasps the fullness and intensity of life in the here and now. Hope, in this sense, resides not in any eschatological expectation of the "fullness of time" but in an openness to what will come. It is "untimely" in the sense that it does not find a false security in either the present or the future.

Great Love and Descensional Reflection

The nature of this attraction is crucial: it is, as Nietzsche puts it early in Book V, the "great love" that is necessary for addressing all "great problems" (GS, § 345).

Nietzsche's affirmative faith is an expression of or, better, is constituted by, love, by an ecstatic, passionate love for "our problem." This faith is not an effort to ground and preserve oneself with answers or ground oneself with certainty, but a questioning even to the point of challenging and undermining one's identity. In this ecstasy we find an indication of the way Nietzsche distances himself from the will to truth, or as David Krell argues, we find the "excess that catapults Nietzsche beyond Platonism" (Krell, 1996, p. 128). The nature of this excess becomes evident in Krell's concept of "descensional reflection."

> From beginning to end, Nietzsche's reflection is descensional, its trajectory decisively earthbound. His thought describes an epochal turn in the history of Western thought from Hegel to Heidegger, which I define provisionally as the descent of reflection from thought on *das Absolute* to thought on *der Abgrund*; the descent of reflection from the death of God to the death of human beings—the descent of reflection in both cases implying the demise of metaphysical logos. (Krell, 1996, p. 78)

Krell's gloss "the death of human beings" reminds us that in thinking the death of God, Nietzsche was also involved in a project of rethinking human subjectivity and human freedom. For Nietzsche, the human being is subject to the ruptures and fissures of the body and necessity. This is not a wholehearted rejection of subjectivity, agency, or intentionality, but is, rather, as Charles Winquist puts it so nicely, a "drift" of subjectivity (Winquist, 1995, p. 13). As an ecstatic form of thinking, descensional reflection is a way in which human beings lose themselves in the abyssal play of the problem. As I will develop in more detail below, any love Nietzsche may have for a new future, a "might/should be" that requires one to overcome the problem of the present, is decisively qualified by a love for what is here and now *as a problem*.

For both Nietzsche and Plato, love drives the search for truth. Two points are crucial here for the development of my argument. First, Nietzsche's descensional orientation decisively modifies Platonic eros in a direction that moves toward Christian *agape*. We should not overstate this modification: since Nietzsche is questioning whether it is at all possible to escape the life-hostility of Platonic and Christian faith, his exceeding of Platonism cannot be conceived in terms of simple transcendence; rather, Nietzsche exceeds faith in the divinity of truth only by immersing himself in the question of whether he remains enslaved to it (Boothroyd, 1995, p. 353). Nonetheless, this shifts the emphasis of this love from communion with the purity of the Ideal (or the Absolute, or God) to a love for the earth by which thought confronts us over and over with our finitude and our questions. This is love that finds its goal in engagement, not in satiation, a love that pushes Nietzsche to invoke a word not often associated with him, *service* (*Dienst, dienen*). In a passage I turn to in more detail below, Zarathustra tells his disciples to "let your gift-giving love serve the meaning of the earth" (Z I, "On the Gift-Giving Virtue"). And in *The Gay Science*, the philosopher, rather than ascending to the heavens, "dances even on the edge of abysses" and considers the dance "his only piety, his 'service of God' [*Gottesdienst*]" (*GS*, § 381). It is not the case, as Nietzsche had seemed to suggest earlier in Book V, that the free spirit who dances on the edge of abysses is free of *all* faith. Such a spirit certainly is free from the fear of the abyss that leads people to grasp after belief and conviction. Nietzsche sees such fear all around him—in Christianity, in metaphysics, in certain atheisms of his day. And free spirits are also free of the despairing vertigo that affects many of those who dare approach the abyss. But the freedom of the free spirit is not primarily negative—not a freedom from—but a freedom that comes when one releases oneself, in beauty and grace, to what is necessary.

The second point to make here is that Nietzsche's descensional orientation is intimately bound up with his untimely faith. If Platonic eros involves an upward trajectory to the finality and transcendence of the forms, Nietzschean love remains vulnerable and open to the now, the future, and all the change and pain in the transition between them. The philosopher is "stretched between today and tomorrow," looking for answers that will only come tomorrow but, at the same time, fully engaged in the problem in the present. For all his rancor and despair at the sight of his contemporaries, Nietzsche knows that to hope for the future at the expense of one's life in the present is to deny life as effectively as any ascetic priest. In his untimeliness, then, Nietzsche gives himself over to the future only as he also affirms and remains bound to the "problem" of his present: fully in the present, he does not grasp after the future but, to use Stanley Cavell's word, "awaits." Learning to await the future requires a new thinking, a kind of receptivity that is open to both present and the future: an awaiting that, as Cavell puts it, "was always the knack of faith" (Cavell, 1995, p. 7).

Part II: Zarathustra on Giving and Loving

"I Love Man"

The question, then: what kind of service is this? That is, even as we distinguish a certain Nietzschean philosophical love from Platonic eros, how does this help us understand Nietzsche's view of the love for other, particular, human beings? The answer, I think, is found in *Zarathustra* and can be articulated through a comparison of Zarathustra's service to the earth with the concept of Christian *agape*. As Timothy Jackson defines it, Christian *agape* is "life-affirming love that involves 1) unconditional commitment to the good of others, 2) equal regard for the well-being of others, and 3) passionate service open to self-sacrifice for the sake of others" (Jackson, 1999, p. 15). As Wirzba and Fraser would argue, such love is life-affirming in its trust and care for the other as he or she is and is particularly attentive and caring with regard to the other's failures and sufferings. That Jackson holds a similar view is evident in his criticism of Augustinian love: he claims that although Augustine certainly wants to honor the scriptural sense of *agape*, Augustine was "so struck by the frailty and sinfulness of others, as well as himself, that he effectively turns away from real persons existing in the present and looks to ideal persons as they will be perfected by God in the future" (Jackson, 1999, p. 69). The question of Zarathustra's "service" has to be raised here because if we eliminate the God and sin language from Jackson's interpretation of Augustine, we arguably get a good sense of Nietzsche's disdainful attitude toward his fellow human beings and his yearning for the *Übermensch*.

Before proceeding to explore this question, though, it is necessary to consider Christian *agape* in more detail, for although Jackson's concerns about Augustine have merit, I would argue that the tension between real and ideal in Augustine is inherent to the complex nature of Christian *agape*. Consider Jackson's definition. Two sorts of tension are evident here, and I think the different possibilities of resolving these tensions are at the heart of differences between Nietzsche and Christianity. First, there is the tension signaled by the difference between a commitment to the "good" of others and the regard for their "well-being." These forms of other-directedness are by no means mutually exclusive, but they can, and often do, conflict because we often deceive ourselves about our own or another's good and seek a certain "well-being" that is grounded in superficial or defensive notions of comfort or happiness. Rowan Williams's caution is relevant here: "If we believe we can experience our healing without deepening our hurt, we have understood nothing about the roots of our faith" (Williams, 1990, p. 11). Kierkegaard, too, is relevant at this point, especially given his deep affinities with Nietzsche's attitude toward their European contemporaries. In *Works of Love*, Kierkegaard focuses on the "up-building" goal of *agape* and stresses the extent to which each person needs to be shocked and shaken out of the complacency of his or her loves and relationships in order to work toward genuine Christian love. In short, Christian love, as neighbor love, must negotiate a tension between loving the other as he or she is, which will include fallible, limited conceptions of happiness or well-being, and as he or she can be in Christ. Because one's love for the other is shaped by a vision of true love in Christ, one might be the source of a certain amount of pain. It is useful to distinguish between Nietzsche's glorifications of heroic, solitary, tragic suffering and agapic compassion directed to the neighbor in his or her ordinary suffering, but in doing so we should not fail to recognize that even Christian compassion can be demanding and hard on the sufferer.

A second tension contained in Christian *agape* concerns the idea of self-sacrifice "for the sake of others." Given the fact that loving the other is the way that one exemplifies and realizes one's own love of Christ—is the "way" to salvation—is it really ever self-sacrifice and *only* for the sake of the other? Even when I make the ultimate sacrifice and give up my life for the sake of the other, I will have my reward. (This speaks directly to the "economic" critique of Christianity we find in Essays II and III of Nietzsche's *Genealogy* and usefully commented on by Derrida in *The Gift of Death* (Derrida, 1995, pp. 82–115). Though it makes sense to say that in such a case I do not give my life *because* I want to be saved but because I love the other, the fact remains that we are talking about self-sacrifice here only in a qualified sense.

A comparison between Nietzschean love and agapic love needs to explore these tensions. This is best accomplished, I think, through a consideration of the narrative of *Zarathustra* and its discussions of gifts and sacrifices, neighbors and friends. It is here, I think, that Nietzsche treats love more thoroughly than in any other text.

The centrality of love in *Zarathustra*, though often overlooked, is signaled in the second section of the prologue. As Zarathustra begins his journey down the mountain, the first person he meets is the "Saint," who asks Zarathustra why he is emerging from his solitude. "I love man," replies Zarathustra. "I bring men a gift." But the Saint warns Zarathustra away from men, saying, "Now I love God, man I love not" (Z, Prologue, § 2). Nietzsche thus begins with a contrast between Zarathustra's descensional love and the saint's ascensional, God-directed love. David Allison relates this contrast to the contrast between Zarathustra and Socrates. Though Socrates in the *Republic* begins by "going down" to Piraeus, he does so only by being "forced" down against his will; Zarathustra, by contrast, "wants to go down" out of "surfeit and superabundance . . . to give the teaching of the overman . . . [which] will be a resplendent vision that will enable humanity to see as with divine eyes" (Allison, 2001, p. 130).

Zarathustra wants to give to humanity. Moreover, as he tells us later in the prologue, this love is self-sacrificial: "I love those who do not first seek behind the stars for a reason to go under and be a sacrifice, but who sacrifice themselves for the earth, that the earth may some day become the overman's" (Z, Prologue, § 4). Yet, this passage raises a question—and returns us to Jackson's concerns about Augustine's love: whom, precisely, does Zarathustra love, and for whose sake? "Man's"? But does this mean human beings in particular, only humankind in general, or only humankind because it is a bridge to the *Übermensch*? Does Zarathustra love "man" only for the sake of the *Übermensch*?

Love and the Gift-Giving Virtue

At the end of Book I, Zarathustra speaks to his "friends" and proclaims that the "gift-giving virtue" is the highest virtue. But contrary to views of genuine giving as "altruistic," Zarathustra considers this virtue to be grounded in "selfishness": not "sick" selfishness that gives economically under threat or out of a desire for a return but a powerful, uncalculating self-love that overflows with gifts. In the context of Book I, Zarathustra claims that healthy giving originates in "the lover's will" (Z I, "On the Gift-Giving Virtue"). He develops this idea of love in Book II. In giving, he says, one should be "too pure for the filth of the words: revenge, punishment, reward, retribution. You love your virtue as a mother her child; but when has a mother ever wished to be paid for her love?" (Z II, "The Virtuous"). A mother, Nietzsche seems to be arguing, may well feel that the boundary between herself and her child is a permeable one, complicating simple oppositions between selfishness and altruism. She gives to the child *of* herself and gives the child, as an act of creation, to itself and to the world—and so also *to* herself. On this model, to be virtuous is to love one's deed, to create and to give, both to others and to oneself, in love. Love thus blurs the boundaries between self and other: in love, there is no sacrifice or surrender of self—no matter how much one gives—precisely to the extent that one *desires* to give and finds oneself loved and empowered in the giving, hence realizes oneself even in "self-sacrifice." In such giving, one does not "sacrifice" *for the sake* of this love and power but out of love. Thus, as Alison Ainly suggests, even though Nietzsche invokes "selfishness" and might, for good reason, be accused of idealizing a self-absorbed selfishness, the image of pregnancy and child also invokes a self that is "already other and already strange" (Ainly, 1988, p. 124).

The discussion of love that links Books I and II also anticipates Nietzsche's first extensive published account of will to power, Book II's "On Self-Overcoming." There, Zarathustra reveals the "secret" confided to him by life: "I am that which must always overcome itself . . . whatever I create and however much I love it—soon I must oppose it and my love; thus my will wills it." Where, exactly, does love stand in relation to this "will"? This discussion of will to power is anticipated earlier in Book II when Zarathustra links love and will to creativity: "Verily, through a hundred souls I have already passed on my way, and through a hundred cradles and birth pangs. Many a farewell I have taken; I know the heart-rending last hours. But thus my creative will, my destiny wills it. Or, to say it more honestly: this very destiny—my will wills" (Z II, "Upon the Blessed Isles"). The Nietzschean self, thus portrayed, finds itself enmeshed in relations of creativity and love that, however crucial and constitutive of the self, are relativized through a deeper connection with a process of power/creativity that Nietzsche calls "will to power." This "will" demands the abandonment of love, which amounts, each time, to an abandonment of self. One must give oneself in love, but one must also abandon that which is created and loved, that into which one has poured oneself and out of which one has created oneself. In short, will-to-power does not "belong" to one. It is a space of alterity within the self, compelling the self always to move beyond itself in acts of giving and creating. At the heart of this movement is a relation between the self—as individual self or ego—and the will to power as that which is not just the deepest heart of the self, but of "life"—it is both within and beyond the self.

Nietzsche here puts the lie to any interpretation of will to power that views it as self-aggrandizing power over others. This is particularly evident in the section following "On Self-Overcoming" where Zarathustra counsels the necessity of overcoming one's "heroic will" and one's pride in self-denial. Such heroic pathos, he claims, is violent and jealous and so cannot discover the blessedness of joy. Overcoming this pathos, finding joy, says Zarathustra, is the way to learning "beauty," "laughter," and "kindness": "And there is nobody from whom I want beauty as much as from you who are powerful; let your kindness be your final self-conquest. Of all evil I deem you capable: therefore I want the good from you" (Z II, "On Self-Overcoming"). Nietzsche's power, on this reading, is not an explosion of dominating will. On the contrary, it involves an ecstatic state in which one "turns away" from oneself and is "will-less," transforming heroism into graceful giving.

Zarathustra's "gift-giving virtue" blurs the boundaries between erotic and agapic love: it is a love full of desire but not a possessive desire to gather riches or benefits for the self, only for the sake of the self, but a desire—both of and not of the self—to give to the other. Like *agape*, which is both of and not of the self insofar as it is God's love working through the self, Zarathustra's love, as expression of will-to-power, takes place when one opens oneself to the giving and creating of a force beyond oneself.

Neighbors and Friends

In some key respects, then, Zarathustra's love is selfless. But to whom or what is it directed? For whose sake does Zarathustra give? Is there any indication that he gives for the sake of the neighbor, or is he simply compelled to give in a "squandering," impersonal way that does not attend carefully to the suffering of the other? Nietzsche certainly is critical of an orientation to the other that he calls "neighbor-love." He argues that neighbor-love conceals hatred for both self and other: as Zarathustra puts it, it is merely "your bad love of yourselves," and it is a way of displacing hatred onto those far away: "It is those far away who must pay for your love of your neighbor; and even if five of you are together there is always a sixth who must die" (Z I, "On Love of the Neighbor"). Moreover, the primary expression of such love for Nietzsche, pity (*mit-leiden*, suffering with, or "compassion"), gets in the way of up-building, for it tears both comforter and sufferer away from themselves. As Nietzsche puts it in *The Gay Science*: "Is it good for you yourselves to be above all full of pity? And is it good for those who suffer?" (*GS*, § 338). His point is that we almost inevitably interpret the suffering of others superficially, that pity "strips away from the suffering of others whatever is distinctly personal."

But this criticism of pity suggests a concern for the "good" of the other (as well as for the comforter) and for the other as she or he really is, that is, for what is "distinctly personal" about the other. Rather than taking Nietzsche's attack on pity as a sign of indifference to others, we should rather see it as part of an effort to cultivate the honest confrontation with oneself and, crucially, to focus on joy rather than suffering. For it is joy, instead of pity, that Nietzsche emphasizes when he considers human relationships: he says that he wants to teach us how to "share not suffering but joy" (*GS*, § 338). The superficial comfort provided by pity is merely escapist because it diverts one from the hard path to oneself and one's joy; it also erases differences between selves, for one comforts by assimilating the suffering of the other to one's own experience, tearing the other away from what is most personal to them. In "friendship," by contrast, Nietzsche finds the possibility for human relationship directed to joy and realization of self because it is based in the recognition of difference between self and other. Friendship, Nietzsche claims, is therefore intimately linked with enmity, not in the sense of envious hatred or in the sense of the "them" that makes possible the comfort of an "us," but in the sense of resistance that refuses to assimilate the friend to oneself, that keeps the differences alive. This is an attentive resistance through which one becomes a means for the other's overcoming. "In a friend one should have one's best enemy. You should be closest to him with your heart when you resist him" (Z I, "On the Friend"). The difference between "neighbor love" and friendship, then, is the difference between running from oneself in "suffering with" the neighbor and engaging in a relationship with the friend of mutual up-building, of working with each other to find one's own joy but also, in reaching for that joy, sharing joy with each other.

So, perhaps in joyful relations with friends there is an element of genuine other-relatedness in Zarathustra's love, at least a real commitment to the "good" of the other. If so, then I can summarize my conclusions to this point as follows. First, Zarathustra's love is selfish (though not self-centered) *and* self-sacrificial; that is, Zarathustra preaches a certain dynamic of self-giving and self-sacrifice that we find in Christian *agape* as well. Second, Zarathustra is committed to the good of the other in the sense that his gifts are aimed at a kind of up-building, a reaching beyond the self for a higher good. Yet so long as such commitment is confined to friends—love as *philia*—we still must distinguish it from Christian *agape*. As Jackson tells us, "*agape* is neither the undervaluation nor the over-valuation of someone's or something's worthiness, since it is self-consciously indiscriminate and other-enhancing" (Jackson, 1999, p. 64). Zarathustra's stress on friendship seems to preclude such indiscriminate giving. Only by answering this question, it seems, can we finally determine what it might mean to "share not suffering but joy," for if Zarathustra confines his love in an evaluative sense, it would lead to the conclusion that, for him, some suffering does not deserve response. But if he seeks to share joy more indiscriminately, then we might argue that the difference between sharing suffering and sharing joy is more a matter of perspective and strategy than of a different kind of love altogether.

Higher Men

I will conclude by arguing that Zarathustra's attitude toward the "higher men" in Book IV exemplifies a love that comes quite close to the affirmative elements of *agape* that Wirzba and Fraser identify. Though it may not be completely in-discriminate, Zarathustra's love is much more compassionate and more attentive to the particularity of the recipient than we might be led to expect from some of Nietzsche's other writings. This difference is, of course, an important one. If we focus on the Nietzsche who speaks in his own voice, in texts after *Zarathustra*, with the possible exception of Book V of *The Gay Science*, then I think we must agree with Wirzba and Fraser on the limits of Nietzsche's love. But I think the

Nietzsche who speaks through Zarathustra tells us something different. This might, of course, reflect a problem with my interpretation of *Zarathustra*. Alternatively, though, we could explain this disjunction via Nietzsche's comments in *Ecce Homo*, where he claims that with the writing of *Zarathustra* "the Yes-saying part of my task had been solved" and that it was then time "for the No-saying, the No-doing" (*EH*, "Beyond Good and Evil," § 1). To make this argument, I must first take note of the context in which Zarathustra's encounter with the higher men takes place, a context in which we see Zarathustra enact the untimeliness and "awaiting" that I have discussed with respect to *The Gay Science*. At the end of Book III, Zarathustra ends the struggle with his "abysmal thought"—the thought of the recurrence of "the man of whom you are weary, the small man" (*Z* III, "On Old and New Tablets"). This resolution takes place in an embrace of the abysmal thought in and through an ecstatic, affirmative experience of the love for life and eternity (Roberts, 1998, pp. 129–37). It is expressed in songs to life and eternity, one of which—I call it "the midnight song"—I return to presently because it is repeated at the end of Book IV. Here, Zarathustra "experiences" a step out of time into an eternity that should be understood not as an endlessness at the end of or above time but a space in the midst of time, constitutive of each moment, in which joy and woe are intimately bound to one another, in which an affirmative love breaks into the present. Throughout the first three parts of the book, Zarathustra has been oriented to the future and has seemed to regret the past and to be seeking a way out of the present. With the embrace of recurrence, though, it becomes evident that his love and affirmation are not just for the future but always also for the now. To "await" the *Übermensch*, then, is also to love and engage the present.

This affirmative pattern is repeated at two points in Book IV, in the sections "Noon" and "The Nightwanderer's Song" (Kaufmann gives the latter section the title "The Drunken Song"): in both, Zarathustra undergoes an "experience" of love outside of time that is firmly tied as both cause and consequence to his encounters with the higher men. That these are all higher men might lead one to argue that, no matter how he loves them, Zarathustra shows a preference for a certain kind of human being and his love is therefore evaluative and not indiscriminate. But this is a motley group that represents a great range of human types, all of whom are in some respects, failures—from a weary soothsayer, to a deceiving ascetic of the spirit, to a pope that has lost his piety, to a group of kings who are themselves in search of a higher man. They are all despairing, without direction, and they see themselves not as Zarathustra's equals but his followers. In other words, they are not at all the strong, gift-giving friends with whom one engages in a mutually up-building relationship that we see in Nietzsche's discussions of friendship. As Zarathustra comes to realize at the end of the book, these are not his "companions." Nevertheless, Zarathustra loves these higher men both in feeling and action.

Prior to the section "Noon," Zarathustra encounters the higher men in their various forms of distress. Particularly important are the last two, the "voluntary beggar" and Zarathustra's own "shadow," for these figures represent two extremes Zarathustra attempts to negotiate. First, he meets the beggar, a "sermonizer on the mount," who wanted to give indiscriminately to humanity but has become disgusted with the envy and greed of rich and poor alike and now preaches only to cows. Zarathustra clearly admires the beggar and the purity of his love but implies that the beggar has not quite figured out the trick to giving (thus, Zarathustra tells him that "right giving is harder than right receiving, and [giving] presents well is an art and the ultimate and most cunning master-art of graciousness" [Z IV, "The Voluntary Beggar"]). Zarathustra then meets his own shadow, who in stark contrast to the beggar's efforts at love has engaged in a nihilistic project of transgression only to end up without a goal, left with an "in vain" (Z IV, "The Shadow"). Zarathustra offers comfort and rest to both these figures and then, in "Noon," undergoes an experience of perfect happiness, conveyed in figures of bliss, love and sensuous pleasure that suggests a way of being somewhere between the beggar's self-defeating love and the shadow's nihilism.

This experience is expressed in language that has strong parallels to the discussion of faith in Book V of *The Gay Science*. There, recall, Nietzsche invokes a wandering and a homelessness not that different from that of Zarathustra's shadow, save for the fact that the "free spirit" dances on abysses tied by "insubstantial ropes." Zarathustra, at "Noon," speaks of himself as a seafaring wanderer who has found rest in a quiet cove, that is, "now near the earth, faithful, trusting, waiting, tied to it with the softest threads" (Z IV, "At Noon"). This rest is not really a sustainable state, but rather a timeless "moment" in the midst of a searching and wandering. (See Slavoj Zizek's provocative treatment of Nietzsche's "High Noon," and the comparison he makes between love in Nietzsche and St. Paul; Zizek, 2003, pp. 81, 114.) These "threads" are links that keep both Nietzsche's free spirit and Zarathustra connected with earth, life, and others even as they experiment and wander in ways as yet unheard of, even as they look to a distant future and new companions. Thus, it is not irrelevant that Zarathustra undergoes his first two experiences of "eternity" after he becomes reconciled with the existence of the "small man" and after his first encounters with the "higher men."

This pattern is maintained with Zarathustra's third ecstatic interlude (in "The Nightwandering Song"). After "Noon," Zarathustra proceeds to his cave to meet the gathered, despairing higher men. The Zarathustra we see in these scenes is compassionate, not in a pitying or even particularly gentle way, but compassionate nonetheless, for he understands the despair of the higher men, both individually and together, and he responds to it by teaching them to laugh, even at himself, and to share joy. The episode in the cave invokes Jesus and Moses, including both a last supper and an "ass festival" in which the higher men, like the Israelites worshipping the golden cow, worship an ass even while Zarathustra preaches "The Higher Man." But in stark contrast to the anger of Moses at the Israelites' unfaithful piety, Zarathustra cavorts and laughs with the higher men.

Amidst this parody and hilarity, he does continue to preach the *Übermensch*: "I have the *Übermensch* at heart, that is my first and only concern—and not man: not the neighbor, not the poorest, not the most ailing, not the best" (Z IV, "On the Higher Men"). But the context here is crucial, for he is complimenting the higher men on their despair, on their not knowing how to live in a time where people are only concerned about utilitarian comfort. Moreover, as his discourse goes on, it becomes less a matter of defining the *Übermensch* and of calculating the worth of a person or of life on the basis of the extent to which it makes the *Übermensch* possible and more a matter of learning to laugh and dance in the present. Zarathustra tells his companions that they will fail but that they should laugh and dance and love as they do so. "This crown of him who laughs, this rose-wreath crown: to you, my brothers, I throw this crown. Laughter I have pronounced holy; you higher men, learn to laugh!" (Z IV, "On the Higher Men"). Thus, even after his discourse on the higher man draws a variety of responses from his companions that seem to miss the point and even to criticize Zarathustra, and even after they become "pious" again and begin to worship the ass, Zarathustra joins in the fun, seeing it not as a betrayal of his teaching but as an indication that they "have become gay again" and have "blossomed" (Z IV, "The Ass Festival").

Again, this engagement with others is the occasion for a mystical interlude. When he sees the higher men dancing with joy, Zarathustra's "spirit fled visibly and flew ahead and was in remote distances and, as it were, 'on a high ridge.' As it is written, 'between two seas, wandering like a heavy cloud between past and future'" (Z IV, "The Drunken Song"). That is, as Nietzsche wrote it earlier in the book, for here Zarathustra returns to the point from which he sang his songs of life and eternity at the end of Book III. Here, at the end of Book IV, he beckons to the higher men to join him in wandering in the night and then repeats to them the "midnight song" of love for woe, joy, and life. Again, Zarathustra finds his deepest contact with his love and his faith in those moments when he is engaged with others, accepting them, comforting them, and sharing joy with them. As the end of the book indicates, Zarathustra still has work to do, a future to seek. But he has found love in the present.

Conclusion

Jacques Derrida has claimed, in a discussion of the messianic, that "as soon as you are open to the future, as soon as you have a temporal experience of waiting for the future, of waiting for someone to come: that is the opening of experience" (Caputo and Derrida, 1997). Beginning with the prologue, Zarathustra voices his hope and expectation for the *Übermensch* and suggests that he loves humanity because they are a means to this ideal. By the end of the book, however, we see that this expectation has had the consequence of opening Zarathustra to his own fears and suffering, and to the suffering and despair of the "higher men." Without being diverted from his hopes, he is able to respond attentively and compassionately to the people before him by sharing his joy. In this sharing of pain and joy, love and hope, he is able to experience the world as "perfect."

Works Cited

Ainly, Alison. 1988. "'Ideal Selflessness': Nietzsche's Metaphor of Maternity." In *Exceedingly Nietzsche*, ed. David Farrell Krell and David Wood. New York: Routledge and Kegan Paul.

Allison, David. 2001. *Reading the New Nietzsche*. Lanham, MD: Rowman & Littlefield.

Boothroyd, David. 1995. "Levinas and Nietzsche: In Between Love and Contempt." *Philosophy Today* 39 (Winter).

Caputo, John, and Jacques Derrida. 1997. *Deconstruction in a Nutshell: A Conversation with Jacques Derrida*, ed. John Caputo. New York: Fordham University Press.

Cavell, Stanley. 1995. "Time after Time." *London Review of Books*, Jan. 12.

Derrida, Jacques. 1995. *The Gift of Death*, trans. David Wills. Chicago: University of Chicago Press.

Fraser, Giles. 2002. *Redeeming Nietzsche*. London and New York: Routledge.

Jackson, Timothy. 1999. *Love Disconsoled*. Cambridge: Cambridge University Press.

Krell, David Farrell. 1996. *Infectious Nietzsche*. Bloomington: University of Indiana Press.

Roberts, Tyler T. 1998. *Contesting Spirit: Nietzsche, Affirmation, Religion*. Princeton: Princeton University Press.

Williams, Rowan. 1988. "The Suspicion of Suspicion." In *The Grammar of the Heart*, ed. R. H. Bell. San Francisco: Harper and Row.

Williams, Rowan. 1990. *The Wound of Knowledge*. Cambridge: Cowley Publications.

Winquist, Charles. 1995. *Desiring Theology*. Chicago: University of Chicago Press.

Wirzba, Norman. 1997. "The Needs of Thought and the Affirmation of Life: Friedrich Nietzsche and Jesus Christ." *International Philosophical Quarterly* 37:4, 148 (December).

Zizek, Slavoj. 2003. *The Puppet and the Dwarf*. Cambridge, MA: MIT Press.

Part Three

Spirit at the Margins
Mimesis, Music, and the Art of Self-Fashioning

Chapter Six

Mimetic Geist

Charles E. Scott

"The whole frame of things preaches indifferency."
—R. W. Emerson

I. What Pascal Lacked

Pascal had a monstrous intellectual conscience, according to Nietzsche, but he did not have what it takes to figure out and determine the history of Western religious sensibility (*BGE*, § 45). Though admirable in its monstrosity, Pascal's intellectual conscience was not made for "the great hunt," for the pursuit of what has happened and is carried in the formation of Western religious awareness and passion. The subject for such a hunt would be an exceptional agency of recognition, naming, affection, and evaluation. The subject that is pursued—Western spirituality—is active in the pursuit: the pursuer is to a degree—a self-endangering degree—the pursued, and the direction is toward a fundamental transformation of not only our recognition of the way Western religious and ethical sensibility began and developed but also and at once the way the recognizing pursuer's awareness began and developed. The danger of major transformation and destruction inheres in the knower as well as in the known.

A conscience different from Pascal's is at issue, one that is no less monstrous but much more devilish, distant, playful, and malicious, a Dionysian conscience that takes delight in its own undergoing and self-overcoming. A sensibility that is Dionysian figures something vastly different from Pascal's. This sensibility is no less sacrificial, no less wounded than Pascal's, but it is without hope for divine promise and presence: the life of Dionysus is at best a mask of gods' (or God's)

105

death and absence. The sensibility is Dionysian (given to self-overcoming *in* its own identity) in part because its own agency is problematic in the pursuit of the problem of religious sensibility, in part because salvation and forgiveness are not at stake, and in part because it dissolves in the force of representation and occurs as a strange mimesis of—virtually an art of—voided presence: a mimesis with no identity to imitate. While Pascal's intellect had with it much that is Dionysian, he, in common, with Western spiritual agency, didn't *know* it and thus didn't know to cultivate it or how to suffer it creatively.

The sensibility of the pursuit is also characterized by a dangerous division: the intention of the pursuit is at cross-purposes with itself. The predisposition toward the pursuit and toward thorough knowledge of spiritual life was forged in the process that produced religious awareness and conscience in Western civilization. The pursuer, after all, has a conscience, even a bad conscience that can understand—more than understand, *know*—Pascal's sense of sin and fall from grace. It is also a conscience that feels badly about that kinship with Pascal's conscience. A dimension of the pursuer's conscience wants betterment, is drawn to sickness, and has a sense for awful divine presence. This sensibility also has another dimension, something like a perspective on its own ethos of religious evaluation and on its own formation that gives goods and bads, divines and evils to appear with the force of identities. This dimension constitutes a perspective that enjoys an indifferent disposition, a liberty of heedlessness, something like freedom from bias before goods and evils, a dimension of unconcern that allows the concern in doing a history of Western religious sensibility a range of freedom and a quality of transformative force unavailable to the disposition in question. I refer to the indifference that characterizes "that vaulting heaven of bright, malicious spirituality that would be capable of surveying from above, arranging and forcing into formulas this swarm of dangerous and painful experiences" (*BGE*, § 45).

"That vaulting heaven of bright, malicious *spirituality*"? What does Nietzsche have in mind by *Geistigkeit*? Certainly a state of mind that is at once historical in its formation and ahistorical in its eventuation. The word suggests "the human soul," a dimension of inner experience as well as *spiritus, anima mens,* and *genius.* Something that is lively and aware, coming to pass, a region with limits, reach, and dimension, with depth, height, and surface, as it were. *Geistigkeit* can connote multiple identities, none of which defines "it." *Geistigkeit* can mean a harbor and a producer of freedom, a site of potential pride and self-confidence as well as of enslavement, self-mockery, and self-mutilation. Western *Geistigkeit* is figured by subjection and dominance, beauty and ugliness, comprehension, foolishness—it names a full range of conscious achievement, failure, and ability.

The aspect of *Geistigkeit* that I want to consider comes to bear in the free spirit (*der freie Geist*). In *Beyond Good and Evil* Nietzsche gave an account of this kind of spirituality prior to his observations on the religious way of being from which I quoted above. The account of the free spirit maps a departure and articulates an agency for the departure from the traditional prejudices imbedded in Western spiritual achievement. In this process his writing embodies not only the common lineage that he shares with Pascal but also a kind of spirituality that Pascal could not bring to creative expression. The aspect of spiritual indifference, one that produces differences in a context of overcoming its own formation, points out indirectly a weakness in many forms of Western spiritual life as well as in Pascal's. It is a weakness that expresses a desire for something personal, even human-like, at the outer borders of spiritual agency, something that saves us from the indifference that permeates living events. This is a dimension of indifference that figures nonetheless in Pascal's sense of number and calculation, the agonizing distance of God, and the soul's implacable need for suffering and abnegation before the requirements of a possible salvation. Nietzsche's Pascal is like a half-waking Dionysus who embodies an only partially reflected sense that indifferent necessity permeates identities and gives them a backdrop and inevitability of oblivion.

The high probability is that Western spiritual enactment carries with it much that follows Pythagorean and Dionysian experience. A certain neutrality often characterizes the lives of Western divinities in their distance and self-absorbed enactments. That is a neutrality that often appears to characterize spiritual freedom before whatever is deathly and time-limited. Such freedom can appear without care, that is, indifferently, in the force of its own enactment. Perhaps we Westerners need to affirm such indifference if we wish to carry out a definitive aspect of our spiritual heritage. If we did affirm it, what and how would we affirm?

II. A Tense Bow

Nietzsche speaks of Pascal's *intellectual* conscience. Recall that one of Pascal's major works has the title *L'Esprit géométrique*: *The Spirit of Geometry*, the *Geist* of geometry. In that work he *showed* the advantages of geometrical procedure in establishing reasonable claims of truth, given that no axioms are provable. And he showed in a second book, *De l'Art de persuader*, that this art requires people to recognize the drastic limits of reason in the formation of reasonable knowledge. In yet a third book, *Expériences nouvelles touchant le vide*, he showed that contrary to the established scientific belief of the time, nature does indeed tolerate a vacuum. So far so good. Pascal was relentless in his critique of easy thought and ill-conceived beliefs as he showed that the source or sources of truth cannot be found in rational activity, and he was equally conscientious in showing that a full skepticism is not really possible for alert human beings. The spirit of the highest form of knowledge, according to Pascal, geometrical knowledge, is found in part in both its ideality and the severity of its limits. The art of the best persuasion carries out the knowledge that first principles are not provable, and we must bring people to experiences of nonrational intention and revelation if we are to find the real beginnings for the certainties that we affirm. And nature, he showed, far from being seamlessly filled with invisible matter, is characterized by empty space.

Such careful, impassioned intellectual work on the limits of the intellect and the probability of space without presence, I assume, won Nietzsche's admiration, even if Pascal were insensitive to the historical development of spirit and its value. Pascal also recognized the profound degree of human spiritual suffering and unhappiness—the misery that comes with Western human life in its uncertainty and mortality. And all of these intellectual accomplishments are unified by two further impassioned claims: people need to hear God, and the only true aid to such hearing is faith in Jesus Christ. Pascal's spirit, so close and so far from a freedom available to it, ending with a calculation of the risks of not believing in the Christian God, developing an art of religious persuasion based on fear and a desire for eternal happiness, filling the vacuum of ignorance and limitation with a horror of unredeemed life and death and, in that horror, with an image of enduring divine, if hidden presence—Pascal is a figure of spiritual tension between recognized, mortal limitation and a tradition-bound affirmation of figures of eternity. It's clearly an art, Pascal's thought, but an art without acceptance of its own historical development or the indifference that is usually necessary for art to be: Pascal's spirit is monstrous in the tension it composes at the heart of his sincerity and conscientious intelligence. His spirit forms a fine image of its greater progenitor, Western spirituality—torn by an attempted affirmation of spiritual freedom in an art the content of which both affirms and denies it. Pascal's art assumes an awful, human freedom from God and Truth at the same time that it affirms God's necessity for that freedom.

Nietzsche writes of spiritual tension in his preface to *Beyond Good and Evil*: "But the fight against Plato or, to speak more clearly and for 'the people,' the fight against the Christian-ecclesiastical pressure of millennia . . . has created in Europe a magnificent tension of the spirit the like of which had never yet existed on earth: with so tense a bow we can now shoot for the most distant goals." This spiritual tension, he says, figures the "need of the spirit." The need is the stretch of Western spirit, its tautness, imbalance, and unrest. This tension composes the nurturance as well as the sickness of free spirit, and, as we shall see, it is a site of disposition without bias to the poles of the tension. This spiritual tension is without care except for its inclination to stretch to a breaking point. This observation suggests that the Western spiritual heritage has a definitive core of life that bends toward its own breaking and that, in the context of Nietzsche's thought, is severely mistaken when it gains the imagery of self-sacrifice in a context of divine reward. It's the threatening force of this tension so apparent in Pascal's spiritual accomplishment, and the failed effort of deviation from the tension in Pascal's faith, that allows him to merit one of Nietzsche's most appreciative adjectives: monstrous.

The tense bow finds its affirmation in "the free spirit." By the adjective *free*, Nietzsche intends a quality of mind that in its passionately interested, critical, and constructive activity reflects a dimension of indifference to most of the images and signs that organized what people have traditionally affirmed as good, evil, and holy. This reflection includes an inscribed indifference to images of free spirits' own moral value. ("The overcoming of morality, in a certain sense even the self-overcoming of morality—let this be the name for that long secret work which has been saved up for the finest and most honest, also the most malicious, consciences of today, as living touchstones of the soul"; *BGE*, § 32.) Moments might well occur when free-spirited activity seems enough for all time, seems to fulfill a destiny in free endeavor considerably in excess of individual creativity. But proper fulfillment of Western free spiritedness happens as people enjoy the pretense of completion while their work moves toward overturning the very identity of "the" free spirit. In this release from the value of so many goods and bads as well as from universality combined with identity, the "vaulting heaven of bright, malicious spirituality" comes to bear. ("[T]here are heights of the soul from which even tragedy ceases to look tragic"; *BGE*, § 26.) The free spirit is now able to arrange things and create formulas of association in the knowledge that "spirit" is a process of appearing and imaging in a force of neutrality that makes all the difference. Let's look more closely at this differential neutrality in the imagery of Nietzsche's thought.

III. The Coming of Images

In *The Birth of Tragedy* Nietzsche describes a thoroughgoing force of influence on Western culture in a preclassical Greek experience of forces of nature and their connection to artistic productivity. Their experience, once given mythical/artistic expression, comes to compose the very disposition of indifference—a prereflective experience of differential neutrality—that is such a significant dimension in Western spirituality as Nietzsche finds it. In *The Birth of Tragedy* he collects the definitive experiences (for our topic) around the images of Apollo and Dionysus and a force of like-making, mimesis.

Apollo, the bringer of dreams, figures in *The Birth of Tragedy* not only as a maker of dreams but also as the shining—the manifesting, the appearing—of dreams. As the Shining One, Apollo suggests the appearing of something that is otherwise invisible in ordinary activity. The preoccupation with invisible reality that so thoroughly saturated Greek experience, both early and late, takes the form of Apollo, who gives invisible realities (past, present, and future) to shine, for example, in the darkness of sleep: nothing but sleep is happening, and then like a shot out of the dark, a dream appears that is free of the constraints of waking life and that radiates a sense of its own, making apparent in itself what is hidden outside of itself, an icon of particular force that must be attended and interpreted carefully because of the power and importance of its appearance. Apollo is the figure of the shining of appearance, not the figure of its content. Like Hermes, the sense of Apollo in this context comes not in the message but in the *appearing* of an otherwise largely invisible reality: not the meaning so much as the shining, the appearing, the breaking in of what is not a matter of common sense. At this point I note the bright, lofty indifference of Apollo to whatever the reality might be, the difference his shining makes, and the striking force that this Greek experience attributes to such occurrences.

Dionysus gives nothing to shine. Chaotic, often indeterminate, deteriorative of forms and orders, and yet vaguely alive and compelling, this strange . . .— is it a grouping of force and nonforce? something like negative power? a figure of contextualized chaos?—Dionysus happens with elision, inessential disintegration, oblivion. Mere passing away. And yet in the experience of passing away, in the slippage and failure of form, Greek people, early and late, found a sense of closeness with vitality, almost by antiphrasis, a resignation proper to suffering mortality, an experience approximate to reconciliation with boundless indifference to whatever matters.

Nietzsche finds in the tension of these two kinds of . . . experiences? forces? lived signs? . . . these two figures of order and disorder, a connection that gave beauty in the form of tragedy to the senseless absence of order and value in the higher and lower reaches of mortal occurrences. In this art, senseless dimensions of sense shine beautifully through human success and failure. Beauty in this context does not abolish anything, certainly not darkness and chaotic fate. Beauty, rather, gives them to shine in a crosshatched, tension-filled, maddening glory of order and chaos that comes to pass with a draw that inclines people to say yes.

Mimesis provides Hellenic context for these two figurations of differential forces. This word describes occurrences when likenesses happen, and it can thereby name a manner of linkage among various occurrences of inception, growth, and decline. On the surface, *Apollo* and *Dionysus* name nonhuman forces of generation and decay, but their many legends add a vast range of subtlety and variation to their qualities. Art works, for example, are like the inception and progress of plants and animals, like the transformative growth and passage of things, insofar as some thing comes from some other thing, and a new thing happens and becomes its own, whether it be a vine, a goat, a boat, a statue, or a drama. Mimesis articulates happenings of likenesses—that boat is like this one, this group of words reminds us of those, the clash of form and disaster in this play is like that of struggling mortals. And the emergence of the boat is like the emergence of a sculpted form. The force of bringing about likenesses makes the differences of similarity, kinship, reminder, imitation, memory, and recognition. It is not especially an ordering force per se—although order without mimesis is not conceivable—but rather one of connection even when the connections do not compose a unity and allow disorder to shine. *Mimesis* also names the kinship of various kinds of making, whether or not the "maker" is a person or something else. The anonymity of mimesis is now the focus, because the indifference of this force to the likenesses it allows is part of—or at least like—the vault of the free spirits' spirituality. How is that so?

IV. A Vault of Mimetic Indifference

Nietzsche established part of the contrast between the free spirit and Pascal by recognizing that Pascal's spirituality fell prey to what Nietzsche wanted to uncover by "the great hunt." The connection I would like to make is that between this process of recognition (the great hunt) and the lineage that Nietzsche sets out to describe, that of the operation of mimesis in the birth (and death) of tragedy. There is a likeness, a kinship, between the lineage and its recognition, and this connection includes mimetic indifference. Mimetic indifference composes forcefully the vault of spiritual life as Nietzsche accounts it. If Nietzsche is accurate, *our* feeling the impact that Greek tragedy had on their experience of being alive requires, if even possible, a mammoth and mind-stretching exercise. What are the dimensions of contemporary experience that are like those of the Greeks who were moved by tragic beauty to want to live in spite of certain suffering, injustice, destruction, and death? Their experience, as Nietzsche imagines it, was in the absence of a sense of foundational meaning for "life." The very process of the performed tragedy—its life—carries no sense of universal meaning or authorship of the world. There is an exhilarating kind of affirmation that possesses none of the unities that images of a singular God or ordered Law impose. The modern charge of "merely aesthetic" against this force of art and beauty comes to Nietzsche as a symptom of spiritual deterioration so profound as to demand from spirits of unusual alertness and resolve (not Pascal's) recognition of the deterioration's inception and formation. But what is the living basis for Nietzsche's images of Greek aesthetic experience? And why would he think (know?) that some gifted spirits could now see at least the outlines of realities in Western sensibility that, by the very obtuseness of that sensibility, are usually invisible? What is the living basis for the great hunt? Especially in the nihilistic age based in the death of a Greek art of tragic affirmation?

We could turn now to any of several genealogies begun by Nietzsche, those of the value of good or of conscience, for example, or of the death of God or depreciation of physical pleasure. But for our present purposes, let's keep mimesis, Apollo, and Dionysus before us to see how, in the forces and collections they figure, we can find a likeness between them and the malicious vaulting sky in Western spirituality. That likeness would be the basic referent we're looking for to show a way whereby Western spirituality composes a tension that intends its self-overcoming (a midway marker of which Nietzsche found in the art and suffering of Pascal). We would show as well a threshold for contemporary access to Greek, tragic affirmation. An indifferent gathering of likenesses among irreducible differences is our key. *Mimesis*, the Greek word, can suggest a relation of dependence: one writer's dependence on another, for example. The word also carries an overtone of the intense attentiveness required by disciplined memory. It also may designate experiences in which a power is exerted that brings likeness and the intimacy of acquaintance that likeness allows. In the context of *The Birth of Tragedy* and Nietzsche's reading of certain aspects of Greek culture, *mimesis* also suggests similarity of images and processes of figured representation. *Mimesis* names a power of imaging and engagement that allows comparison, complex recognition, interdependence among differences, as well as differences among similarities. The power of mimesis (faceless, without identity) also functions now in the emergence of images as they happen with similarity and difference. Mimesis takes place, for example, in the formation and interaction of signs and symbols, in any thing's sense and recognition. And when attended to, mimesis lets us know that our sensible worlds—wherever there are connections of likes— are like works of art, even though no particular person or subject can rightly be named as their creator. Mimetic power, seemingly like that in Greek experience, continues today as constitutive of relational events and hence as intrinsic to oc- currences of recognition. It is a force of likeness, no matter what happens to be alike. This kind of power is indifferent to consequences, purposes, and values, like a neutrality of relational force. It would be a primary *geistige* factor in rec- ognizing Christ as savior, God as dead, and Pascal as monstrous.

As in other of Nietzsche's observations, one of his thoughts here is that powerful functions carry with them memories and imbedded dispositions. Non- voluntary mimetic occurrences, I have said, have in them memory of what some Greeks appear to have affirmed: powers of connection and kinship among things (including images) show nothing of fundamental justice, singular identity, or purpose. Mimetic power is without preference among options. As the force of likeness, it is like a sheer vaulting heaven, invisible to those without eyes to see. This lack of identity in mimesis, reflected so well in some Greek drama, com- poses a vault above the comparatively low ceiling of Pascal's agonized efforts to form a hope that human limitations are juxtaposed with another dimension of revealed and beneficent reality. Affirmation of this lack of identity in the force of likeness is also the site of genesis for a different kind of conscience, one that intends in a traditional way to be honest but now with an honesty that it knows is like a work of art, a mimetic event that presents and re-represents in the un- biased disposition of the power of tragedy. This unbiased disposition (mimesis) is a kind of *Geistigkeit* for Nietzsche, not like a person, divine or human, but like nothing other than the happening of likenesses, likenesses that come to form and degenerate into other likenesses. This kind of *Geist* doesn't mean a thing. Imaging, likening, re-presenting, expressing, figuring—something like art—take place as people come to know things and see with all manner of connections, kinships, and differences. Recognitions happen in the indifferent forces of like- ness with formation and disappearance: a vault of alert eventuation with no one there but formed and deformed likenesses. Something like real masks.

People can hear no resonance with human compassion in Greek tragedy, where art, the gift of mimesis, joins the forces figured by Apollo and Dionysus—a grand simulacrum of the fate of all individuals. Tragedy as a functioning form carries the loss of whatever meaning it might also possess—dispossesses such meaning in Dionysus' power—and leaves the questions: is being alive worth the effort? With the loss of everything, can you live without the promise, even the hope, of restitution? Tragedy is a living memory of the possibility of what Nietzsche called a pessimism of strength, of "an intellectual predilection for the hard, gruesome, evil, problematic aspect of existence, prompted by well-being, by overflowing health, by the fullness of existence" (*BT*, "Attempt at Self-Criticism"). This kind of pessimism, before the possibility of which Pascal's own monstrous and unhealthy spirit failed, and in the force of which begins the great hunt for recognition of Western spirituality's generation and decay—this kind of pessimism lies embedded in the occurrence of tragedy before it can be denied. Such denial seems to be peculiar to a spiritual flight from tragedy—*down* from tragedy, we might say, when we have the vaulting heaven in mind. This refusal of a manner of *geistige* life by a manner of *geistige* life composes a very powerful tension—a tension whose occurrence we can now say is memorial, a history-bearer, one that in its power moves toward a release of itself in new images, new configurations of force, new manners of living.

That release in the forms of new knowledge is, of course, one of Nietzsche's intentions. One aspect of the new knowledge is an account of the tensions that compose his Western *geistige* life. Both the account and the knowledge to which it contributes take multiple forms, many of which are not compatible or consistent with the others and are indifferent to many customary connections of compatibility. We might follow this indifference to traditional connections as one way to the vaulting heaven. Or we could follow Nietzsche's style of breakage and interruption, his dismissal of sacred axioms or his occasional accomplishment of laughter before the values that he most cherishes. Whatever the way, we can find in his work the vaulting differential of mimetic indifference in the tragic confluence of powers of formation and deformation.

Who cares whether likeness and difference are indifferently mimetic in their relations? Not many philosophers in this country, at least. We philosophers in the United States have found worthy causes to espouse, many "–ists" by which to identify ourselves, not to mention intellectual pieties, both religious and nonreligious. We are busy with our philosophical-ethical good deeds, optimistic in our pursuit of political efficacy and timeliness. Very likely some of our most trenchant philosophical differences will be bridged by people's joining good causes, whether on the left or right of the spectrum, as we look to make a difference in our society by dint of careful analyses and descriptions and by alignments with those who need our gifts—especially with those who might put our thought to work in agencies and committees. Perhaps political differences will replace distinctly philosophical differences as the axis for argument and differentiation;

and Western philosophy in this country, not entirely alien to its medieval heritage, will take its cues from sources that are not philosophical. Proper espousal and belief (as though they were not *geistige* events), not new arts of expression, new principles of aesthetic order, might become the goal of thought—with little sense for a vast, largely invisible neutrality at the historical core of our sympathies and affiliations. No sense of fate. An optimism with little awareness of the forces that play in it.

One ingredient in such a state of mind might be the exercise of slight care in reading the tradition that, though formative of our powers to know and represent, seems largely past. Strong espousal requires the courage of convictions (not their relentless interrogation or suspension), a kind of sincerity and seriousness not found among the complacent. Such sincerity and seriousness are also not found on the edges of Nietzsche's noncomplacent thought where his mimetic art is most forceful. Nietzsche might be accurate in his description of the resources of creative alertness in Western culture: what is sometimes called spirit in the West with admirable ambiguity is formed in a tragic struggle of forces best designated by figures and not concepts, forces that engender likenesses and their rules of connection, and forces that are often expressed in tensed forms of self-refusal. Were he accurate, we could say that our good will in philosophy, our desire to work for good causes, would mask conflicted currents of spirit that defy all "—ists" and make probable that our endeavors are like a satyr play after tragedy, certainly a relief after so much hopelessness but captured by histories that we enact and cannot know outside of alert engagement with mimetic power.

Or perhaps Nietzsche is only half right. Perhaps our desire for proper beliefs, our well-intentioned humanitarian philosophies, and our likeness mediated by "—ists" now effect a sky-change, a cosmic shift in Western *Geistigkeit*. Far from blindly fulfilling a destiny of misaimed and tragic tension, we are now engaged in a Great Reconstruction, one that makes a vault of optimism, with mistakes, perhaps, but without a fateful tension. Perhaps we are entering a time of extroversion that witnesses the turning of *Geist* into an *ungeistige* world, better for people and only vaguely appreciative of another world's discovery that beauty can make a life worth living.

Chapter Seven

Nietzsche on Music*

Richard Schacht

> Formerly philosophers were afraid of the senses. . . . Having "wax in one's ears" was then almost a condition of philosophizing; a real philosopher no longer listened to life insofar as life is music; he *denied* the music of life—it is an ancient philosopher's superstition that all music is siren's music. (*GS*, § 372)

> Suppose that one assessed the *value* of a piece of music according to how much of it could be counted, calculated, and expressed in formulas: how absurd would such a "scientific" assessment of music be! What would one have grasped, understood, known of it? Nothing, really nothing of what is "music" in it! (*GS*, § 373)

Two of the greatest loves of Nietzsche's life were language and art—and more specifically, literature and music. He drew heavily on his intimate knowledge of both in his philosophical thinking. Much has been made of his reliance upon models and metaphors drawn from language and literature. The poststructuralists have even taken him to have construed reality as textuality, and Alexander Nehamas summed up his interpretation of Nietzsche's thought in the subtitle of his *Nietzsche: Life as Literature*. It seems to me, however, that while there is something to these interpretations, they do not do justice to a different and deeper

---

* A shorter and somewhat different version of this paper, under the title "Nietzsche, Music, Truth, Value, and Life," was presented at a symposium of the North American Nietzsche Society (NANS) at the 2002 Pacific Division meeting of the American Philosophical Association and appeared under that title, along with the other contributions to the symposium, in the NANS issue of *International Studies in Philosophy* 35/3.

dimension and direction of Nietzsche's thinking; that, of these two great loves of his, language and art, the influence upon his thought of his sense of art was the greater; and that, rather than "life as literature" the epigraph *"life as music"* would be closer to the mark. My thesis in this essay is that in his thinking about human life and even about truth and value more generally Nietzsche is often guided (in the language of *The Birth of Tragedy*) by "the spirit of music" and the paradigm of music and is best understood accordingly. And it seems to me that when he is read and heard in this way the results are both interpretively important and philosophically interesting.

I

It took Nietzsche some time to work his way to the point that he could appropriate and make use of the model of music in this way; for he first had to overcome both his Schopenhauerian metaphysical construal of it and his Wagnerian valorization of it. He had begun by following Schopenhauer in taking music to have a special status, setting it apart not only from the other arts but also from language and the concepts it enables us to form, owing to its purported special reflection or expression of the dynamic reality underlying all appearances that he had called "will." He subsequently abandoned the Schopenhauerian metaphysics of "the world as will and representation"—and with it, the metaphysics of music as something that is neither "representation" nor "will" itself but, rather, a kind of "language of the will" unmediated by perceptual or conceptual representations, to which a deeper kind of "truth" (as correspondence) may therefore be accorded than is even possible for representations of either sort.

But in the end Nietzsche did not simply replace Schopenhauer's metaphysical "world-will" with such psychological phenomena as "feelings," "passions," and other such "affects." Rather, he moved toward an understanding of life and the world on the model of music itself, having something like its basic character, and along the lines of which the ideas of what it means for something to be real, or to be true, or to have value, are to be recast and retrieved—while music itself, on the other hand, was likewise reinterpreted as a piece of life, capable of significantly affecting the rest of the lives of creatures like ourselves in which it can figure, in varying ways.

In a sense, of course, Nietzsche had had something like this idea from the beginning, for a version of it is in plain view in *The Birth of Tragedy* (*BT*), quite independently of the Schopenhauerian metaphysics of the world and of music, in his conception of the fundamentally Dionysian character of life, which gave birth to both music and dance through its eruptions in the intoxicated frenzy of Dionysian revelry. He could and did retain this basic idea even as he moved away from its Schopenhauerian interpretation in terms of "will" as the "in-itself" of the world, endlessly expressing itself in the objectifications and representations in which everything in the world and all experience of it consist. He replaced that metaphysics with a philosophical psychology, biology and cosmology that might be thought of as a scientifically informed but interpretively supplemented naturalism, drawing on forms of experience to which the sciences are strangers and to which they are methodologically blind. He aspired to a postmetaphysical reinterpretation of life and the world that takes account of, incorporates, and does justice to everything that the sciences discern—*and then some*, supplemented by what can be comprehended with respect to human life from a variety of further perspectives and associated human phenomena.

Music is one such phenomenon, and a richly illuminating one at that. From *BT* onward, and in his later writings no less than at first, Nietzsche drew upon the phenomenon of music as a source of insight with respect to our human reality and possibility, while also drawing upon his emerging picture of our human resources and constitution to advance the understanding of music. There are few better examples of his methodological perspectivism in action than his alternating efforts to look at music in what he refers to in the "Attempt at a Self Criticism" (*SC*) that he added to his 1886 reissue of *BT* as "the optic of life" (*BT, SC*, § 4) and to look at life in the "optic" of music.

II

It is essential to recognize and bear in mind that Nietzsche thinks first and foremost of music being *made*, rather than simply listened to. The essence of dance obviously is *dancing*, rather than (voyeuristically) watching others dance. And so also for Nietzsche the *Urphänomen* of music is that of bursting into music-making, primordially in the form of bacchic-choric singing. He takes such singing to be a psychosomatic expression of ecstatic frenzy—like dancing, with which it was originally united. And even though it has been much subdued and refined in the course of its history, it still reaches and moves us (when it does) at this same elemental level. That is the basis of its ability to reach across lines of cultural difference, for it is not so much a universal *language* as an expression of vital excitement to which we are primed to resonate from the depths of our own vital nature.

I would further suggest that Nietzsche took music-making to be paradigmatic of human *spirituality*. It is a metamorphosis of vital energies that have their source in physiological states and processes but are sublimated and transformed in an expression that surpasses the bodily, even while remaining inseparable from the body. Music perfectly illustrates Nietzsche's points when he has Zarathustra say first (in "On the Despisers of the Body"): "body am I entirely, and nothing else; and soul is only a word for something about the body" (*Z* I:4), and then (in his very next speech, "On Enjoying and Suffering the Passions"): "Once you had wild dogs in your cellar, but in the end they turned into birds and lovely singers" (*Z* I:5). Indeed, music does more than illustrate his points; it is suggestive and supportive of them. For the example of music shows how all spirituality can be "only a word for something about the body" and yet be a matter of a kind of transformation of the bodily that makes a profound difference, involving the attainment of a kind of reality and significance that bodies like ours in their original and merely vital state did not have and would not otherwise now have.

One could make something like this point (as Hegel in fact does) by means of an analogy with works of plastic art. But for Nietzsche music is a better choice, owing to its inherently dynamic character. The living of life is more akin to music being made than it is to works of plastic art either being made or being viewed. What making music and living life both involve is only incidentally related to the production of any sort of relatively fixed and enduring object. Both, of course, require the existence of relatively fixed and enduring objects (at a minimum, bodies with certain characteristics, in working order), and both may feature their production (in the case of music, such as scores and records); but their production is not what either is centrally about. And just as music is not a mere matter of sound-making, human living is not a mere matter of vital functioning. What makes sound music has to do with what is done with sounds that can be made; and for Nietzsche something of the same sort obtains with respect to the living of human lives. What makes life human has to do not merely with its biological reality but, rather, with the character of the lives lived. And the potential for variation in both cases is enormous, qualitatively as well as morphologically.

Music is philosophically fascinating for Nietzsche because it is obviously, undeniably, and importantly *real* and yet highly contingent, insubstantial, relational, and ephemeral; because it is intensely physiological and yet—at its best, at any rate—sublimely spiritual; because it happens by way of physical events, and yet what it is all about is happenings that merely have these events for their presupposition and certainly cannot be comprehended in terms of them as such. It makes manifest that reality has not been limited to physicality; that "translating man back into nature" does not mean translating everything human back into the language of the sorts of processes that are the domain of the natural sciences; that there is more to the phenomenon that may still be called by the name of "soul" than the biologically describable human body, even if it is also the case that "soul is only a word for something about the body"; and that there are or can come to be values and qualitative differences that amount to something more and other than anything that can be expressed purely quantitatively or analyzed purely functionally.

Music, for Nietzsche, vividly expresses and indeed epitomizes the kind of thing life is and has in it to become. The plastic arts are quintessentially "still lifes"—frozen glimpses of life that radically distort it even as they may idealize it. Indeed, they are more like death than life—akin to the memorializations of the once-living in lifeless paint or marble. At their very best they only create the illusion of life. Music, on the other hand, like its kindred art, dance, is actually a kind of refinement and extension of the surge and flow of life itself, and it is far superior to dance in getting below life's skin and connecting with what makes us tick. Even the literary arts, although surpassing the plastic arts in this respect, fall far short of it. And their medium of language has characteristics that render its relation to life a considerably more complex and problematic one for Nietzsche, with which he wrestled throughout his productive life. Music was also on his mind from beginning to end, and to follow the course of his tempestuous love affair with it is to achieve a very illuminating perspective on a number of the most important elements of his thought.

III

From the moment the musically minded and talented young Nietzsche discovered Wagner's music, while still in his teens, he came under its spell; then, while still a student at Leipzig, he came under that of the Master himself. He remained obsessed with both for the rest of his life, even after his early adoration of them gave way to alienation and then turned to antipathy. He dedicated *BT* to Wagner, by whom it was inspired, and whom above all it was intended to impress, and he declared in his dedicatory preface to it, clearly with Wagner's musical *Gesamtkunstwerk* above all in particular in mind: "I am convinced that art represents the highest task and the truly metaphysical activity of this life." In the book itself he contends that "the non-imagistic Dionysian art of music" originates in the "physiological phenomenon" of "intoxication" (*BT*, § 1) but that it is far more than just another physiological phenomenon. So he cites and then approvingly elaborates "Schopenhauer's doctrine" that music is to be understood "as the language of the will unmediated" ("*Wir verstehen also, nach der lehre Schopenhauers, die Musik als die Sprache des Willens unmittelbar*"; *BT*, § 21).

Music, moreover, is held not only to have a special kind of metaphysical status and truth (by virtue of its correspondence to the world's "true reality," to which it is truer than any words or images can possibly be), but also to have a crucial sort of significance by virtue of that status and truth. For it—and "tragic myth," to which "the spirit of music" has given birth—makes it possible for us to experience the "primordial joy" that Nietzsche here takes to be the key to our being able to affirm life notwithstanding its harshness, without being either devastated by Dionysian wisdom (with respect to the plight of all individual existence in this world) or shattered by Dionysian ecstasy. It does this by administering the latter to us in doses we can take and by enabling us to learn how to find joy even where there is pain and so to come to positive terms with life in this world on the only conditions it offers. It thus figures crucially in the central idea of *BT*, which is that "existence and the world" can come to "appear justified" *only* as "an aesthetic phenomenon."

> There is only one direct way to make [this idea] intelligible and grasp it immediately: through the wonderful significance of *musical dissonance*. . . .
> Only music, placed beside the world, can give us an idea of what is meant by the justification of the world as an aesthetic phenomenon. The joy

> aroused by the tragic myth has the same origin as the joyous sensation of
> dissonance in music. (*BT*, § 24)

In short, for the Nietzsche of *BT*, "music and tragic myth are equally expressions
of the Dionysian," by "transfiguring" our experience and sense of ourselves in
relation to the world: "both play with the sting of displeasure, trusting in their
exceedingly powerful magic arts; and by means of this play both justify the existence of even the 'worst world'" (*BT*, § 25). They thus cultivate in us a capacity
to affirm this life in this world, not only at its best but even at its worst, by making it possible for us to resonate to the world's own fundamental nature through
musical phenomena that reflect that nature in a manner attuned to our sensibility. Music, which is expressive of and akin to the world's underlying nature,
mediates and thereby facilitates our experience of and identification with that
nature, making possible an overcoming of the alienation from it to which our
various other prosaic and unmusical forms of consciousness and identities have
given rise. It is not works of art or literary characters into which we must strive
to turn ourselves to achieve Dionysian self-realization and life-vindicating joy;
rather, it is something like pieces of music and their further expressions in song
and dance.

The idea and ideal of rendering life more fully and truly "musical" in a
sense became Nietzsche's theme song, the refinement and elaboration of which
occupied him for the rest of his productive life. It was a theme with many variations and on which he made many an experiment—some turning out better
than others, as is only to be expected. And it was spun out again and again in
ways involving the kindred forms of song and dance, reflecting the registers
of thought and action in which the music of human lives must at least for the
most part be played. His next major treatment of it was in the fourth of his
Untimely Meditations (*UM*), *Richard Wagner in Bayreuth* (*RWB*), written four
years later (1876).

What is most important for present purposes about this curious encomium
to Wagner, at once exaggerated and strained (as his break with Wagner neared),
is Nietzsche's attempt to rid himself of the Schopenhauerian metaphysical bag-
gage with which he had encumbered his account in *BT*. What music now is held
to express (at least when it is at its best) is *"authentic feeling,"* although it also is
held to stand in a significant relationship to "nature" (presumably now conceived
postmetaphysically and perhaps even naturalistically, albeit Romantically): "this
music is a return to nature, while being at the same time the purification and
transformation of nature." More specifically, in such music *"there sounds nature transformed into love"* (*UM:RWB*, p. 215). As such "it becomes judge over
the whole visible world of the present" and, in particular, over the whole world
of human society, which Nietzsche joins Wagner in thinking leaves a great deal
to be desired in some respects, just as mere nature leaves much to be desired in
others.

IV

Two years later, however, in the first volume of *Human, All Too Human* (*HAH*), Nietzsche abandoned even this Romantic-naturalistic revision of his earlier estimation of music's special nature, wondrous powers and enormous significance, carrying his naturalistic reassessment of it much further and debunking his own (as well as Schopenhauer's and Wagner's) earlier view of it. Only a few of its 638 aphorisms and reflections make any mention of it at all, and only one is devoted to it. And that one marks a 180-degree turn:

> *Music*—Music is, of and in itself, not so significant for our inner world, nor so profoundly exciting, that it can be said to count as the *immediate* language of feeling; but its primeval union with poetry has deposited so much symbolism into . . . the varying strength and volume of musical sounds, that we now *suppose* it to speak directly *to* the inner world and to come *from* the inner world. . . . In itself, no music is profound or significant, it does not speak of the "will" or of the "thing in itself"; the intellect could suppose such a thing only in an age which had conquered for musical symbolism the entire compass of the inner life. It was the intellect itself which first *introduced* this significance into sounds. (*HAH* I, § 215)

Nietzsche repeats the same basic point and takes it even further in the second installment of *HAH*, published a year later, in which he accords it a highly contingent and derivative status: "Of all the arts that grow up on a particular cultural soil under particular social and political conditions, music makes its appearance *last*, in the autumn and deliquescence of the culture to which it belongs." And after remarking (memorably) that therefore "all truly meaningful music is swan-song," he goes on to drive home the point: "Music is thus *not* a universal language for all ages, as has so often been claimed for it, but accords precisely with a measure of time, warmth and sensibility that a quite distinct individual culture, limited as to area and duration, bears within it . . ." (*HAH* II:I, § 171).

This belittlement of music at its usual best (and castigation of it at its more common worst) carries over into Nietzsche's next two books, *Daybreak* (*D*) and the first edition of *GS* (*GS*, 1882). There is one passage in *Daybreak*, however, in which he offers a glimpse of his own version of a "music of the future" that would be more highly estimable (and very different indeed from Wagner's *Zukunfts-musik*). Strangely enough—or perhaps not so strangely, in light of his growing antiromanticism—it involves the wedding of music with the very kind of intellectuality toward which Nietzsche's own thinking was evolving:

> Our music, which can transform itself into everything has to transform itself because, like the demon of the sea, it has in itself no character: . . . —why should it not in the end discover that brighter, more joyful and universal sound which corresponds to the *ideal thinker*?—a music which knows how to *be at home* only floating up and down among the broad

> soaring vaulted arches of *his soul*? . . . So let it then show that it is possible
> to feel these three things at the same time: sublimity, deep and warm il-
> lumination, and the joy of perfect consistency." (*D,* § 461)

This passage is of interest in a number of respects—for the light it sheds on the
character of the thought of the type of thinker Nietzsche at that point was striving to become, under the banner of the "free spirit," and also for the picture of
which it offers a first sketch of a kind of spirituality in which intellectuality and
musicality are intimately intertwined, as well as for its hints concerning a possible
reconceptualization of music. For now it is taken to be the distinctive expression
of nothing whatsoever, having "in itself no character" and no essential relation
to anything in particular either about the world or about ourselves. Instead, it
is suggested to be but a medium in which any sort of spirituality can express itself—and yet a distinctive medium, affording human spirituality possibilities of
development and expression that can make a significant difference to the sort
of thing it can become. This rather formalistic conception, however, while very
different from Nietzsche's first word on the subject, is not his last.

Having caught sight of this possibility, Nietzsche was moved to ever more
strident denunciations of the use of the expressive powers of music to stimulate
surges of strong emotions, produce intoxication, and (worse still) addict people
to them, to the detriment of their constitutions and lives. Acerbic remarks to this
effect in his books of this period (e.g., *GS,* § 86) gave way to scathing polemics
toward the end of his productive life directed against the music of the Germany
of his century in general and of Wagner in particular. So, for example, in the
"Attempt at a Self-Criticism" (added to *BT* in 1886), he wrote contemptuously of
"contemporary *German music,* which is romanticism through and through, and
the most un-Greek of all possible art forms—moreover, a first-rate poison for the
nerves," which has the dangerous (especially to Germans) "double quality of a
narcotic that both intoxicates and spreads a *fog*" (*BT, SC,* § 6). But he also continued to reflect on the way in which music and the other arts have contributed
to the resources we now have to draw upon through their transformations and
enrichments of our capacity for experience.

For example: near the end of the fourth and final part of the 1882 version of
GS, immediately before one of the most important sections in the entire volume
(*GS,* § 335, in praise of science precisely for what can and must be learned from it
if we are to "become those we are"), we find a complementary section that bears a
revealing title; while its point goes well beyond music—not only to the other arts
but to life itself—it is from music that Nietzsche obviously learned it:

> *One must learn to love.*—This is what happens to us in music: First one
> has to *learn to hear* a figure and melody at all, to detect and distinguish
> it. . . . Then it requires some exertion and good will to *tolerate* it in spite of
> its strangeness. . . . Finally there comes a moment . . . when we sense that
> we should miss it if it were missing, and now it continues to compel and

enchant us relentlessly until we have become its humble and enraptured lovers. . . . But that is what happens to us not only in music. That is how we have *learned to love* all things that we now love. . . . Love, too, has to be learned. (*GS*, § 334)

These, for Nietzsche, are points of the utmost importance, and they may fairly be said to be his springboard into *Thus Spoke Zarathustra* (*Z*), the great accomplishment of his next three years (1883–85)—and of which he wrote in *Ecce Homo* (*EH*), "Perhaps the whole of *Zarathustra* may be reckoned as music" (*EH*, "Why":Z, § 1). Without the ability to "learn to love" at least some of what life has to offer and we are able to create, for Nietzsche, and without the capacity to embrace it as an aesthetic phenomenon regardless of whether it has any sort of truth or reality apart from our lives and experience, our plight would indeed be a sorry one, and Schopenhauer would carry the day. But for Nietzsche and his Zarathustra, Schopenhauer and his nihilistic pessimism do not have the last word. They can be overcome, and the key to their overcoming is not the actual Schopenhauer "as educator" (as his *Schopenhauer as Educator* might lead one to believe he thinks) but, rather, *art* as the higher education of the human spirit, with music in a leading role and *Thus Spoke Zarathustra* as the *Bildungsroman* of higher-human spirituality. And *Zarathustra* is filled with episodes of song and dance that contribute greatly to the conveying of its meaning.

V

The Nietzsche who began to publish in prose again three years later, with the appearance of *BGE* (in 1886), had only three more years remaining to him before his collapse. He had little to say about music in any of the works he published during the first two of those years (though much in the final year of his productive life), but the significance of what he does say about it in them is considerable. It is in *BGE* that he quips: "In music the passions enjoy themselves" (*BGE* 106), thereby suggesting a return to a version of his earlier view that music is expressive of something having to do with our affective nature. And the one more substantial section devoted to music in this "Prelude to a Philosophy of the Future" (as *BGE* is subtitled) is of no little interest, for in it Nietzsche again takes up the subject of a kind of music that would be far better paired with the kind of philosophy and spirituality he heralds and champions than that of the tradition that had culminated in Wagner:

Against German music all kinds of precautions seem to me to be indicated. Suppose somebody loves the south as I love it, as a great school of convalescence, in the most spiritual as well as the most sensuous sense, as an uncontainable abundance of sun and transfiguration by the sun that suffuses an existence that believes and glories in itself: well, such a person will learn to be somewhat on his guard against German music, because in corrupting his taste again it also corrupts his health again.

> If such a southerner . . . should dream of the future of music . . . , in his
> ears he must have the prelude of a more profound, more powerful, per-
> haps more evil and mysterious music, a supra-German music that does
> not fade away at the sight of the voluptuous blue sea and the brightness of
> the Mediterranean sky . . .—a supra-European music that prevails even
> before the brown sunsets of the desert, a music whose soul is related to
> palm trees and feels at home and knows how to roam among great, beau-
> tiful, lonely beasts of prey— (*BGE*, § 255)

Such a music, Nietzsche goes on to observe, would "no longer know anything of
good and evil"; it would have escaped the orbit of past and present moral (and
religious and metaphysical) interpretations and evaluations and would instead
be in the service of a more promising sort of life and spirituality—of which he
gives a deliberately provocative but lamentably inadequate and misleading sketch
here. As problematic as it is, however, this passage does hint significantly at an
idea that warrants pursuing—as he himself indicated in the new preface added
to *BT* when he republished it a year later, asking: "what would a music have to
be like that would no longer be of romantic origin, like German music—but
Dionysian?" (*BT, SC*, § 6).

VI

Nietzsche turned again to the subject of music in the new "Fifth Book" of an
expanded edition of *GS* that he published in 1887, and I shall dwell upon what
he has to say about it there at some length. First, however, I shall complete my
overview by commenting on the remarkable outpouring of discussion of it that
one finds in his writings of the next and final year of his productive life (1888).
In *Twilight of the Idols* (*TI*), the first (and most temperate) of his books of that
year, he discusses music and the arts more generally in almost clinical terms, as
psycho-physiological phenomena of a peculiar but interesting and serendipitous
nature, accounting for them in resolutely naturalistic terms. He thereby at once
makes sense of their occurrence and takes them down off of their pedestals, while
yet also attempting to do justice and give new credit to their extraordinary character and exceptional possibilities for the enhancement of life. He writes:

> Music, as we understand it today, is also a total excitement and a total dis-
> charge of the affects, but even so only the remnant of a much fuller world
> of expression of the affects, a mere residue of the Dionysian histrionicism.
> To make music possible as a separate art, a number of senses, especially
> the muscle sense, have been immobilized . . . so that man no longer bodily
> imitates and represents everything he feels. Nevertheless, that is really the
> normal Dionysian state, at least the original state. Music is the specializa-
> tion of this state attained slowly at the expense of those faculties which
> are most closely related to it. (*TI* IX:10)

To those who love music but for whom anything that has such a genealogy is thereby no longer deserving respect and esteem, this sort of account will appear distressing and threatening. And indeed it is Nietzsche's intention in this book to suggest the hollowness of a good many of the "idols" he discusses in it. In this instance, however, as in a number of others, his purpose is a different one: to shatter common fond illusions with respect to some such cherished things—but also to encourage and help those who are up to it to get over their disillusionment and to develop a new respect and appreciation for these things that will give their love of them not only a new lease on life but also a firmer foundation. So, for example, it is in the same work that he famously remarks that "Without music, life would be an error" (*TI* I:33).

In *The Case of Wagner* (*CW*) Nietzsche returns anew to the idea (first intimated in *BT*) that humanity at its best is much like music at its best and indeed is at its best when it actually becomes the sort of phenomenon that music at its best is—which moreover is a transformation made possible paradigmatically precisely by music at its best. He even goes so far as to say: "Has it been noticed that music liberates the spirit? gives wings to thought? That one becomes more of a philosopher the more one becomes a musician?" (*CW*, § 1). But there is a worrisome corollary for Nietzsche (as, rather ironically, there had been for Plato, his philosophical opposite number): the resonance of our nature to music likewise has the consequence that music at its worst can have a detrimental effect upon the character and quality of one's humanity surpassing the consequences of the sheer absence of any music at all in one's life. If he is right, the corruption of music can mean not merely the impoverishment but also the corruption of life.

That is precisely the theme of Nietzsche's diatribe against Wagner here: "Wagner represents a great corruption of music," he writes. "He has guessed that it is a means to excite weary nerves—and with that he has made music sick." He thereby "makes sick whatever he touches"—and so he "corrupts our health—and music as well" (*CW*, § 5). In his hands, music not only is "a mere means" but a dangerously debilitating one, in a double respect. For he has the genius to be able to turn it into a powerful artificial stimulant, "calling back into life those who are half dead," and for whom it becomes a preferred substitute for genuine vitality (*CW*, § 5), and further into a seductive and addictive narcotic for those who crave escape or relief—as he himself had found it to be: "If one wants to rid oneself of an unbearable pressure, one needs hashish. Well then, I needed Wagner." As such, he readily allows that Wagner's music at its "best" is unsurpassed: "To this day I am still looking for a work that equals the dangerous fascination and the gruesome and sweet infinity of *Tristan*—and look in all the arts in vain" (*EH* II:6). But that is not exactly to commend it.

In *CW*, Nietzsche further laments that Wagner represents "*the emergence of the actor in music*" and the ascendency of "the theater" and its mendacious manipulation of the audience's emotions at the expense of "the integrity of musicians, their 'authenticity'"—not to speak of the potential counterpart genuine ("truer" and "higher") humanity of those in the audience—in a manner to which he had not been sensitive in *BT* and to which he is now strongly antipathetic. So he concludes with an impassioned statement of "the *three demands* for which my wrath, my concern, my love of art has this time opened my mouth," to wit:

> That the theater should not lord it over the arts.
> That the actor should not seduce those who are authentic.
> *That music should not become an art of lying.* (*CW*, § 12)

By "the arts," Nietzsche clearly has in mind music in particular. By "those who are authentic," he clearly means those who have it in them to attain to the "highest" and "truest" or most genuine form of humanity—which, as has already been observed, has the character of its counterpart form of musicality. And, in light of his various reflections on art as something like "the cult of the untrue" (*GS*, § 107), in which "the lie is sanctified" (*GM* III, § 25), it is of particular interest that he here makes much of the point (as his parting shot) that music can and should be what it is and do what it does in a manner that is honest and above-board. More specifically, it should have no part of the sort of "lying" he is here imputing to "the theater" in general and to Wagner's myth-making, "infinite-meaning"-mongering theatricality in particular (and to Pauline Christianity in *Der Antichrist*).

This may well be an echo, in transmuted and reauthenticated form, of the idea he had appropriated from Schopenhauer in *BT* that music stands in a different and more deeply truthful relation to the basic character of the reality of which we are a part than do the plastic and dramatic arts with their exaggeration of the status and significance of form and individuation in it. But now it is no longer the Dionysianism of *BT* that Nietzsche takes to be the whole truth of this life and this world. For the Dionysianism of the later Nietzsche has acquired an Apollinian side that is no less genuine an expression of its primordial character than its unruly *Ur*-Dionysian counterpart, and it is precisely their tension and interplay that is for him the spice of life—and of music. And it is precisely the strength of the former in temperance of the latter that he cherishes of life, wants of music, and misses in Wagner:

> What we others, we *halcyons*, miss in Wagner—*la gaya scienza*; light feet, wit, fire, grace; the great logic; the dance of the stars; the exuberant spirituality; the southern shivers of light; the *smooth* sea—perfection— (*CW*, § 10)

VII

Let us now consider several things Nietzsche has to say about music in Book Five of the 1887 second edition of *The Gay Science*. The music-life connection figures centrally in them. In a section on Nietzsche's kind of philosophy that bears the heading "Why We Are No Idealists," for example, it is interesting to observe how he makes his point:

> Formerly philosophers were afraid of the senses. . . . Having "wax in one's ears" was then almost a condition of philosophizing; a real philosopher no longer listened to life insofar as life is music [*insofern Leben Musik ist*]; he *denied* the music of life [*die Musik des Lebens*]—it is an ancient philosopher's superstition that all music is siren's music. (*GS*, § 372)

Nietzsche could hardly say any more clearly and directly that he considers life—certainly human life in particular, and perhaps life more generally as well—to have something of the *character* of music and to need to be so construed and interpreted if it is to be at all adequately comprehended. And in the very next section he goes even further. I consider the entire section to be of great importance both for the understanding of Nietzsche and for what it has to say—about music, and also about a good deal more, which he takes the case of music to illuminate It bears the heading "'Science' as Prejudice" ('*Wissenschaft' als Vorurteil*).

> That the only justifiable interpretation of the world [*Welt-Interpretation*] should be one in which *you* are justified because one can continue to work and do research scientifically in *your* sense (you really mean, mechanistically?)—an interpretation that permits counting, calculating, weighing, seeing, and touching, and nothing more—that is a crudity and naivete, assuming that it is not a mental illness, an idiocy. . . . Suppose that one assessed the *value* of a piece of music according to [*schätzte den Wert einer Musik danach ab*] how much of it could be counted, calculated, and expressed in formulas: how absurd would such a "scientific" assessment ['*wissenschaftliche' Abschätzung*] of music be! What would one have grasped, understood, known of it [*Was hätte man von ihr begriffen, verstanden, erkannt!*]? Nothing, really nothing of what is "music" in it! [*von dem, was eigentlich 'Musik' an ihr ist!*] (*GS*, § 373)

The implication is clear: for Nietzsche, the same may be said of "the world"—and more particularly, of life—as of music. For his whole point in making reference to music as he does is to draw upon what he takes to be the similarity of the two cases. And I take him here to be indicating quite clearly that he considers it to be meaningful to speak of truth, knowledge, and value—certainly with respect to music, and by implication with respect to life and the world as well, by way of analogy. And that is not all. But let us go one step at a time.

First, it is evident from this passage that Nietzsche is quite prepared to grant that there are things about music (and about life and the world more generally) that admit of being "counted, calculated, and expressed in formulas." Some such descriptions will be true, and others will not; and he does not deny or even question the possibility of their coming to be humanly known through the relevant sorts of "scientific research." So that is already something. But that is not all. For the whole point of the passage is to insist that there is *more to it*—and indeed more to particular "pieces of music," as well as about music generally—than what is true of it on that level of description, and indeed more to it that can come to be known, even if not in the same ways. "What is *music* in it" is something that may not be obvious to anyone and everyone whose ears are working or who can make the appropriate measurements, but it is something that *must* be "grasped, understood, known" if one's comprehension of it is to be anything more than "crude and naïve"—and it is something that someone with the appropriate sensibility *can and should* be able to discern. Those who are not capable of such discernment are missing something in the music. Nietzsche is not content simply to make this point; he hammers it home by reiteration, using three different cognitive verbs in succession for emphasis: it is precisely what is most important about the music that they will not have *"begriffen, verstanden, erkannt!"*

Nietzsche himself is by no means so "crude and naïve" as to be thinking, however, that music is some sort of metaphysical realm of musical *Dinge an sich*, to which the musically minded have privileged cognitive access. Rather, music is fundamentally a kind of *happening* that we are able to tune in on precisely by *being in on it*. It is nothing apart from the sorts of activities and experiences in which we can involve ourselves, but as the sort of event that it is, in which we are able to participate, its reality is at once palpable and knowable. And our knowledge of it, if we know it well enough to know what Nietzsche is talking about, is fundamentally a kind of knowledge by *acquaintance*—and in the first instance, the acquaintance of *involvement*. Turning that knowledge into statements with the descriptive resources of ordinary natural languages can never be done adequately, and the prospects for capturing it in the nets of scientific analysis and discourse are even dimmer. But it is knowledge nonetheless, and there is a kind of truth at stake in it that is worth more than any other for creatures like ourselves who are in need of richer fare than either the merely natural, the purely rational, the rigorously analytical, or the simply practical can provide.

That is the link of truth and knowledge here to *value*. Nietzsche makes it clear in the passage under consideration that "the *value* of a piece of music" is bound up with the very kind of thing that is missed when one fails to "grasp, understand and know . . . what is 'music' in it." And that has to do with aspects of the kind of thing musical experience *is* that are discernible only from inside the circle. It can only be discerned by firsthand acquaintance and after appropriate preparation, but it is no less real for that. One has to have developed the requisite sensibility for such things to register at all, and the cultivation of that sensibility, hand in hand with the associated development and refinement of the abilities and practices and institutions, is the double-chambered heart of the reality of music and of art more generally as a sphere of human life.

And there is more. Nietzsche appears to be suggesting here that music can do even more for us than suggest how meaningful and interesting sorts of truth, knowledge and value can be conceived, and how they might be extended by analogy and extrapolation to life and the world more generally, philosophically important though this may be. For it further is suggested to show the way to the actual expansion and enrichment of their actual *domains of reference*—and this is of great human as well as philosophical significance. This idea has its most important application in the matter of value, but it applies with respect to truth and knowledge as well. Consider first the matter of truth—and more specifically, what kinds of ways there are in which things can be said to be (or come) true. By way of the transforming enhancement of human life to which music contributes, things can *come true* with respect to human reality in ways that were neither possible nor even conceivable once upon a time, even if they may well *not* be so for much of humanity even now, or ever, and even if they may only be so at all for a little while. Owing to them, as he says elsewhere in another context, "the aspect of the earth [*der Aspect der Erde*]" is "essentially altered [*wesentlich verändert*]" (*GM* II, § 16)—not permanently, to be sure, or pervasively either, but nonetheless really. Human reality has become a different reality in connection with which different sorts of truth-conditions have come to obtain and to be satisfiable and to be satisfied.

I am suggesting that Nietzsche thinks of music as having opened up a new and important sort of human possibility associated with a form of life and human activity that may either have or lack—and may either promote or hinder—a kind of *genuineness* in relation to something that matters about the larger life from which it springs and in which it figures. Music, in short, is the birthplace of a sensibility the refinement of which establishes the possibility of distinguishing meaningfully between a new sort of authenticity and its absence. And because it connects centrally rather than merely peripherally with what fuels as well as forms human life, music thereby sets the stage for the emergence of this sort of truth as a real possibility and issue in human life more generally, which may either be realized or neglected, and opens up a previously nonexistent sort of vulnerability. Hence the importance of "the case of Wagner" for Nietzsche.

It should be obvious from *GS*, § 373, how Nietzsche considers music to make a difference with respect to knowledge. As the sensibility it cultivates schools us in our capacity for the kind of "knowledge by acquaintance" that the comprehension and appreciation of "what is *music* in music" require, it equips us with a cognitive ability differing from those acquired in other ways. This makes it at least possible to bring our musically-educated intelligence to bear upon things other than music, to grasp what this enables us to discern. It may even tempt us to do so. This is a temptation Nietzsche himself constantly felt, and the attempts to which it prompted him led him to conclude and suggest that much is to be gained thereby.

VIII

Music, one might say paraphrasing Zarathustra, is only a word for something about sound—about the making and the hearing of sound. Both are intimately bound up with a certain sort of physiological and neurological constitution and involve the happenstance that certain states of creatures with such a constitution have an experiential dimension that admits of modification. And yet *music* is a word for something pretty remarkable about sound that sets some sounds quite apart from others—even if only in ways that are meaningful only to those who are attuned to them. Sound in general has both an experiential reality and other sorts of reality, including features that can be "counted, calculated, and expressed in formulas" and investigated by subjecting it to various sorts of "scientific research." And so does music.

These other sorts of reality are real enough, and the results of such research into them may be true enough—as far as they go. But they do not constitute the reality of "what is 'music'" in music. That reality is not merely subjective in the sense of being entirely a matter of how a person happens to think or feel about it, but it is a reality of a relational and contextual sort, having to do with *the sort of experience it is*. And it is *the sort of experience it is* that endows the realities associated with it with the meaning and significance they have and make them (by extension) not just sound but "the sounds of *music*." Without that which can be "counted, calculated, and expressed in formulas," at least in the neural states of brains like ours, there is and can be no musical reality. But what is decisive with respect to the question of which such states (in brains and typically in the surrounding and impinging world as well) are *musical* states—not to mention the question of their quality and "value"—is the experience they make possible.

This, for Nietzsche, is also how to think about "'soul' as a word for something about the body" (*Z* I:4) and about *consciousness* as a word for something about our brains and nervous systems and sense organs and about *spirituality* as a word for something about our affects. It is how to think about their reality— and also about the reality of the sorts of values that can and do come to pertain to them. For like musical values, these values too have a naturalistic basis, and yet are no more reducible to what can be captured and articulated in terms of features that can be "counted, calculated, and expressed in formulas" than what makes "a piece of music" a piece of *music*. The qualitative difference is as profound as that which distinguishes music from mere sound—and it is a difference of a fundamentally similar sort.

Our spirituality, to the extent that we attain to some measure of it, might be thought of as *the musicalization of the sounds of our lives*, which themselves have already been transformed into something considerably more than mere noise by way of the genealogy of our humanity (on which Nietzsche speculates in *GM*). The transformation of sound into music is something that actually has come to be humanly possible. As it did so, humanity became capable of the sort of spirituality associated with it. And whatever broader spiritualization has become humanly possible, once this process got off the ground, may plausibly be supposed to be variations on the same basic theme.

Nietzsche had begun in *BT* by associating music with the psycho-physiological phenomenon of intoxication and by conceiving of it as a kind of ecstatic outburst into both sound and movement, tending to shatter artificial constraints and forms of all kinds. He remained very much aware of its power to both express and stimulate feelings and emotions. Indeed, one of his chief charges against Wagner was that by capitalizing upon its ability to function as a stimulant he made it "a first-rate poison for the nerves" (*BT, SC,* § 6) and an addictive one at that, thereby "corrupting" both music and the life it touches. Yet Nietzsche also came to be greatly interested in the contrasting features of music, without which it would not be music at all but, rather, mere chaotic noise and frenzy: rhythm and harmony. These are ordering features, seemingly more Apollinian than Dionysian; yet they are the keys to the transformation of noise and frenzy into music and dance. It is precisely the imbalance of these features, intensifying stimulation at the expense of regulation, that Nietzsche found so dangerously seductive in Wagner.

So when we find Nietzsche championing Bizet (and *Carmen*) against Wagner (and *Tristan*), it is because he has come to recognize (in a Kantian manner of speaking) that, while form without passion may be empty, passion without form is meaningless. Or rather (and worse), passionless form may be deathly, but formless passion can be deadly. To be healthy (not to mention life-enhancing), music must have an effect that is tonic rather than toxic, and to do so, it needs to accord with our need for the attainment of *form*, as well as for the excitation and expression of whatever energies we may have at our disposal. It must move us; but it must do so in a way that is conducive to the strengthening and refinement of that fundamental disposition to the ordering transformation of everything within our power that he came to call "will to power" as it plays itself out both within ourselves and beyond ourselves. That is what "perfection" amounts to for creatures like ourselves; and music is at once a way in which we are able to try our wings impelled by its promptings and a schooling for us as we do so.

Thus the "music of the future" Nietzsche envisions is by no means to be de-Apollinianized, his characterization of it as Dionysian notwithstanding. So he poses the question (claiming rather dubiously to have been doing so even in *BT*): "what would a music have to be like that would no longer be of romantic origin, like German music—but *Dionysian*?" (*BT, SC,* § 6). He complains of Wagner that "he simply did not require the higher lawfulness, *style*," and "never calculates as a musician, from some sort of musician's conscience." And for this reason, he says, "Wagner's music is never true" (*CW,* § 8). He provides an indication of his answer to his question when he writes that what "we *halcyons* miss in Wagner" is "the great logic; the dance of the stars; the exuberant spirituality; the southern shivers of light; the *smooth* sea—perfection" (*CW,* § 10).

Nietzsche conceives of "perfection" in music along these lines, and his remarks in *GS,* § 368, to which I have already drawn attention indicate that he does so because he conceives of "perfection" in *life* similarly. Music is at its best when it serves to "quicken" us, enhancing our vitality and the optimality of our entire psychosomatic state, and "gilds" our lives by means of the "golden and tender harmonies" it shows us to be attainable in them. It can affect us in this way because we resonate to it, and we resonate to it because it is a projection of our very vital nature, given the sort of form in which that nature finds its greatest satisfaction.

"In music the passions enjoy themselves," Nietzsche writes (*BGE*, § 106), for in music they are enabled to do so in a manner involving both their intensification and their control, each contributing to that enjoyment. That is something we learn through music to do in our lives, if we learn it at all. And it is only music that has the power of bringing even the dissonances of life within the compass of the enjoyable, enabling us to find a kind of perfection even there. For as Nietzsche had contended in *BT*, "Only music, placed beside the world, can give us an idea of what is meant by the justification of the world as an aesthetic phenomenon"—namely, "through the wonderful significance of *musical dissonance*," which reveals the possibility of a sublimating appropriation of the Dionysian phenomenon of frenzy, "with its primordial joy experienced even in pain" (*BT*, § 24). It is a long way from such frenzy to the sort of perfection to which he refers in his characterizations of what is lacking in (and wrong with) Wagner, but music itself has been the medium in which humanity has managed to traverse that way.

Music, for Nietzsche, can serve as a model for us in this fashion—as a token of a kind of reality to which we can aspire, embodying a kind of value that we can at least to some extent attain—because he considers it to be a kind of alter ego. It is, that is to say, a kind of objectification of the rudiments of our own psychic life, which has been sufficiently distanced from us to be capable of a separate development that has proceeded in certain respects well ahead of and beyond our own and from which we now have the possibility of benefiting. This line of reflection led Nietzsche to speculate on the psycho-physiological genealogy of music, taking it off its romantic pedestal and (along with our human nature itself) "translating it back into nature." He does so not to belittle it, however, by suggesting that it amounts to nothing more than it was in its very naturalistically human beginnings, but rather to establish its deep relationship to fundamental elements of our very humanity—and so to lay a new foundation for its full and high appreciation.

If Nietzsche is at all close to the mark here, the relation of music's nature to our own is indeed an intimate one, and if music could have originated in this manner, so could a good deal else. And on the other hand, by originating in this manner and so becoming capable of development "as a separate art," it then became capable of playing a significant role in our own subsequent development into a creature whose existence is far worthier of "justification" and affirmation "as an aesthetic phenomenon" than it would have been otherwise. This observation permits a much more significant and interesting reading than is customary of Nietzsche's apparent mere quip in the very same book that "Without music, life would be an error" (*TI* I:33). For in this context, what he is saying is that the emergence of music in human life is associated with a transformation of human reality that matters greatly with respect to its affirmation as well as its comprehension. Without music, life would be more trouble than it is worth, but thanks in no small measure to the difference music makes, it is more than worth the trouble.

IX

Value in music for Nietzsche thus clearly amounts to more than mere biological or vital value, even if (like all value for him) it ultimately requires to be understood in terms of "value for life." For something can be of such value if it makes a difference to the affirmation of life, whether by *enhancing its aspect* in ways that render it more enticing and so amenable to affirmation or by *enhancing the capacity for affirmation* of those who may or may not be up to it. And music can and does work in both of these ways. A world with music in it is a different world (for those capable of noticing) than a world otherwise the same but without it would be, and a sensibility schooled by music is capable of strong responses to features of such a world that will otherwise be invisible or mere curiosities. And as each feeds into the other, their dynamic can powerfully affect the disposition of those fortunate enough to be in on it.

Other parts of human life and human culture can do so as well. But none taps as deeply as music into both the world's nature and our own, which here are brought into an alignment and attunement that sets up a distinctively energizing resonance in us, which draws upon and funds back into our vitality but also sublimates and transfigures it. This is the possibility that grounds what Nietzsche calls his "Dionysian value standard." And it is the heart of his claim that a kind of meaningfulness attaches to this transformation of vitality into an existence-vindicating aesthetic phenomenon that redeems nature from meaninglessness and is itself *Übermenschlichkeit*, "the meaning of the earth" (*Z* I:P:3).

Music is thus deeply instructive with respect to the way in which Nietzsche fundamentally conceives of value. Neither music nor value has any existence beyond and independently of this life in this world; neither is reducible to anything that can be "counted, calculated, and expressed in formulas"; and while both have fundamentally to do with dynamics of life naturalistically conceived, neither can be done justice in such terms alone. If one seeks something to relate them to "objectively," there is nothing more to be found than the various forms of life in the world and the ways in which they configure and reconfigure themselves and elements of their environments. What matters about both only becomes discernable from perspectives within and upon these forms of life from which sense can be given to qualitative distinctions. And for Nietzsche the key to the development of both, beyond the level of merely vital functions, is the emergence of the possibility of creative transformations of the natural in ways independent of all biologically and social-functionally specific imperatives. Music and value both have outgrown their sources, even if they remain anchored in them or cut loose from them at their peril. Both present the spectacle of life making something more of itself than merely more life—and so, as Nietzsche likes to put it, of its self-overcoming.

If such talk is not to one's liking, however, one can put the matter differently—as Nietzsche himself is sometimes wont to do. Let it be supposed that all that matters about music is really and truly a function and expression of certain very complicated socio-neuro-physiological conditions and processes, as they have come about and go on in the course of human events. For Nietzsche this would not matter; for it would not affect what *does* matter—namely, the sorts of experience we have, the kinds of music-making that have come to be humanly possible, the ways in which different sorts of music can and do affect us, and the fact that music has a future that is just as meaningfully open as it ever has been.

And Nietzsche surely could and would say the same about values and the "value-creation" of which he so often speaks, along with all enhancements of life. It is indeed conceivable that, just as *soul* is only a word for something about the body, *creativity* and *Übermenschlichkeit* are only words for something about the exceptional psycho-somaticities and life histories of some human beings. But even if that turns out to be so, musical composition and performance and experience will be neither harder nor easier, and neither richer nor poorer, whatever the case may be. We therefore will have nothing to feel sorry for ourselves about if this is somehow discovered to be so. We then should just get on with it, in the spirit of Zarathustra at the end of Part Four of *Zarathustra*, who gives "pity for the higher man" and "for suffering" the back of his hand, and exclaims: "Am I concerned with *happiness?* I am concerned with my *work.* . . . And he left his cave, glowing and strong as a morning sun that comes out of dark mountains" (Z IV:20).

And so I shall conclude, in the spirit of Prince Vogelfrei (to whom Nietzsche gives the last word in *BGE*), with a Nietzschean version of a familiar ode's last lines, which seems to me to be as apt as it is tempting. I like to think that Nietzsche would not take it amiss.

Truth is music, music truth:
That is all ye know on earth,
And all ye need to know.

Chapter Eight

Nietzsche and the Transfiguration of Asceticism

An Ethics of Self-Fashioning

Steven V. Hicks and Alan Rosenberg

I. Introduction

Nietzsche evinces a general concern for the problem of human suffering and its implications for the ultimate meaning of being human. He is dissatisfied, however, with traditional philosophical and religious attempts to deal with pain and suffering. In particular, he attacks the Christian moral tradition and what he terms its "ascetic ideal" as offering only escapist solutions to the very real problems of human suffering. As Nietzsche sees it, by enshrining the belief that the best life is one of self-denial and by devaluing the importance of natural, human life in favor of an "otherworldly home of value," traditional ascetic morality provides a means of self-escape that both trivializes the significance of human suffering and leads to nihilism.

In what follows, we shall examine a series of concepts centered around Nietzsche's understanding of the formation of the modern, postmoral individual—the so-called "man of the future"—who, in Nietzsche's words, "will redeem us not only from the hitherto reigning [ascetic] ideal but also from that which was bound to grow out of it, the present nausea, the will to nothingness, nihilism" (*GM* II, § 24). The point of departure for our inquiry will be Nietzsche's intriguing claim in *Genealogy of Morals* that "the most terrifying aspect of two thousand years of training" in Judeo-Christian morality is that humanity, to date, has no alternative to the life-denying "ascetic ideal" as a strategy for dealing with human suffering (cf. *GM* III, § 27). This sweeping claim applies even to those experimental "free thinkers," "free spirits," and "honest atheists" such as Nietzsche himself, since, as he says, "this [ascetic] ideal is precisely their ideal too; they themselves still embody it today" (*GM* III, § 24). In Nietzsche's view, our morality has "overwhelmingly negative value" as a hindrance to the enhancement of life and to what Nietzsche sees as the individual's creative task of "rendering life significant, important, [and] worthy of his or her own respect and exuberance" (Geuss, 1999, p. 18; Allison, 2001, p. 246). But is a life-enhancing alternative ideal to the "hitherto reigning ascetic ideal" to be found in Nietzsche's writings—one that, perhaps, he intentionally veiled, or "masked," or did not fully recognize himself? Can we identify an "opposing ideal" that is not based, like the ascetic ideal, upon lies, false causal notions, "metaphysical comforts," and transcendental devaluations of the natural world but that instead would allow humanity "to learn the art of *this-worldly* comfort": to learn "to do without [transcendental] meaning in things . . . to endure to live in a meaningless world precisely because one fashions a small portion of it oneself" (*BT*, *"Attempt at Self-Criticism,"* § 7; *WP*, § 585A)? "On this one point," Nietzsche says, "it behooves me to remain silent, or I shall usurp that to which only one younger, 'heavier with a future,' and stronger than I has a right . . . *Zarathustra the godless*" (*GM* II, § 25).

What we wish to suggest in this essay is that by focusing on the complex issue of what it means, in Nietzsche's words, to "self-fashion" (*sich schaffen*) in an otherwise meaningless world, we may point the way beyond the ascetic ideal toward a viable alternative—one more open-ended, nondogmatic, and which Nietzsche cannot therefore dogmatically commend to his readers but which his readers must somehow discover for themselves (cf. *TI* IX: 49). What we also wish to suggest is that the attempt to move beyond the ascetic ideal must nonetheless mobilize "the more scrupulous 'hermeneutics of desire' fostered in the Christian [ascetic] tradition" itself (see Roberts, 1998, p. 95). In other words, the "new form of morality" that Nietzsche envisions is still closely related to traditional forms of ascetic practice involving, among other things, strenuous modes of "self-discipline, self-surveillance, and self-overcoming" imposed upon "the powers of the passions and the instincts" (see *GM* III, § 16; *WP*, §§ 914–915; see also Thiele, 1990, pp. 146–147). Paradoxically, it is only by means of such a "transfigured" or "re-naturalized" asceticism that the postmoral "men of the future" will be able to discern and oppose the life-denying "ascetic ideal" in order "to affirm the world" (*HAH* I, § 29). But the "transfigured" techniques and practices remain themselves, largely, ascetic ones (see Roberts, 1998, p. 95). By exploring the creative tension between such transfigured ascetic techniques on the one hand and aesthetic/artistic procedures on the other and by utilizing what Nietzsche terms this ascetic "artists' cruelty"—"this delight in imposing a form upon oneself as a hard, recalcitrant, suffering material . . . this uncanny joyous labor of a soul voluntarily at odds with itself"—Nietzsche hopes to open up a space within which a new, life-affirming "ethics of self-fashioning" can occur (see *GM* II, §§ 10, 18).

II. Nietzsche and the Idealization of Asceticism

In the *Genealogy of Morals,* Nietzsche argues that Western culture, ever since the decline of the "tragic age" of the Greeks, has been dominated by, and dependent upon, moral values associated with Platonism and Christianity and their idealization of asceticism. He insists that it has been so dominated by the ascetic ideal that it will be difficult to wean Western culture away from these "negative" and "reactive" values "without a cultural transvaluation of staggering proportions" (see Magnus, 1986, p. 51). Why did the ascetic ideal triumph? It gave human suffering a meaning, and according to Nietzsche, any meaning for "senseless suffering" is better than none; people would rather "will nothing than not will at all" (*GM* II, § 7; III, § 28). The real issue for human beings is the meaning of the tragic suffering that, to a large extent, is simply inseparable from the human condition. For more than a millennium, the "ascetic ideal" responded to what Nietzsche calls our "metaphysical need" for meaning, that is, our need to create comforting illusions "in the midst of no [fixed] meaning at all" (Scott, 1990, p. 45). By "metaphysical need" (*metaphysisches Bedürfnis*) Nietzsche has in mind a historically developed need for "enduring continuants and constants" that we imaginatively construct in order to avoid (or at least assuage) the pain associated with flux, change, and temporality (see *BGE,* § 2; *GM* III, §§ 23–27; *BT,* "Attempt at Self-Criticism," § 7; *HAH* I, § 26; see also May, 1999, p. 124). Human beings developed over time a psychological need for a "fixed" framework that would transcendentally ground the world and give "total" meaning to our intricate web of feelings, affects, perceptions, beliefs, and practices. We developed (historically) a need for a "horizon" that will "stand fast" and that will impose meaningful structure on certain difficult experiences (involving pain and death), answer certain recurring questions (e.g., "Why do we suffer?" "Why do we die?"), and which in doing so, will allow us (psychologically, emotionally) to actively participate in the world. By claiming as it does that the best life is one of self-denial, and by devaluing the natural, human world in favor of some "afterworld" (which supposedly bestows a "transcendent" value on this "ephemeral" world), the ascetic ideal responds to this metaphysical/psychological need. It satisfies our "human, all too human" need for what Nietzsche terms "metaphysical comfort" (*der metaphysische Trost*), especially the comforting metaphysical illusion that "we can ultimately escape 'the world' and all its predicates such as fate, suffering, imperfection . . . and time" (see *BT,* § 7; see also May, 1999, p. 124). In this way, Nietzsche claims, the ascetic ideal eventually became the only (transcultural) ideal that made pain and suffering bearable—even desirable—by giving it meaning. Suffering becomes the sign of a promise that, "at some point, in some other realm of existence, suffering will end once and for all" (Roberts, 1998, p. 35).[1]

While its overt message is that this world, our everyday world, has no value and ought to be denied in favor of some "true world," the ascetic ideal still gives us a feeling that there is, after all, something worth living for, something that can satisfy our psychological need for a sense of power and effectiveness in the world. The adherent of the ascetic ideal gets a sense of power from self-denial by believing in a "true word" beyond this one "toward which one moves through self-denial" (Roberts, 1998, p. 79). Nietzsche argues that the "self-contradiction" represented by the ascetic ideal is that, in fact, it is a disguised form of the "will-to-preserve-life" (*GM* III, § 13). While devaluing human life, the ascetic ideal paradoxically functioned not to destroy that life but to preserve it by encouraging "mastery" and self-discipline over it (see *GM* III, § 15). For a long time, the "life-denying" ascetic ideal actually served a "life-enhancing" function: it spurred one's willingness to go on, to keep acting, and to keep willing. It worked to overcome depression and disgust with life and had "the positive value of seducing inherently weak and despairing creatures who would otherwise have been tempted to do away with themselves into continuing to live, by giving their suffering (which actually resulted [in part] from their own weakness) an imaginary meaning" (Geuss, 1999, p. 18). And Nietzsche is quick to point out that "any meaning"—even a fantastic "otherworldly" metaphysical meaning based upon "gross misapprehensions"—is better than none at all (see *GM* III, §§ 13, 20, 28).

Moreover, Nietzsche argues that the ascetic ideal functioned historically to preserve life by successfully altering the direction of the "*ressentiment*" that resulted, in part at least, from "socialized man's" being forced to live under the constraints of civil society. For example, he argues that the ascetic priest successfully altered the direction of the resentment of "socialized man" back on himself, thus making the sufferer the object of his own rancor (see *GM* III, § 15). In this way, the sufferer comes to blame himself for his own senseless suffering, and society is protected from the potential "ticking bomb" of vengefulness, bad conscience, and rancor against life (cf. *GM* III, § 14). Such redirected resentment also had the added bonus of giving humanity "depth," "intelligence," a sense of "evil," thus making us, for the first time, "interesting animals" (see *GM* I, §§ 6–9). It forced people to develop an "inner world," or "soul," within which they could "oppose themselves," thus creating "favorable conditions under which [they could] expend all [their] strength and achieve a maximal feeling of power" (*GM* III, § 7). It provided humanity with the creative "womb of all ideal and imaginative phenomena" (*GM* II, § 18). Ascetic morality has thus been "a useful morality" for weak, suffering humanity: "one that allowed the maximal life-enhancement possible for *them* (given their naturally limited possibilities); it was a trick life itself used to outwit the weak and preserve itself under difficult circumstances when drastic measures were the only ones that would work" (Geuss, 1999, p. 18).

The problem with the ascetic ideal is that, while it cultivates truthfulness and introspection (e.g., Christian confession about self and world), it is "a form of valuation which requires its devotees to make claims and have beliefs that won't stand up to truthful introspective scrutiny (such as that moral action arises from altruistic sources)" (Geuss, 1999, p. 21). Hence, the ascetic ideal eventually "draws its inference against itself" and thereby "dissolves" itself (*GM* III, § 27). Its "will to truth" eventually destroys its own comforting illusions—the "other-worldly" myths, "the lie involved in the belief in God"—without offering any alternative, redeeming, life-affirming visions (*GM* III, § 27). "The awe-inspiring catastrophe of two thousand years of training in truthfulness" is that the ascetic ideal is bringing to an end its own life-affirming fantasies, and there is nothing on the horizon to take its place. Humanity today can no longer get what it really needs from the ascetic ideal—a feeling of power and effectiveness in the world—except by denying or ignoring the cornerstone of that ideal, namely, the "will to truth" (*GM* III, § 27). And those with a "will to truth" cannot simply go back to an explicit acceptance of the ascetic ideal once they accept the "truth" that their "will to truth" is itself an expression of the ascetic ideal. We would feel foolish instead of powerful in embracing a life-denying ideal once we accepted the truth that our real motive for embracing it was to get a sense of power and vitality necessary to feel better about life, and thus, to continue living (see Clark, 1990, pp. 184–187, 191–192, 234). Hence, there is an urgent need for a new ideal.

Nietzsche argues that no alternative ideals to the life-denying ascetic ideal currently exist. All of the likely candidates—such as "science," "modern art," "traditional atheism," and "utopian" social and political movements—can be shown, upon analysis, to be bound up with the ascetic ideal in complex and subtle ways (for more on this see *GM* III, §§ 5, 23–25; see also Hicks, 2003, pp. 82–85).[2]

Nietzsche believes that modern humanity desperately needs a new ideal, for the inevitable demise of the ascetic ideal will lead to cultural dislocation and general social malaise: nihilism will be the result of the self-dissolution of previously accepted values (cf. *WP*, §§ 2, 3, 12; for more on this issue see Hicks, 2003, pp. 76–85). As David Owen and Aaron Ridley observe: "Nietzsche argues that the self-destruction of the ascetic ideal threatens to undermine our capacities for 'self-discipline,' 'self-surveillance,' and 'self-overcoming,' and our disposition to truthfulness precisely because we now lack an overarching goal in the service of which these capacities and this disposition are cultivated" (Owen and Ridley, 2000, p. 149).

But what, if any, alternative vision does Nietzsche advocate in the service of which our ethical capacities and dispositions could be cultivated and reshaped non-nihilistically? Certainly his numerous suggestions are not very clear or well developed. For example, he talks obscurely of "wedding the bad conscience to all *unnatural* inclinations," and he somewhat obliquely advocates "re-naturalizing" the ascetic ideal (meaning, presumably, applying its disciplinary techniques and practices to our everyday lives), so that we do not turn the activity of valuing, which is necessary for life, against life (see *GM* III, §§ 1, 24; *WP*, § 915). Nietzsche clearly wants to show how the idealized ascetic compulsion to alienate human beings from themselves (and value from the world) is a historical product of contingency (e.g., the contingency of the "metaphysical need"); moreover, he wants to suggest ways to overcome this compulsion. While the ascetic ideal offers us a transcendental meaning for life and a metaphysical solace (*Trost*) for suffering,

Nietzsche wants to find a "de-transcendentalized" meaning created and forged in the process of living itself. He wants to find a way to "harness" human suffering, to show its place in the overall economy of human life, in order to turn us toward life so that we can fashion our lives as immanently valuable in spite of pain and suffering. As he says, it is the "discipline" and cultivation of suffering that "has created all enhancements of human kind so far achieved" (*BGE*, § 225; see also § 62). Nietzsche believed that the "noble" pre-Socratic Greeks had achieved such an enhancement of life out of their suffering via the creation of Attic tragedy. And he clearly hopes to discover a "new nobility" that can recapture a way of living that is immanently valuable, a way of life rewarded by its own creativity and vibrancy (cf. Higgins, 1987, p. 131). But as Ridley observes, Nietzsche will have to construct his ideal for human living out of the capacities (internalization, depth, intelligence, truthfulness, etc.) that "two millennia of asceticism have bequeathed to us" (Ridley, 1998, p. 11). Simply put: how do we now come to accept ourselves and find joy in our lives as the "interesting animals" the ascetic ideal has made us?

While short on specifics, Nietzsche's preferred model for doing this is the "Dionysian artist-philosopher" who is committed to the "art of living" as a process of self-fashioning, self-interpreting, self-overcoming, revaluing, and transfiguring, and who finds his only goal in the constant "once more" (eternal recurrence) of the process of self-creation as an expression of "gratitude and love": a "dithyrambic . . . art of apotheoses" that says "yes to all that is questionable and terrible in existence" (*GS*, § 370; *TI* IX: 49). But what exactly does Nietzsche's dithyrambic art of living entail? As we shall see in the next section, it first entails using ascetic "techniques" against the "ascetic ideal" so as to "steel our hearts" against our own transcendental illusions and consolations.

III. The "Gymnastics of the Soul": Nietzsche's "Transfigured Asceticism"

In Book Three of the *Genealogy*, Nietzsche argues that the ascetic ideal is largely the result of centuries of Christian theorizing about suffering and of priestly attempts to gain "dominion over suffering" (cf. *GM* III, § 15; *TI* VI: 6). As Nietzsche sees it, the "metaphysical need" to construe one's life (and one's suffering) as meaningful is simply a corollary of being a self-conscious animal (see Ridley, 1998, p. 39). The ascetic priest responded to this need by offering humanity "metaphysical comfort," that is, by projecting "a whole mysterious machinery of salvation into [human] suffering" (*GM* II, § 7). The priest's idealized ascetic view of the world was really a bid for power within it—an attempt to gain mastery over suffering as the most profound and basic condition of life. In this way, the ascetic priest gave a comprehensive answer to the question of the meaning of life and in doing so successfully "preserved" human life. But, Nietzsche insists, it was "preserved" at a cost, namely, the devaluation of this-worldly existence: "The real significance of any action is [now] a matter of how it is evaluated from a [transcendental] perspective that lies outside of time. . . . [As such] we divorce ourselves from a sense of real interaction with the larger world" (Higgins, 1988, p. 144).

If the priestly Christian interpretation of asceticism is the result of centuries of theorizing about suffering, then, in principle at least, it can be gotten rid of and replaced with a more affirmative interpretation, one that, in Zarathustra's words, "remains faithful to the earth" and to "the art of *this-worldly* comfort" (*Z*, Prologue; *BT*, "Attempt at Self-Criticism," § 7). Of course, this is easier said than done, and Nietzsche is clear that it does not automatically follow that we can effectively change any particular historical context (or perspective) in which we now find ourselves. Such a change is likely to be difficult and may, in fact, require a long and complex historical process to be brought about.[3]

Still, Nietzsche argues optimistically that "the [metaphysical] needs which religion has satisfied and philosophy is now supposed to satisfy are not immutable; they can be *weakened* and *exterminated*" (*HAH* I, § 27). For example, the "Christian distress of mind that comes from sighing over one's inner depravity" is, according to Nietzsche, an "acquired, time-bound" need that philosophy "can be employed either to satisfy [via the ascetic ideal] or to set aside." In Nietzsche's view, "we now have absolutely no need of these [idealized ascetic] certainties regarding the furthest [fixed] horizon to live a full and excellent human life" (*HAH* I, § 27; *WS*, § 16). Yet to "set aside" such contingent metaphysical needs and "to effect a transition here, to relieve the heart over laden with feelings [of distress]," requires a great deal of work, discipline, and concerted effort on our part. In particular, Nietzsche insists that we must first wrest asceticism away from the prevailing idealized negative Christian interpretation—this "saintly form of debauch"—that tries to extinguish the passions rather than to elevate and spiritualize them (*GM* III, § 1). But how is this to be accomplished?

One way to do it, Nietzsche suggests, is to go back to the original pre-Pauline understanding of "asceticism" as an *askēsis*: literally, a "spiritual exercise" or "gymnastics" of thought brought to bear on itself, intended not to deny the world but to help transform the way one experiences both the self and the world (cf. *WP*, §§ 207, 914–915; see also Hadot, 1995, p. 128; 2002, pp. 122–126). In the *Antichrist*, Nietzsche claims that the idealized interpretation of asceticism was something largely "invented" by Saint Paul as a particular interpretation imposed on the life of Jesus (cf. *AC*, § 42). Paul's interpretation contains various dogmatic propositions about the immortality of the soul, freedom of the will, the need for redemption, the Day of Judgment, and similar ideas, all designed to satisfy our need for comforting illusions and transcendental consolations for suffering (cf. *AC*, §§ 39–43; *WP*, §§ 167, 175, 213; also see Geuss, 1999, pp. 9–17; Higgins, 1987, pp. 50–51). But Nietzsche thinks that Paul's interpretation represents a crude "psychological misinterpretation" and reversal of Jesus' ascetic way of life, "whose real nature could not for a long time be understood and described as it really was": namely, as a spiritual *askēsis,* or mode of working on the self and educating oneself against oneself, similar to what Hadot has recently termed the "spiritual exercise" or "gymnastics" of the self (see *WP*, § 207; *GM* III, § 13; see also Hadot, 1995, p. 128). Asceticism, understood as *askēsis,* was originally defined by a series of serious and concerted efforts to train, study, and discipline the self. As Nehamas observes, "the purpose of the complex exercises of which *askēsis* consisted was not to deny the pleasures—of sex, food, of worldly ambition—but to avoid excess. The point was not to be mastered by pleasure but to become its master and therefore to become the master of oneself as well" (Nehamas, 1998, p. 179). Ascetic limitation was viewed as "indispensable for any creative process" (Safranski, 2002, p. 201). And as Nietzsche sees it, this "most needful gymnastic" is still indispensable "if one wants to preserve in oneself the joy of being one's own master" (*WS*, § 305).

In his various writings, Nietzsche stresses the need for ascetic discipline and practice—for what he terms a "noble self-control"—not to deny or devalue the world but to "affirm the world" and to "take possession of [ourselves]" (see *BGE*, § 283; *HAH* I, § 29; *EH*, "Human, All Too Human," § 1). He repeatedly stresses the positive role of ascetic procedures in contrast to the negative (Pauline) "idealization of asceticism" (see *GM* II, § 3). Ascetic procedures, as opposed to the ascetic ideal, are directed to the end of self-cultivation and not self-denigration. He often characterizes ascetic practices ("poverty, chastity, humility") as prudential options for "imposing a form upon ourselves as hard, recalcitrant, suffering material" and for realizing "the most favorable conditions under which [we] can expel all [our] strength and achieve a maximal feeling of power" (see *GM* II, § 18; III, § 7). Such ascetic practices were originally intended (in their pre-Pauline mode) to provide us with opportunities for working on ourselves, improving ourselves, and "giving style" to ourselves, which Nietzsche declares is the "one most needful thing" for humans (see *GS*, § 290). For example, Nietzsche often stresses the positive role ascetic procedures played historically as "memory devices" for rendering a few important ideas "inextinguishable, fixed, and unforgettable," thus freeing them from competition with all others (see *GM* II, § 3). Adopting such ascetic techniques was not the same thing as adopting the priestly ascetic ideal of denying this world in favor of a transcendent one. Rather, the end to which ascetic practices were originally directed was something "immanent," something within the ascetic's own life, something useful, productive, and even enjoyable, namely, making oneself the object of one's own consciousness and will, reflecting on oneself with a view to changing oneself. As Nietzsche likes to say, "a certain asceticism, the severe and cheerful continence with the best will, belongs to the most favorable conditions of supreme spirituality" (*GM* III, § 9). By contrast, the Pauline ascetic ideal extrapolates from these ascetic procedures in order to posit a "denigration" of "that which one opposes in oneself." It moves from a life-affirming spiritual *askēsis* to "the loathing for everything fleshly," and as such, it constitutes a retreat from life (for more on this see Ridley, 1998, pp. 59–73).

"In place of the [Christian] aim of denial," Nietzsche now proposes "making asceticism natural again . . . the aim of strength; a gymnastics of the will; abstinence and periods of fasting of all kinds, in the most spiritual realm" (*WP*, § 915). Nietzsche hopes to recover philosophical possibilities from the past—in this case, the ancient understanding of asceticism as a "most needful gymnastics" and spiritual mode of working on the self—in order to use them in the present to open up alternative (non-nihilistic) spaces for future discourse and disclosure, and for thinking and acting differently in the world. "We can profit from a philosopher of the past," Nietzsche writes, "only insofar as he can provide an example of a type of philosophical life to be achieved." And this example "must be supplied by his outward life and not merely in his books—in the way, that is, in which the [pre-Socratic] philosophers taught, through their bearing, what they wore and ate, and their morals, rather than what they said or wrote" (*UM* III, §3; also see *PPP*, pp. 44–48).

As David Konstan recently observed, "ancient philosophy was not the narrowly intellectual discipline it is today, but professed to exist for the purpose of changing the way its adherents lived their lives" (Konstan, 2004, p. 26). The philosophers of antiquity were concerned less with theory than with imparting the practical spiritual training (*askēsis*), discipline, and education (*paideia*) that would allow individuals to "orient themselves in thought, in the life of the city, or in the world" (Davidson, 1995, p. 21). The object, as Foucault observes, was "to learn to what extent the effort to think one's own history can free thought from what it silently thinks, and so enable it to think [and act] differently" (Foucault, 1990, p. 9).

This ancient understanding of philosophy as *askēsis,* or spiritual training, is, at least in part, what Nietzsche has in mind when he speaks of philosophy as "the art of transfiguration" or the "art of living" (cf. *HAH* I, § 27; cf. also Safranski, 2002, p. 202). As he remarks in a note from 1881, "so far as praxis [the 'praxis' of philosophy] is concerned, I view the various moral schools [of ancient philosophy] as experimental laboratories in which a considerable number of recipes for the art of living have been thoroughly practiced and lived to the hilt. The result of all their experimenting belongs to us today, as our legitimate property," that is, as material to be utilized in fashioning a "noble," affirmative way of life for ourselves (*SW* IX, pp. 654–655). Nietzsche was particularly impressed by the possibility of using what he saw as the "ephectic bent" of ancient philosophy—its analysis, doubt, and suspension of judgment—to help accomplish the ends of self-cultivation. While the ascetic ideal demands a non-ephectic rejection of the whole world, Nietzsche's "Dionysian artist-philosophers" will use ascetic discipline to preserve their skeptical, experimental propensities. They will use ascetic techniques to free themselves from their present (nihilistic, decadent) condition in order to "bring something home to themselves," to become "most truly themselves" (see *GM*, Preface, and *Z* IV. 1). For too long, Nietzsche thinks, modern philosophers (of the Kantian and Schopenhauerian persuasion) have taken refuge in the ascetic ideal and masked their ephectic/experimental bent in an ascetic cocoon. They have lived under the idealized ascetic compulsion to expel value from the world we actually live in to some "unintelligible beyond" (the noumenal world, the world of "things-in-themselves"). By contrast, Nietzsche's Dionysian "philosophers of the future" will seek to still the life-denying voice of the ascetic ideal by adopting a certain ascetic discipline and by being "reflexively ephectic" in the face of the future (see *GM* III, § 12; see also Ridley, 1998, p. 117).

By urging us to rethink the genealogical history of the ascetic ideal and by asking us to reexamine a series of "exemplary models" from philosophy's ancient past (and to be guided by these models), Nietzsche hopes that we can eventually regain a more positive, life-enhancing, pre-Pauline understanding of asceticism as a spiritual *askēsis* and as "the nature, need, and instinct" of "the most spiritual human being" (see *UM* III, § 1; *GM* III, § 13; *AC*, §§ 21–23). He also hopes that, in this way, we can eventually overcome the "metaphysical need" in ourselves and recover the ancient understanding of philosophy as "the art of living," or the art of being "reflexively ephectic." This "soul artistry" calls for ascetic procedures but not the ascetic ideal (see Ridley, 1998, pp. 76–77, 117; see also Davidson, 1995, p. 21; Safranski, 2002, p. 348). In Nietzsche's view, such a transfigured asceticism—the "cheerful asceticism of an animal become fledged and divine, floating above life rather than in repose"—provides "optimal conditions for the highest and boldest spirituality," as well as "favorable conditions" for "being here and for being human," that is, for "evolving to be our [better] selves" (see *GM* III, §§ 7–9, 13; *EH*, "Why I Am So Clever, § 9; *EH*, "Birth of Tragedy," § 3; see also Safranski, 2002, p. 269; also Allison, 2001, pp. 141–142, and Conway, 1999, pp. 40–42). Ascetic procedures, combined perhaps with certain more modern (Kantian) aspirations for autonomy and self-determination, are instrumental, as Nietzsche sees it, to refining our instincts, harnessing our creative drives, and integrating a maximum number of conflicting drives into a "manifest wholeness" of character (see *BGE*, §§ 210–212; see also Nehamas, 1998, pp. 178–179; May, 1999, pp. 102–103). And the point of giving such a coherent unity and "style to one's character—a great and rare art"—is to make oneself affirmable, thereby avoiding "the great nausea," the idealized ascetic hatred of self and world: "For one thing is needful: that a human being should attain satisfaction with himself, whether it be by this or that poetry and art. . . . Whoever is dissatisfied with himself is continually ready for revenge, and we others will be his victims" (*GS*, § 290).

As Nietzsche observes in *Ecce Homo,* "what I [am] fundamentally suggesting here . . . is something altogether different . . . an unequaled problem of education, a new concept of self-discipline, self-defense to the point of hardness, a way to greatness and world historical achievement" (*EH*, "The Untimely Ones," § 3). This "altogether different" education aims at fashioning a "new self"—a self that has the "strength of will" to generate new "non-nihilistic" values for itself and for its community (cf. *WP*, § 585A). This is especially important in what Nietzsche thinks is our modern "decadent" era, when humanity teeters on the "abyss" of nihilism and can no longer generate affirmative values for itself (for more on Nietzsche's notion of "decadence," see Safranski, 2002, pp. 309–310; see also Geuss, 1999, pp. 56, 174, 192). Under such conditions, ethical success will entail some painful (ephectic) self-reflection and severe ascetic self-discipline: "Only great pain is the ultimate liberator of the spirit. . . . Only great pain, the long, slow pain that takes its time—on which we are burned, as it were, with green wood—compels us philosophers to descend into our ultimate depths" (*GS,* Preface, § 3).

Here, as elsewhere, Nietzsche is given to hyperbole. Still, his point is well worth considering: a healthy "soul" in a decadent era will necessarily be ascetic. It will constantly have to negate or deny conventional states or emotions in order to attain higher ones. It will constantly struggle to ascetically transform or rise above lower values in order to achieve higher ones, and it will have to do this as a condition for its being able to say "Yes" to the world. This expanding ascetic tension in the "soul," stretching it across a gradation of opposed values, is maximally life-enhancing and is conducive to achieving mastery and power over the self (see May, 1999, pp. 102–103). "This [ascetic] tyranny . . . has *educated* the [human] spirit" (*BGE,* § 188).

Nietzsche even goes so far as to suggest that ascetic self-discipline is now a "moral imperative" of nature or, at the very least, a "first imperative of prudence" (see *BGE,* § 188; *EH,* "Why I Am So Clever," § 8). As Margaret Miles interprets this, for Nietzsche "ascetic practices are methods, not goals"; they are methods whereby one struggles with oneself to renounce the "timely" (decadent) present so that one can fashion an "untimely" life for oneself and a "will to be true to oneself" (see Miles, 1981, p. 161; see also Safranski, 2002, p. 330). Such "transfigured" ascetic methods help generate particular ways of understanding and acting on ourselves that involve both renunciation and creation, that is, fashioning ourselves in terms of self-imposed limits and constraints (see *EH,* "Why I Am So Clever," § 8). As such, they are essential to fashioning what Nietzsche likes to call our "second nature" (i.e., our freer, stronger, more sovereign "spiritual" nature) without devaluing or denigrating (per the ascetic ideal) our given "first" (human-all-too-human) biological nature. In Nietzsche's words, "Only those who exercise self-control can know self-regard," and only those who know self-regard can "become who or what they are," namely, "the poets of their own lives" (see *EH,* "Human, All Too Human," § 1, and "Why I Am So Clever," § 9; see also Safranski, 2002, pp. 188, 349).

IV. Nietzsche and the "Small Things"

So far we have argued that ascetic procedures are integral to Nietzsche's work of overcoming the life-denying voice of the ascetic ideal in order to find a life-affirming alternative vision for the modern world. We have also examined his attempts to recapture certain philosophical possibilities and strategies from the past to aid him in his efforts. These include the cultivation of an "ephectic self-relation" as well as a "noble self-control" in the "art of living." But does Nietzsche offer any concrete suggestions as to how we might begin to implement these strategies? One clue is to be found in an unlikely place: in what Nietzsche likes to call "the small, everyday things" generally considered "matters of complete indifference" to philosophy. As he observes in *Human, All Too Human,* "the closest things, for example, eating, housing, clothing, social intercourse are typically not made the object of constant impartial, and general [philosophical] reflection: because these things are accounted degrading—they are deprived of serious intellectual and artistic consideration" (*WS*, §§ 5–6). But Nietzsche responds:

> These small things—nutrition, place, climate, and recreation . . . are inconceivably more important than everything one has taken to be important so far. Precisely here one must begin to relearn [asceticism]. What mankind has so far taken seriously have not even been realities but mere imaginings . . . lies prompted by the bad instincts of sick natures that were harmful in the most profound sense: all these concepts of "God," "soul," "virtue," "sin," "beyond," "truth," "eternal life"—the greatness of human nature, its "divinity," was sought in them. All the problems of politics, social organization, and of education have been falsified through and through because . . . one learned to despise the "little" things, which means the basic concerns of life itself. (*EH*, "Why I am So Clever," § 10)

As Stauth and Turner correctly observe, "insufficient weight" has been given to Nietzsche's insightful comments on the "small things," especially as they relate to his own notion of asceticism (cf. Stauth and Turner, 1988, pp. 16–17, 24–26). For example, in the passage just quoted from *Ecce Homo,* Nietzsche implies that the first step toward liberating ourselves from the "metaphysical need" (and its life-denying ascetic ideal) is to redirect the focus of our ascetic self-scrutiny (our *askēsis*) away from the "big things" on which it has been focused for centuries, the so-called "first and last things" of metaphysics, back to those "small things" we are given in life. In other words, the first step by which we overcome the "negative" ascetic ideal consists not in abandoning its techniques and practices but in redeploying them to fashion a "wholeness of character" out of the limited resources we are given in life; that is to say, out of the "small everyday things," the "closest things of all": "our mode of life, in the division of the day, in for how long and with whom we enjoy social intercourse, in work and leisure, commanding and obeying, feeling for art and nature, eating, sleeping, and reflecting" (*WS*, § 6). We render our everyday life a "testing ground" or "workshop," as it were, for ascetic discipline, focus, and self-control (see Safranski, 2002, pp. 28–46). And we do this, not to transcend or deny the self and world but to enhance them: to "'become the persons' we are [potentially]" (*GS*, §§ 270, 335; *EH*, "Why I Am So Clever," § 9). As Nietzsche says, "Be yourself! But know that all you are now doing, thinking, and desiring is not you yourself" (*UM* III, § 1). In other words, if you do not learn how to master the "small things" in your life, the danger is that you will be completely mastered by them in such a way that your creative energies will be completely drained. For example, your life will be consumed by your job or by your computer or by a culture of advertisement, mass media, and popular entertainment. "The reason for this is that when defensive expenditures, be they ever so small, become the rule and habit, they entail an extraordinary and entirely superfluous impoverishment. Our great expenses are composed of the most frequent small ones . . . and energy gets wasted on negative ends" (*EH*, "Why I Am So Clever," § 8).

In the *Untimely Meditations*, Nietzsche makes it clear that it was an impassioned attention to the "small things" in life that he found so admirable about the pre-Socratic philosophers. As he says, the "courageous visibility" of the way of life of the pre-Socratic philosophers gave them an "experiential richness" that made their lives meaningful and valuable. And to be aware of such richness in all the moments of one's life is to be serious about life in all its parts, even the smallest and most mundane parts: "it is to love life for its own sake" (*UM* III, § 3; cf. also Higgins, 1987, pp. 235–242). By contrast, it is "feigned disrespect . . . for all the things closest to them" that leads the "ascetic priests," "metaphysicians," and the "despisers of the body" to "transform the earth for so many into a vale of tears" (see *WS*, § 6; *Z* I.4). Such "afterworldly" proponents of the ascetic ideal—from Christian optimists to Schopenhauerian pessimists—seduce us into being "unfaithful to the earth" by focusing exclusively on the "big things" (God, Eternity, the Will, etc.). They seek a "true world" in contrast to this one—"a world in which one does not suffer; for contradiction, dependence, and change cause suffering"—in order to bestow meaning and value on "this world, our world" (see *WP*, § 585A). They have enough, "more than enough understanding," Nietzsche says, but "it is employed in the wrong direction" toward the "big things," the "first and last things" of metaphysics, and "artificially diverted away from these smallest and closest things" (*WS*, § 6). From their perspective, "the requirements of the individual, his great and small needs within the twenty-four hours of the day, are to be regarded as something contemptible or a matter of indifference" (*WS*, § 6). For them, "the world as it ought to be (the afterworld, the "true world") exists; and this world (the world of the "small things") in which we actually live, is an error—this world of ours ought not to exist" (*WP*, § 585A). But Nietzsche asks, "What kind of man reflects this way?" His answer: "an unproductive, suffering kind, a kind weary of life."

> But if we imagine the opposite kind of man, he would not need to believe in what has Being; moreover, he would despise it as dead, tedious, indifferent—The belief that the world as it ought to be is, really exists, is a belief of the unproductive who do not desire to create a world as it ought to be. They posit it as available already, and they seek ways and means of reaching it. "Will to truth"—as the impotence of the will to create. . . .
> This same species of man, grown one stage poorer, no longer possessing strength to interpret, to create fictions, produces nihilists. A nihilist is a

man who judges of the world as it is, that it ought not to be, and of the world as it ought to be, that it does not exist. According to this view, our existence (action, suffering, willing, feeling) has no meaning: the pathos of "in vain" is the nihilists' pathos. (*WP*, § 585A)

As Nietzsche sees it, the "nihilist's pathos" is a response to the fact that "man is the as yet undetermined animal," a self-conscious animal subject to "an excess of failures, of sickness, degeneracy, infirmity, and suffering necessarily" (see *GS*, § 1; *BGE*, § 62). The "teachers of metaphysical purpose" (Platonists, Ascetic Idealists, etc.) gave comfort to such "undetermined animals," whose suffering would have otherwise seemed pointless, by relating their suffering to the "big things" (God, salvation of the soul, "service to the State"). But Nietzsche makes clear that "the true world invented by Plato" has been abolished in the modern era, and when the "true world" is abolished "the apparent world is also abolished, and man is left with the task of discovering how to live with the world that remains," namely, the world of the "small everyday things" (see *TI*, IV; see also Lampert, 1986, p. 21). Now we must learn how to live without "metaphysical comfort," without "healing, comforting worlds of illusion," without "these totalistic interpretations and introductions of [metaphysical] meaning" (see *WP*, § 585B; *GS*, §§ 84–87). "It is a measure of the degree of strength of will to what extent one can do without [fixed] meaning in things [i.e., in the 'big things,' the 'first and last things'], and to what extent one can endure to live in a meaningless world precisely *because* one learns to fashion a small portion of it [i.e., the 'small things'] oneself" (*WP*, § 585A).

Thus, to combat the nihilism of the ascetic ideal, Nietzsche insists:

We must first become good neighbors to the closest things [the "small things"] and cease from gazing so contemptuously past them at clouds and monsters of the night. In forest caves, in swampy regions and under cloudy skies—this is where man has lived all too long, and lived poorly. . . . There he has *learned to despise* the present . . . and life and himself—and we, who see in the *brighter* fields of nature and the spirit, we too have inherited in our blood something of this poison of contempt for what is closest [for the "small things"]. (*WS*, § 16)

If we are to overcome this "contempt for what is closest," we must learn how to be the "poets of our life—first of all in the smallest most everyday matters" (*GS*, § 299). As Nietzsche says, "the lack of self-mastery in the small things brings about a crumbling of the capacity for great things" (*WS*, § 305). We must "learn from the artists while being wiser than them in other matters." We must learn the "artistry of the soul" and "fashion something that was not there before," namely, "a character with style—a grand and rare art" (*GS*, §§ 290, 299, 301; see also Ridley, 1998, pp. 78–95). But what exactly does this mean?

As Nehamas observes, this means that we must learn to create for ourselves, out of the "small things" we are given, "a life that, despite and perhaps because of the pain and suffering it will inevitably contain, will constitute such an achievement that [we] would be willing to live through it again, down to the smallest detail." But how is this possible? Nehamas says it is possible only if we first learn to fashion ourselves into an "object so organized [like a work of art] that every single part of it is equally essential and in which, therefore, any alteration would bring about a breakdown of the whole"; and this means cultivating "essentially [an] aesthetic attitude toward life and the world" (Nehamas, 1985, p. 136). Here we see the influence of Schiller, Goethe, Stendhal, and Hölderlin on Nietzsche's ethical thought. Meaninglessness is rendered tolerable only when life is beautified. And life is beautified, Nietzsche thinks, only through "this secret self-ravishment . . . this delight in imposing a form upon oneself as hard, recalcitrant, suffering material" (*GM* II, § 18). This "artists' cruelty," directed backward "in the labyrinth of the breast to use Goethe's expression," creates for itself "an abundance of strange new beauty and affirmation, perhaps even beauty itself" (*GM* II, § 18). As Nietzsche sees it, beauty is primarily "a state of the soul: it is the result of going to work on oneself, of interpreting oneself, of exercising upon oneself that artist's violence" (Ridley, 1998, p. 89). It is also a matter of resisting resentment, a task that requires great discipline and strength: "weak characters without power over themselves hate the constraint of style" (*GS*, § 290). Nietzsche regards Goethe as perhaps the best example of a "soul artist" that Europe has produced:

> He [Goethe] did not retire from life but put himself into the midst of it; he was not fainthearted but took as much as possible upon himself, over himself, into himself. What he wanted was *totality*; he fought the mutual extraneousness of reason, senses, feeling, and will (preached with the most abhorrent scholasticism by *Kant*, the antipode to Goethe); he disciplined himself to wholeness; he *fashioned* himself. (*TI* IX: 49)

Such artists of the soul will "give style to their character" by surveying "all the strengths and weaknesses of their nature and then fitting them into an artistic plan until every one of them appears as art. . . . In the end, when the work is finished, it becomes evident how the constraint of a single taste governed and formed everything large and small" (*GS*, § 290). As David Owen suggests, "becoming what one is" can be likened to the process of creating a work of art in which "the achievement of self-mastery is revealed as the constraint of style given content" through taste, heuristic imagery, and rigorous self-interpretation (Owen, 1995, p. 111). "Soul artists," such as Goethe and Stendhal, will seek "to form a totality out of [themselves], in the faith that only in the totality everything redeems itself and appears good and justified" (*WP*, § 95). They will constantly experiment with various images and metaphorical depictions of alternate (non-decadent, non-nihilistic) forms of life that they, in turn, can impose on themselves, use to reconfigure and enhance themselves, and in doing so attain satisfaction by interpreting themselves anew. Such exemplary figurative/metaphorical models can also help others achieve an intimation of a form and meaning that they, in turn, can appropriate in their own terms and use for their own "self-enhancement and creative self-expression" (see Safranski, 2002, pp. 216, 299). In the absence of any metaphysical consolations, Nietzsche claims it is only "as an aesthetic phenomenon [that] existence is still *bearable* for us" (*GS,* § 107; for more on the "figurative dimension" of Nietzsche's thought, see Hicks and Rosenberg, 2003).

Nietzsche's "soul artistry" or "aesthetics of existence" entails a "nonmoral asceticism," which Nietzsche relates closely to the "spiritual power and the practice of philosophy" (see Nehamas, 1985, pp. 114–117; see also Roberts, 1998, pp. 81–95; Thiele, 1990, pp. 146–147). "Spirit is the life that cuts into life: with its own agony it increases its own knowledge. Did you know that?" (*Z* II.8). Moreover, "every attainment, every step forward in knowledge, follows from courage, from hardness against oneself, from cleanliness in relation to oneself" (*EH,* Preface, § 3); and only if one is severe against one's heart can one aspire "to have integrity in matters of spirit" (*AC,* § 50).

V. Ascetic/Aesthetic Self-Fashioning: Liberating the Self

Nietzsche wants us to use the tools we have ready to hand (ascetic procedures, the "small everyday things," etc.) to change ourselves, educate ourselves against ourselves, and to discover new and noble ways of living. His "altogether different" education—his ascetic/aesthetic education—is directed to the end of self-cultivation and not self-denigration. It aims to cure the ills of the ascetic ideal and to redeem us "not only from the reigning ideal but that which was bound to grow out of it, nausea, will to nothingness, nihilism" (*GM* II, § 24). But Nietzsche also makes clear that the movement of this ascetic/aesthetic education will necessarily be from a situation of "nondifferentiation" of the self (in the "herd," in the "crowd," in the "timely present") to differentiation of the self from others (differentiation of an authentic self from the "voice of the herd"; cf. Taylor, 2000, p. 182). In numerous places in his writings, Nietzsche argues that the goal of most existing social and cultural arrangements is simply to "distract" us from ourselves so that we lose ourselves in the undifferentiated "crowd" (e.g., in mass media and mass politics). As such, we "cease to be aware" of our selves as unique individuals. "Through this process, the individual becomes so identified with or integrated within the social totality of which he is a member that all sense of personal uniqueness and self-responsibility evaporate. The result is mass, herd, or crowd existence" (Taylor, 2000, p. 57).

> "All loneliness is guilt"—thus speaks the herd. And you have long belonged to the herd. The voice of the herd will still be audible in you. And [if] you say, "I no longer have a common conscience with you," it will be a lament and an agony. (*Z* I.17)

Nietzsche thinks that all of us have "internalized" the "voice of the herd," and it is "still audible" within us. Therefore, "the worst enemy" we shall encounter in our attempts to fashion ourselves will always be ourselves. We "lie in wait" for ourselves, "in caves and in woods" (Z I.17). As Kierkegaard says, "no one wants to be I, but pulls in his antennae and becomes third person, 'the public,' 'they'" (Kierkegaard, *Journals and Papers*, cited in Taylor, 2000, p. 58). Any attempt to fashion a new and authentic self demands, in Nietzsche's words, "the hardest self-love and self-discipline" in order to defend oneself against one's "old self," that is, against the "voice of the herd" within us (see *EH*, "The Untimely Ones"). But why should anyone desire to cultivate this "hardest self-disciple" and "instinct of self-defense" in the first place? Nietzsche's answer:

> Because he [the self-fashioner] realizes that he is in danger of being cheated out of himself, and that a kind of agreement exists to kidnap him out of his own cave. Then and only then does he bestir himself, prick up his ears, and resolve: "I will remain my own!" It is a dreadful resolve . . . for now he will have to descend into the depths of existence with a string of curious questions on his lips: Why do I live? What lessons have I to learn from life? (*UM* III, § 4)

> Why this hardness, this suspiciousness, this hatred for your own virtues? Now he [the self-fashioner] dares to ask aloud and hears in reply something like an answer. "You shall become master over yourself, master also over your virtues. Formerly *they* were your masters; but they must be only your instruments beside other instruments." (*HAH*, Preface, § 6)

According to Nietzsche, we all tend to interpret our everyday experiences in terms of categories, concepts, and attitudes that are common to everyone. We tend to follow "what is familiar . . . what we are used to," but this familiarity (or "timeliness") inhibits our receptiveness to creative ("untimely") insights and alternatives and thus prevents us from "becoming who or what we are," from becoming our "better selves" (see *GS*, § 355). "Your true nature [or self] doesn't lie buried deep within you but immeasurably high above you, or at least above that which you usually take yourself to be" (*UM* III, § 1). Our goal lies in the "peaks," as it were, "in the great individuals, the saints and artists" (see Safranski, 2002, pp. 269 and 297). By contrast, it is the "voice of the herd" that "cheats us out of ourselves" and keeps us from scaling the peaks and "taking possession of ourselves" (cf. *EH*, "Human, All Too Human," §1). We typically allow ourselves "to be swept along by mass movements" or by a culture of advertisement and celebrity, "swirling in the social mainstream." Thus, we "lose [our] moorings and drift with the ever changing currents of the day" (Taylor, 2000, p. 58).

As Nietzsche sees it, there is an urgent need for liberation. We need to be liberated "from what in [our] nature does not belong to [us]," namely, from the undifferentiated "voice of the herd." It is this need for liberation, to be lifted above the "tumult of everyday existence," that prompts us to undertake the arduous task of "self-fashioning" in the first place (see *EH*, "Human, All Too Human," § 1; see also Safranski, 2002, p. 257). Only by attempting such a task does "the free, ever free spirit begin to unveil the riddle of that great liberation which had until then waited dark, questionable, almost untouchable in his memory" (*HAH*, Preface, § 6). Liberation requires acts of transgression— transgression against the prevailing (idealized ascetic) moral conventions and prejudices of the day. It requires us to gain "mastery" over what Zarathustra calls "the people's table of values" so that "a new table of values" can eventually emerge (cf. *Z* I.8). It requires us to gain mastery over ourselves so that we can "become free" of the herd and begin to take "possession of our selves" as genuinely "free spirits." "The term 'free spirit' here . . . means a spirit that has *become free,* that has again taken possession of itself" (*EH*, "Human, All Too Human," § 1). Such "self-mastery" and "self-possession" is what "distinguishes those who assume responsibility for giving style to their lives from those who do not; and this, Nietzsche observes, is a 'grand and a rare art'" (Alderman, 1977, p. 64). But this "grand and rare art" can only be accomplished through those "transfigured" ascetic procedures that provide us with the "bulwark against the unendurable," that is, against the decadent, nihilistic present (see *CW,* Preface; *Z* I.1; see also Safranski, 2002, p. 257). It is only through a cheerful transfigured *askēsis*—an "exercise of the self on the self by which [we attempt] to develop and transform [ourselves] and attain a certain mode of being" in the world—that we first "create the freedom to create a self," that is, "create the creature" we are seeking to discover (see Foucault, 1997, pp. 281–301; see also Alderman, 1977, p. 104). For Nietzsche, as for Kierkegaard, it is with the individual person, or the "care of the self," that ethics has preeminently to do, and therefore "any endeavor to compromise or undermine that paramount insight must be sternly resisted" (Gardiner, 1988, p. 86).[4]

At the same time, however, Nietzsche does not advocate a romantic kind of isolated individualism. In Book Five of the *Gay Science,* Nietzsche says that "the human being . . . who wants to behold the supreme measures of value of his time must admittedly first overcome this time in himself—this is the test of his strength—but equally, not only his time but his prior aversion and contradiction against his time, this suffering from his time, his un-timeliness, his romanticism" (*GS,* § 380). While Nietzsche clearly sees the modern ethical dilemma as being that of the individual self inauthentically "dispersed" in the social totality (or "herd" mentality) of the decadent present, it does not follow that he is endeavoring to arrive at an isolated or "romantic" *Einzelner* as the remedy to our modern discontents. Instead, his analysis, like Hegel's, attempts to reach a new intersubjectivity of "spiritual community," or what Nietzsche likes to term a community of "free spirits," "revaluers," and "hyperboreans" (cf. *AC,* §1). As Nietzsche sees it, strong, postmoral individuals who fashion new non-nihilistic/non-decadent modes of life for themselves can have the greatest positive effect on the life of culture and on the social and political world at large (cf. Nehamas, 1998, pp. 141, 168). By ascetically overcoming the "ascetic ideal" in themselves, by learning to confront "senseless" suffering head on, they can make for themselves a "character with style" and thus create an alternative voice (to the "voice of the herd") that others can then appropriate in their own terms and use for their own creative purposes. In this way, the self-fashioner can help to generate, for himself and for others, "a philosophy of life in which the critique of what we are is at one and the same time the historical analysis of the limits imposed on us and an experiment with the possibility of going beyond them" (Foucault, 1984, p. 50; see also Rabinow, 1997, xxvii–xxxvii).[5]

VI. Conclusion: An Ethics of Self-Fashioning?

Nietzsche believes that the ascetic ideal is now engaged in the final stages of its own self-destruction and that an impending nihilism will be the legacy of the modern world. In response to the immanent collapse of the ascetic ideal, Nietzsche proposes an experimental self-fashioning in which one does not take oneself as a given "in the flux of passing moments" but as an "object of a complex and difficult elaboration," consciously making "[one's] body, [one's] feelings, [one's] passions, [one's] very existence a work of art" (see Foucault, 1984, pp. 41–42). The outcome of this "complex elaboration" is "a self-referential dynamics of enhancement where life is its own purpose, designed to investigate and elicit the possibilities inherent in it" (see Safranski, 2002, pp. 28, 35–37, 45–46, 328; see also Conway, 1999, pp. 40–43). "Ever questioning and questionable, as if life were nothing but cracking nuts, and thus we are bound to grow day-by-day more questionable, worthier of asking questions, perhaps also worthier—of living" (GM III, § 9). But what, if any, alternative ideals emerge out of this "self-referential dynamics of enhancement"?

This question is a vexing one, for the "awe-inspiring catastrophe" of the gradual self-overcoming of the ascetic ideal is that its own self-destruction seems to preclude the possibility of anything's ever taking its place (see GM III, §§ 27–28). As Ridley astutely observes: "only *another* 'closed system of will, goal, and interpretation' could possibly take its place; and it is precisely in the realization that *any* transcendentally self-justifying account of existence must be unintelligible that the last inference of asceticism consists. Thus, when it overcomes itself, the ascetic ideal doesn't merely vacate the playing field, it abolishes it as well" (Ridley, 1998, p. 124). As a consequence, any prospective "counter-ideal" must be limited to a proposal of something immanent, something (non-transcendentally) grounded "in our ambitions for ourselves as denizens of 'this world, our world'" (see Ridley, 1998, p. 126). As Nietzsche sees it, this situation holds great promise as well as great peril for the modern world. The great promise is that now, in light of the collapse of the ascetic ideal, we are free to "create the creatures" we are seeking to discover. The great peril is that if we cannot fashion some sort of "noble" life-affirming meaning for ourselves (in the face of no fixed, transcendentally grounded meaning at all), then nihilism beckons. But does Nietzsche have anything concrete to offer on the score of a counter-ideal that would allow us to affirm life for what it is after the collapse of the ascetic ideal? Does he give us anything to go on in our attempts to imagine what a truly immanent ideal of living might be like?

In *Ecce Homo,* Nietzsche claims that a "counter-ideal was lacking— until Zarathustra" (*EH,* "Genealogy of Morals: A Polemic"). But what counter-ideal, if any, does Zarathustra offer us? There seem to be only two serious candidates for the alternative ideal that Zarathustra teaches: (1) the "Overman" (or *Übermensch*) ideal, and (2) the ideal of affirming eternal recurrence (see Clark, 1990, p. 253).

At first glance, the Overman ideal would seem to provide the perfect framework for consummate self-fashioning—one associated with notions of self-overcoming, sublimation, self-mastery, creativity, self-perfection, and the joyful affirmation of life (cf. Magnus, 1988, pp. 168–170). The Overman seems to articulate a noble, immanent ideal of living that contrasts positively with both the ignoble decadence of the "last man" of modern culture and the ascetic resentment and vengefulness of modernity's "small men."

Yet by the time we reach Book IV of *Zarathustra,* Zarathustra himself is forced to recognize that his *Übermensch* ideal is simply a variation on the old ascetic ideal he despises. For while Zarathustra preaches the positive value of this life as opposed to all "afterworldly" views, in practice his Overman ideal allows him to value human life, not immanently, but only as a means or bridge to a "beyond," to a "superhuman" life. For Zarathustra, the "meaning of the earth" is only found in striving toward a goal that is not grounded in "this world, our world" (cf. Higgins, 1988, p. 143). Rather than being "faithful to the earth" and its "small things," Zarathustra admits, "I should not know how to live if I were not a seer of that which must come" (Z II.20). As Maude Clark interprets this:

> The value of human life ... derives completely from its status as a means to the Übermensch, the negation or overcoming of the merely human. Here we have the same pattern we find in the case of the ascetic ideal: Human life is accorded value as a means to something that is its own negation. (Clark, 1990, p. 273)

Worse still, the Overman ideal seems to express the same reactive mode of resentment (e.g., against time, against the past, against the "it was," etc.) that Zarathustra associates with the "wisest of all ages," namely, the Platonists, ascetic priests, Pauline Christians, and similar groups. For while it allows Zarathustra to affirm life despite his suffering, it does so at the cost of resentment and imaginary revenge against those he perceives to be the cause of his suffering, namely, the "small men." According to Zarathustra, the "small men" promulgate ascetic values that accuse and devalue human life. They find value in life only by accusing and condemning human life and depriving others of the ability to affirm life. But ironically, the Overman ideal also implies that human life has value only reactively as a means to condemn something: "he [Zarathustra] denies value to the small man, but also to human life itself, except as a means to its own negation" (Clark, 1990, p. 277). And when Zarathustra's "abysmal thought" forces him to imagine his enemy (the small man, the Last Man) recurring again and again, nausea and disgust overcome him. As Giorgio Agamben observes, "whoever experiences disgust has in some way recognized himself in the object of his loathing and fears being recognized in turn. The man who experiences disgust recognizes himself in an alterity that cannot be assumed . . ." (Agamben, 1999, p. 107). Thus, when Zarathustra finally recognizes the abysmal truth behind his Overman ideal, he also comes to recognize his own life as devoid of intrinsic value: he sees that "he contains the small man within himself" (Clark, 1990, p. 277). He cannot assume a counter-framework for genuine self-fashioning and self-enhancement that is itself still based on an idealized ascetic revenge against life.

It would seem, then, that we are left with only one viable alternative to the ascetic ideal—the ideal of affirming eternal recurrence. And indeed, at the end of the *Twilight of the Idols,* Nietzsche characterizes himself as "the teacher of the eternal recurrence" (*TI* X: 5). But what exactly is this alternative ideal, and moreover, how is it linked with the dynamics of self-fashioning? What would it mean to "self-fashion" in accordance with the "rule" or "ideal" of "eternal recurrence"?

On our reading, eternal recurrence is not intended as a cosmological theory but as a figurative/metaphorical view of the self. As Nehamas suggests, this view does not "presuppose the [literal] truth . . . that the world, or even that one's own life, eternally repeats itself" over and over again. Rather, "what he [Nietzsche] is interested in is the attitude one must have toward oneself in order to react with joy and not despair to . . . the thought that one's life will occur, the very same in every single detail, again and again and again for all eternity" (Nehamas, 1985, p. 151). This is the guiding attitude, we suggest, of Nietzsche's "soul artists" (such as Goethe) who "divide themselves against themselves," who go to work on themselves and on the "small things" in their lives and who attempt to create something out of their own self-overcoming: a character with style. This is the affirmative attitude of the authentic self-fashioner who lives within the tragic, with suffering and death as the inevitable conditions of life, and who faces the tragic dimensions of life through the "spiritual exercise" of affirming eternal recurrence in order to transfigure and enhance life: "in order to be oneself the eternal joy of becoming" (*EH,* "Birth of Tragedy," § 3).

That Nietzsche yearns for such an immanent counter-ideal for self-enhancement is beyond question. But as Rüdiger Safranski suggests, his various attempts to link "eternal recurrence" with the "dynamics of enhancement" are never altogether clear or successful (see Safranski, 2002, p. 326). We conclude this essay by offering the following observations concerning the important link between eternal recurrence and Nietzsche's ethics of self-fashioning.

First, to fashion oneself in accordance with the ideal (or "rule") of eternal recurrence is to be joyfully willing to engage in the same activities again and again, even though one has no hope of any final "fixed state" or goal ever being achieved (see *WP,* § 708). As Nietzsche sees it, the highest affirmation of life would be to style a self that one finds valuable, not just as a means to an end beyond the process of living but as grounded in meaningful day-to-day living, that is, as grounded in the "small things" of life. Instead of seeing one's life as valuable only as a means or bridge to some further goal (e.g., bringing the Overman into existence), one must find intrinsic worth in the art of living one's life. Doubtless this will require all of the efforts at "self-overcoming" that Zarathustra associates with the Overman ideal but minus the condemnation of life and imaginary revenge against those who fail to live up to the ideal. As we've seen, Zarathustra is tempted to nihilism by the "abysmal thought" that the "small men" or the "Last Man" will recur eternally. But Nietzsche implies that the very "nobility" of the sovereign individual—the nobility of the ethical self-fashioner—resides in his or her capacity to affirm even the endless repetition of the Last Man. It is this capacity that provides "the catalyst of the *overcoming* of nausea which constitutes Zarathustra's greatest moment," as well as the "spur" that pushes us beyond ourselves in order to "become who or what we are" (see Ridley, 1998, p. 151; see also Higgins, 1988, p. 143). Viewed in this light, eternal recurrence is almost a "regulative" idea in the Kantian sense, a stimulus conducive to the further enhancement of life (see Schacht, 1983, pp. 261, 266).

Second, to live our lives immanently in terms of affirming eternal recurrence would require each of us to cultivate a certain "lightness of being," a "playfulness" and "repetitiousness," that Nietzsche associates with the "child spirit" of Zarathustra's "Three Metamorphoses": "The child is innocent . . . a new beginning, a game, a self-propelled wheel, a first movement, a sacred 'yes.' For the game of creation, my brothers, a sacred 'yes' is needed, the child now wills his own will" (*Z* I.1). In his early essay *Philosophy in the Tragic Age of the Greeks,* Nietzsche even alludes to eternal recurrence as "the greatest of plays" and the "innocent game of the aeon" (*PTG,* §§ 6–8). Thus, to "self-fashion" in accordance with this ideal is like playing an experimental, pedagogical game: "roughly like a child's game or an artist's creative play-impulse" (*PTG,* §19). Here, Maude Clark draws a useful analogy with the familiar "marriage game." In the "marriage game" we pose the whimsical question to ourselves: "If I had it to do all over again, would I still marry the same person?" Taken literally, the marriage game involves a number of unrealistic confusions and assumptions (just as the literal "cosmological reading" of eternal recurrence probably involves a number of unrealistic confusions and assumptions). For example, the marriage game requires you to ask yourself "would I, knowing what I know now, go through an experience identical to one in which I knew much less than I now know?" Nonetheless, the game does succeed in testing one's underlying attitude toward one's marriage (cf. Clark, 1990, p. 269). So too with self-fashioning in accord with the "rule" of eternal recurrence: it offers us a "selective principle" operating in the "service of strength" (*WP,* § 1058). It offers us a "test," as it were, for determining whether or not we have the "strength of will" to reject "the metaphysical need" for comforting illusions and to endure to live in a "meaningless world" precisely because we have "learned to fashion a small portion of it" ourselves (see *WP,* § 585A). It offers us an experimental, metaphorical strategy in which we take our willingness to relive our life over and over—even those aspects that entail suffering and that seem impossible to embrace—as a measure of the strength, affirmation, and positive valuation we place on our actual (nonrecurring) life. To test one's strength and affirmativeness in this metaphorical way, one must be willing to "play the game"—one must be willing playfully to imagine the recurrence of one's life as continuous with and therefore as adding suffering and joy to one's present life situation (cf. *Z* I.1). And to "win" at the game, one must learn to fashion or create a self who would be able to respond with joy to the demon's famous proclamation in the *Gay Science*: "This life as you now live it and have lived it, you will have to live once more and innumerable times more." As Nietzsche sees it, the demon's proclamation poses a challenge to our ability to imagine what a truly immanent ideal of living would be like. "Would you not throw yourself down and gnash your teeth and curse the demon who spoke thus? Or have you once experienced a tremendous moment when you would have answered him: 'You are a god and never have I heard anything more divine'" (*GS*, § 341). Nietzsche leaves little doubt that most of us would respond by gnashing our teeth. But what would be required of each of us if we are to respond with joy to the demon's proclamation? What would it take to "crave nothing more fervently" than eternal recurrence (*GS*, § 341)? What would be required "in order to be oneself the eternal joy of becoming, beyond all terror and pity" (*EH*, "Birth of Tragedy," § 3)?

Certainly, it would require us to "love the whole process" of living so much that we would be willing to relive eternally even those aspects of life that we do not, and perhaps cannot, love. Contrary to Nehamas's claim, this doesn't mean that we have to *prefer* the exact recurrence of history, with all its pains and sufferings, to an otherwise identical history without suffering, for this would be tantamount to "preferring suffering for suffering's sake," and hence a relapse into the idealized ascetic denigration of life (cf. Nehamas, 1985, pp. 148–169; Clark, 1990, pp. 277–286). Rather, Nietzsche's counter-ideal requires only that, when confronted with the demon's proclamation, we shall have styled the kind of self who can affirm it *and* who would experience joy at its prospect. So characterized, the ideal of affirming eternal recurrence is a strategy for articulating what it would mean to find intrinsic value in our temporal (nonrecurring) life and for accepting the prospect of finitude and death in a way that doesn't undermine the joyful affirmation of that life. In this sense, it is (potentially) "the greatest cultivating idea" as well as the "touchstone of our strength and affirmativeness" (*WP*, §§ 1053, 1056).

Hadot observes that "the authenticity of existence consists in the lucid anticipation of death, and it is up to each of us to choose between lucidity and diversion" (Hadot, 1995, p. 96). In this context, affirming eternal recurrence is very much a lucid "spiritual exercise" (*askēsis*), or "training for death," in the Socratic sense. And "training for death," as Socrates likes to say, is "the training for life" (see Hadot, 1995, p. 97; see also Hadot, 2002, pp. 122–125). To fashion oneself via the *askēsis* of affirming eternal recurrence entails keeping one's finitude "in front of one" at all times, in living one's life and in the choices one makes in life. Rather than interpreting one's present life and life choices "reactively" à la the ascetic ideal (e.g., as burdened by the legacy of a guilty or resentful past), the doctrine of eternal recurrence interprets them proactively and lucidly as "raw material" to be appropriated and used "in aspiring toward some individually determined vision of greatness" (Higgins, 1988, pp. 145–146). But again, what sort of choices and what "vision of greatness" does Nietzsche commend us to aspire toward?

Nietzsche insists that this question is impossible to answer in advance and will require different things of different people, depending upon context: "This is my way; but where is yours—thus I answered those who asked me 'the way.' For 'the way'—that does not exist" (*Z* III.11). Life is not a single monolithic thing, and our ethical characters and commitments will often vary (cf. Safranski, 2002, p. 202). Admittedly, the basic goal of self-fashioning is always the same: to "become who or what we are," to "evolve to be our [better] selves" (see *EH*, "Why I Am So Clever," § 9, "Birth of Tragedy," § 3; *GS*, § 270). But the ideal of fashioning ourselves according to the "rule" of eternal recurrence does not function dogmatically or categorically. As Nietzsche says, "to commend a goal is something quite different; the goal is then thought of as something which lies in our own discretion" (*D*, § 108). The counter-ideal he commends is more open-ended, more of a rule of thumb or a prudential imperative: "So live that you would desire to live again; this is your duty" (see Danto, 1980, pp. 212–213). So fashion yourself that you would be willing to be (or act) exactly the same way an infinite number of times. Heeding this, Nietzsche hopes that modern humans might stop feeling resentment and rancor against life. In place of a transcendent vision of another world, the "rule" of eternal recurrence "rules out" even the possibility of an "afterworld," and instead refers us back to what we are immanently in this world and to what we might become.

Likewise, the self one fashions by affirming the rule of eternal recurrence will always be significantly different from other selves—something new, unprecedented, and uniquely individual. Ethical self-fashioning, as Nietzsche envisions it, is essentially an individual project, and even exemplary selves (such as Goethe, or Nietzsche himself) are not to be imitated per se but rather appropriated in our own terms and used for our own creative and uniquely individual purposes. As Zarathustra likes to tell his disciples, if they have yet to find themselves, they have found him too soon (cf. *Z*, Prologue, and I.22) Similarly, one's attempt to follow Nietzsche's ideal of affirming eternal recurrence will always culminate in an encounter with one's own (discretionary) attempt to fashion an authentic life for oneself. And there is no spelling out in advance just what the transfigurative effects of this discretionary attempt will be. We cannot say ahead of time just what kind of self will be fashioned in the process. Nor can we say with certainty what "new table of values" (if any) will emerge from one's attempt to construct "a narrative unity of the self, constant with the 'rule' of eternal recurrence" (Owen,

1995, p. 112). We only know that, whatever the transformative effects may be, they should always be based in "gratitude and service" to life rather than resentment and revenge against it (see Clark, 1990, p. 284).

So understood, Nietzsche's ideal of affirming eternal recurrence is a means for inciting us to attain a new, life-affirming orientation toward ourselves and toward the world. It is a heuristic image, or metaphorical device, for seducing us to "live a life of truthful self-surveillance and self-overcoming" and for cajoling us to "practice that noble 'discipline of suffering' which permits [us] to say yes to as much of existence and the world as [we] can bear" (Ridley, 1998, pp. 153–154).

Works Cited

Agamben, Giorgio. 1999. *Remnants of Auschwitz: The Witness and the Archive.* New York: Zone Books.

Alderman, Harold. 1977. *Nietzsche's Gift.* Athens: Ohio University Press.

Allison, David B. 2001. *Reading the New Nietzsche.* Lanham, Boulder, New York, Oxford: Rowman and Littlefield, Inc.

Clark, Maudemarie. 1990. *Nietzsche on Truth and Philosophy.* Cambridge: Cambridge University Press.

Conway, Daniel. 1999. "Annunciation and Rebirth: The Prefaces of 1886." In *Nietzsche's Futures,* ed. John Lippitt. New York: St. Martin's Press.

Danto, Arthur. 1980. *Nietzsche as Philosopher.* New York: Columbia University Press.

Davidson, Arnold I. 1995. "Introduction: Pierre Hadot and the Spiritual Phenomenon of Ancient Philosophy." In Pierre Hadot, *Philosophy as a Way of Life.* Oxford: Blackwell.

Foucault, Michel. 1997. "The Ethics of the Concern of the Self as a Practice of Freedom." In *Michel Foucault: Ethics, Subjectivity, and Truth,* ed. Paul Rabinow. New York: The New Press.

———. 1990. *The Use of Pleasure,* trans. Robert Hurley. New York: Vintage Books.

———. 1984. "What Is Enlightenment?" In *The Foucault Reader,* ed. Paul Rabinow. New York: Pantheon Books.

Gardiner, Patrick. 1988. *Kierkegaard.* Oxford and New York: Oxford University Press.

Geuss, Raymond. 1999. *Morality, Culture, and History: Essays on German Philosophy.* Cambridge: Cambridge University Press.

Hadot, Pierre. 1995. *Philosophy as a Way of Life,* trans. Michael Chase. Oxford: Blackwell.

———. 2002. *What Is Ancient Philosophy?,* trans. Michael Chase. Cambridge, Mass.: The Belknap Press of Harvard University Press.

Hicks, Steven V. 2003. "Nietzsche, Heidegger, and Foucault: Nihilism and Beyond." In *Foucault and Heidegger: Critical Encounters,* ed. Alan Milchman and Alan Rosenberg. Minneapolis and London: University of Minnesota Press.

———, and Alan Rosenberg. 2003. "Nietzsche and Untimeliness: The 'Philosopher of the Future' as the Figure of Disruptive Wisdom." *The Journal of Nietzsche Studies* 25 (Spring): 1–34.

Higgins, Kathleen Marie. 1987. *Nietzsche's Zarathustra.* Philadelphia: Temple University Press.

———. 1988. "Reading Zarathustra." In *Reading Nietzsche,* ed. Robert Solomon and Kathleen Higgins. Oxford: Oxford University Press.

Kierkegaard, Søren. 1941. *Concluding Unscientific Postscript,* trans. D. F. Swenson and Walter Lowrie. Princeton: Princeton University Press.

———. 1968. *Fear and Trembling* and *Sickness Unto Death,* trans. Walter Lowrie. Princeton: Princeton University Press.

Konstan, David. 2004. "Parrhesia: Ancient Philosophy in Opposition." In *Mythos and Logos: How to Regain the Love of Wisdom,* ed. Albert A. Anderson, Steven V. Hicks, and Lech Witkowski. Amsterdam and New York: Rodopi.

Lampert, Laurence. 1986. *Nietzsche's Teaching.* New Haven and London: Yale University Press.

Magnus, Bernd. 1988. "The Deification of the Commonplace: *Twilight of the Idols.*" In *Reading Nietzsche,* ed. Robert Solomon and Kathleen Higgins. Oxford: Oxford University Press.

———. 1986. "Nietzsche and the Project of Bringing Philosophy to an End." In *Nietzsche as Affirmative Thinker,* ed. Yirmiyahu Yovel. Dordrecht: Martinus Nijhoff.

May, Simon. 1999. *Nietzsche's Ethics and His War on "Morality."* Oxford: Clarendon Press.

Miles, Margaret. 1981. *Fullness of Life: Historical Foundations for a New Asceticism.* Philadelphia: The Westminster Press.

Nehamas, Alexander. 1998. *The Art of Living.* Berkeley: University of California Press.

———. 1985. *Nietzsche: Life as Literature.* Cambridge, Mass.: Harvard University Press.

Owen, David. 1995. *Nietzsche, Politics, and Modernity.* London: Sage Publications.

———, and Aaron Ridley. 2000. "Dramatis Personae: Nietzsche, Culture, and Human Types." In *Why Nietzsche Still: Reflections on Drama, Culture, and Politics,* ed. Alan Schrift. Berkeley: University of California Press.

Rabinow, Paul. 1997. Introduction to *Michel Foucault: Ethics, Subjectivity, and Truth.* New York: The New Press.

Ridley, Aaron. 1998. *Nietzsche's Conscience: Six Character Studies from the "Genealogy."* Ithaca, NY: Cornell University Press.

Roberts, Tyler. 1998. *Contesting Spirit: Nietzsche, Affirmation, Religion.* Princeton: Princeton University Press.

Safranski, Rüdiger. 2002. *Nietzsche: A Philosophical Biography,* trans. Shelly Frisch. New York and London: W. W. Norton.

Schacht, Richard. 1983. *Nietzsche.* London and New York: Routledge.

Scott, Charles E. 1990. *The Question of Ethics: Nietzsche, Foucault, Heidegger.* Bloomington and Indianapolis: Indiana University Press.

Stauth, Georg, and Bryan S. Turner. 1988. *Nietzsche's Dance: Resentment, Reciprocity, and Resistance in Social Life.* Oxford: Basil Blackwell.

Taylor, Mark C. 2000. *Journeys to Selfhood.* New York: Fordham University Press.

Thiele, Leslie Paul. 1990. *Friedrich Nietzsche and the Politics of the Soul.* Princeton: Princeton University Press.

Notes

1. "In the human need to find meaning throughout the whole of material and spiritual existence, the ascetic ideal has given unity and purpose to the world: it has given *meaning* to the world and to the individual who suffers from that world" (Allison, 2001, p. 242).

2. Simply put, they all embody what Nietzsche terms the "will to truth"—the faith in truth as having an unconditional value, as being "that for the sake of which" everything else in life can be sacrificed. This "unconditional will to truth," Nietzsche says, is just the latest expression of "faith in the ascetic ideal itself, even if as an unconscious imperative" (*GM* III, §§ 23–24). Nietzsche insists that it is not the practice of science, or the capacity of human knowledge to inform us of the truth, that is at issue here. Indeed, for Nietzsche, the practice of science enjoys enormous advantages in explanatory power and predictive success over any of its alleged competitors (cf. his note "Long Live Physics!" in *GS*, § 335). Rather, it is the uncritical commitment to the unconditional value of truth—along with all of the self-denial involved with that commitment—that Nietzsche equates with the ascetic ideal (cf. Clark, 1990, pp. 184–187). Thus Nietzsche argues that scientific materialism, traditional atheism, and utopian socialism all involve themselves in various idealized forms of asceticism: denying oneself the comforting belief in God, taking a stand against natural desires and practical inclinations, etc., and they do this *not* in order to make life intrinsically worth living but just for the sake of truth. Hence, they "sacrifice God for nothing" (see *BGE*, § 55; see also *GM* III, § 3). Nietzsche fears that the old morality of resentment is simply acquiring a new set of underpinnings from the modern scientific ideal. Unconditional faith in science as a systematic, complete, and inestimably valuable view of things threatens to take over the old unconditional faith in God as the new "ground beyond criticism" for life-denying values. As Nietzsche sees it, this "scientific faith" in ultimate explanation is still just a "metaphysical faith" animated by the selfsame idealized ascetic attempt to devalue the real, immanent world (see Ridley, 1998, pp. 98–99).

3. There are, of course, no guarantees that we will be successful in bringing about such a change. Kant, for example, having criticized traditional metaphysical thinking, concluded that, after all, we are as likely to give up our "metaphysical researches" as we are to give up breathing. See his *Prolegomena to Any Future Metaphysics,* § 367.

4. For both Nietzsche and Kierkegaard, the main "ethical interest is in one's own reality," in becoming our "better selves" (see Kierkegaard, 1941, p. 228). "For though it [the self] is itself, it has to become itself . . . and in as much as it has to become itself, it is a possibility" (Kierkegaard, 1968, p. 168). All attempts by the "crowd" to objectify this ethical reality (or possibility) via socially established rules, norms, or imperatives are viewed by Kierkegaard and Nietzsche with deep suspicion.

5. "Nietzsche's point is this: just as the performance of a noble action is partially constitutive of a noble life, so too the living of a noble life is partially constitutive of a noble humanity: in seeking to live noble lives ourselves (self-overcoming), we help to bring about the goal of a noble humanity, that is, we contribute to the self-overcoming of humanity" (Owen, 1995, p. 119).

Part Four

Natural and Cultural Expressions of Marginal Forces
Nietzsche on War, Ecology, and Geophilosophy

Chapter Nine

Nietzsche and Ecology

A Critical Inquiry

Michael E. Zimmerman

More than two decades ago, I published an insufficiently critical essay that interpreted Martin Heidegger as a forerunner of deep ecology (Zimmerman, 1983). A decade later, in the light of disturbing revelations about the entwinement of Heidegger's thought with National Socialism, I had to retract important elements of my earlier claims (Zimmerman, 1993, 1994). When I was invited to discuss how yet another conservative German philosopher's work might be pertinent to ecology, I resolved not to repeat the problems found in my early interpretation of Heidegger. Because other writers, in particular Graham Parkes, have argued effectively that Nietzsche's thought is in some ways compatible with contemporary environmentalism, I do not feel obligated to repeat their insightful analyses (Hallman, 1991; Parkes, 1994, 1998; Stack, 1992). Anyone familiar with Nietzsche's work knows that he deeply appreciated the natural world and that he defined humankind (*der Mensch*) at least partly in terms of naturalistic categories. In what follows, however, I will argue that there are also considerable *difficulties* in the way of any uncritical reading of Nietzsche as a proto-ecologist (see Acampora, 1994).

Perhaps the greatest difficulty is that Nietzsche's major concern as a thinker differed from that of contemporary environmentalists, many of whom believe that human behavior is profoundly harming the biosphere. Despite the remarkable achievements of nineteenth-century European industry, few people at that time—including Nietzsche—believed that humans could destroy the conditions necessary for human life. In the 1880s, atomic weapons were not on the conceptual horizon, much less on the tips of ICBMs; human population was a fraction of what it is today; industrialism had not spread too far beyond Europe and parts of North America; rapid species extinction was only beginning; and vast areas of land were not only uncharted, but also regarded—however naively—as virtually "untouched" by human hands. In view of his critique of animal abuse, his interpretation of humankind as a natural organism, his frequent use of metaphors drawn from natural phenomena in order to describe humankind and its possibilities, and his passion for swimming and hiking, it is easy to see how one can regard Nietzsche as anticipating today's environmental attitudes. While condemning Christianity (and similarly otherworldly religious and metaphysical traditions) for despising the body and nature, he seems to have envisioned a this-worldly *transfiguration* of the human body that would correspond to his affirmation of nature. "Remain faithful to the earth," proclaimed Zarathustra, Nietzsche's prophet of a future and higher humankind.[1]

Despite all this and more, Nietzsche would have had serious reservations about certain aspects of contemporary environmentalism. He would have been deeply suspicious of romantics yearning to restore a supposedly Edenic human past. He would have criticized the seriousness, the spirit of gravity, and the ascetic attitude discernible in many contemporary environmentalists. He would have loathed the utilitarianism and social justice ideals that inspire much of today's Green movement. Perhaps most importantly, he would have criticized the kind of anti-anthropocentrism that guides much of today's environmentalism. Because "ecology" has contemporary political, cultural, and scientific meanings that did not obtain in the 1880s, the politics of nature today differ considerably—although by no means completely—from German politics of nature more than a century ago. The "nature" about whose fate Nietzsche and many other leading intellectuals, scientists, and ideologues were most concerned was not *biospheric* nature but, rather, *human* nature.

These days, environmentalists are informed by the science of ecology, which studies the relationship between organisms (including human beings) and their organic and physical environment. Informed by scientific ecology, mainstream environmentalists maintain: 1) that human well-being and survival depend on maintaining vital ecological relationships among the interconnected constituents of the biosphere; 2) that the enormous expansion of both industrialization and human population is undermining vital ecological relations, harming human (and nonhuman) health, and extinguishing species at a rapid rate by destroying relatively "wild" habitat; 3) that humans must make changes in their behavior, attitudes, and institutions in order to limit threats to human well-being and the well-being of other life forms; and 4) that the attitude most in need of change is *anthropocentrism*. This attitude, deeply rooted in major Western religious and philosophical traditions, provides ideological justification for the concept of progress that legitimates the use of industrial technology to dominate nature. Given the importance of anti-anthropocentrism in Anglo-American environmentalism, in what follows I will focus on how Nietzsche might have evaluated such anti-anthropocentrism. As we will see, Nietzsche's major concern was how to avoid degeneration and *nihilism*, not how to avoid environmental destruction and *ecocide*.

I begin by discussing Nietzsche's complex approach to the notion, inspired by Darwin's revolution, that man should conceive of himself merely as a clever animal rather than as a soul-endowed being specially formed by the biblical Creator. Nietzsche makes clear, however, that man is not just one among other animals but instead the "over-animal" (*HAH* I, §40). His effort to "reanimalize" man, however, is closely bound up with problematic concepts of race, breeding, and degeneration that were widely shared at the time. Next, I examine his claim that anthropocentrism has been destroyed by astronomers who have demonstrated the insignificance of the human animal. In fact, however, Nietzsche contends that science does man little service if it fails to provide him with a justification for his existence. Man *needs* to believe in his own special status. The death of God is an earth-shattering event precisely because it threatens man with cosmic meaninglessness, which Nietzsche feared would throw European man—already degenerate, because out of touch with his animal instincts—into suicidal despair. After explaining in more detail why, for Nietzsche, man is the exceptional animal that invents a world suitable for enhancing human power, I show the extent to which he embraced a certain conception of "progress" that validates human domination of the planet. Such domination is undertaken not merely to preserve the human species but primarily to enhance the human *Typus* by generating a few exceptional individuals who can "justify" human existence. Finally, I argue that Ernst Jünger and Martin Heidegger offer a plausible, though controversial, reading of Nietzsche's Overman as heralding the culmination of 2,500 years of metaphysics, which takes the form of technological domination of the planet. Nietzsche's *naturalistic* anthropocentrism can be interpreted in a way that is decidedly at odds with current environmental thinking. What follows is *one* way, not *the* way, to understand Nietzsche's pertinence for ecology. I hope that my approach helps to inspire constructive debate.

I. Nietzsche's Qualified Reanimalization of Man

In naturalizing humanity, Nietzsche focused on *human* nature, which he defined not only in terms of organic heritage and constitution but also in terms of character, race, psychology, moral capacity, and evolutionary possibility. For Nietzsche, "reanimalization" of man and "return to nature" involved *not* the recovery of simpler times but instead an *ascent to something higher, freer, more terrible* (*TI*, "Skirmishes," 48). Such ascent requires recontacting long-suppressed instinctual energies but *without regressing* to the social formations, cultural levels, and psychological traits consistent with unmediated expression of such energies. Channeling instinctual energy into the modern consciousness enormously deepened by centuries of the ascetic ideal might make possible the step *beyond* herd man toward the higher man, even the Overman. Although Nietzsche often criticized arrogant anthropocentrism, then, his major concern was about the health and destiny of *humankind*. Here, he revealed his continuing attachment to the Western notion that humans bring forth historical, conceptual, artistic, and moral domains that cannot be understood solely in terms of naturalistic categories. Indeed, in "Schopenhauer as Educator," he remarks: "And if all of nature presses toward the human being, then in doing so it makes evident that he is necessary for its salvation from animal existence and that in him, finally, existence holds before itself a mirror in which life no longer appears senseless but appears, rather, in its metaphysical meaningfulness" (*UM* III, § 5). So as to underscore our entwinement with animal being, however, Nietzsche closes with a question: "Where does the animal cease, where does the human being begin?"

As noted earlier, many environmentalists criticize anthropocentrism, a belief-system originally fostered by Biblical religions but later put on life-support by agnostic and atheistic Enlightenment moderns. Anthropocentrists believed that humankind stands atop the terrestrial (and perhaps even cosmic) pecking order. Hence, humans are morally justified in treating nonhuman nature however they choose, including as an instrument for human ends. Religious believers once used the term *soul* to name the special trait that elevates humans over other animals, but moderns speak of "mind" or "rationality" or "linguistic capacity." Nietzsche states in *The Antichrist*:

> We no longer derive man from "the spirit" or "the deity"; we have placed him back among the animals. . . . Man is by no means the crown [nor the purpose] of creation: every living being stands beside him on the same level of perfection. And even this is saying too much: relatively speaking, man is the most bungled of all the animals, the sickliest, and not one has strayed more dangerously from its instincts. (*AC*, § 14)

This passage would be music to the ears of some environmentalists. A false note, however, is sounded in the sentence that immediately follows: "But for all that, he is, of course, the most *interesting* [animal]." In his "modest" attempt to naturalize humankind, and in his critique of shame about the human body and its instinctual demands, Nietzsche did *not* make the mistake of overlooking how dramatically *different* man is from other animals! Man is the "over-animal" because he has developed an exceptional moral and evaluative capacity. Real "progress," we are told, would occur if man left behind the instinct for violence and lust for punishment—"gifts" bestowed on humans by *other* animals—and developed instead a greater capacity for justice (*WS*, § 183; *HAH* I, §§ 43, 44, 452).

Yet, did not Nietzsche proclaim that progressive (socialist, democratic, modern) man is degenerate and effeminate precisely *because* he weakens the vital instincts—including hostility—required for healthy existence, and promotes instead the ignoble goal of pain-free happiness (*TI*, "Skirmishes," 37)? Yes, he did, much to the delight of far right-wing ideologues who promoted racist social Darwinist attitudes.[2] Concerns about degeneration, however, were by no means limited to right-wing thinkers. Likewise, racist explanations for such degeneration (miscegenation) were widespread among European intellectuals, *including* some who would have regarded themselves as progressive. At the time, major questions were: Is there a common human nature, or instead are there different races that on the one hand have some something in common but on the other hand can and should be rank ordered in terms of their capacities and weaknesses? If there is no God in whose eyes all humans are equal, should we turn to the social hierarchy at work in the animal world for clues about organizing human society? Is the European (white, Aryan) race of human animals degenerating and thus becoming uncompetitive with other races?

Interrelating with one another in complex ways, social Darwinism, naturalism, racial concepts, and concerns about degeneration shaped the politics of nature in late-nineteenth-century Europe. Consider this: the man who in 1866 coined the term *ecology*, Ernst Haeckel, was an influential German scientist and nature-mystic, as well as a racist and social-Darwinist (see Gasman, 1971; Staudenmeier, 1995). Soon the idea would emerge that land was healthy if tended by purebloodied people who have been affiliated with it for centuries. The Nazi version of this idea is summarized in the slogan, *Blut und Boden*. Efforts to combat racial degeneration, concern about which reached near-hysterical levels in some groups, were not confined to Europeans. Americans played a crucial role in developing the science of eugenics to combat degeneration. Nazi ideologues made extensive use of this research in setting up their own infamous programs (Kevles, 1985; Kuhl, 1994). Many notables, including Nietzsche, Theodore Roosevelt, and Lord Baden-Powell (founder of the Boy Scouts) expressed grave concern about the disappearance of "manly men." To be sure, some social critics blamed urbanization, industrialization, and material deprivation—not miscegenation—for sapping the virility of Western men. Miscegenation, however, was uppermost in the minds of many of those seeking an explanation for the decline of European vitality and virility. By comparison, so it was widely believed, growing populations of purebloodied *non*-whites retained their vigor and thus would eventually out-compete European humankind, even if nonwhites were originally "inferior" to Europeans. Racist theorists claimed that European blood was particularly debilitated when mixed with that of the allegedly semihuman Africans, the Asiatic hordes (including the Slavs, who were allegedly always threatening to overwhelm the continent), and of course the Jews.

Arguably, Nietzsche's most important concern was how to halt degeneration of European (and German) man. To his credit, he often publicly castigated anti-Semites who warned against allowing German blood to be contaminated by that of Jews. Indeed, he often maintained that hybrid races—products of miscegenation—were more vigorous. Hence, an appropriate admixture of (the right kind of) Jewish blood could help not only to restore the degenerating German *Volk* but also to promote the "good European" who synthesizes the strengths of various European peoples. Nietzsche's frequent expressions of admiration for Jews, however, were sometimes linked to the observation that their remarkable cultural longevity could be traced in part to their racial purity (*BGE*, § 251), in contrast with mongrelized (and thus *sometimes* degenerate) peoples (*BGE*, § 200). Although having arisen from several different races, as did the ancient Greeks, the Jews kept their bloodlines relatively unmixed for many centuries. That there was a *physiological* dimension to Nietzsche's conception of race cannot be wished away by those who prefer to emphasize its cultural component (see, for example, Scott, 2003). Nazi ideologues often not only distorted his views, of course, but also omitted his admirable tirades against anti-Semitism. Nevertheless, his free use of race-based categories, his references to physiological degeneration, and his frequent talk of breeding a nobler race, strike discordant notes among most contemporary readers who know that National Socialists used similar categories to justify exterminating "degenerate" elements of the population—elements that were described as subhuman, as vermin. When blended with racism and social Darwinism, naturalism can become an extremely potent and dangerous political ideology.

Until recently, liberal white American environmentalists might have asked: what does any of this have to do with *our* concern to prevent wild habitat loss in order to slow the extinction spasm now taking place? Indeed, they would have summarily dismissed suggestions that racialism or even racism was influencing their attitudes and practices. About fifteen years ago, however, African-Americans, Hispanics, and other minorities began to assert that their communities—many of which were poor and located in urban areas—were negatively affected by what is now called "environmental racism." Environmental justice advocates charged that mainstream environmental organizations: a) were composed almost entirely of white people, b) tended to ignore urban pollution, land use issues, and installation of toxic waste dumps in areas that disproportionately affected poor and nonwhite groups, c) focused primarily on preserving "wilderness," and d) sometimes adopted anti-immigrationist views consistent with racist or ethnocentric organizations on the grounds that nonwhite immigrants could not be trusted to "preserve" the land.

Until recently, anti-anthropocentrism led many environmentalists to assume that humans were a pestilence upon nature; hence, only "virgin," or "untouched," land was pure and worthy of being called wilderness. Precontact America was regarded as such a wilderness, to which "original" condition the land ought to be restored, if possible. Some anthropologists, however, have not hesitated to charge that *racism* underlies such attitudes, which depict Native Americans—who in fact *substantially* altered North America for millennia—in what can be regarded as at best a demeaning manner. Forty years ago, O. C. Stewart wrote:

The fact that even the more historically minded American ecologists have started their evaluation of the influence of man upon nature with the landing of the Pilgrims follows from the view that American Indians were part of nature like other animals. Aborigines could be ignored more easily than buffalo as forces of nature[!]. . . Not only scientists but all whites of European ancestry have always found it difficult to take the Indians seriously enough to learn from them. The relationship between Indians and whites started with the assumption that the Indians were only part of the natural environment. This logically led to the point of view that the American natives had nothing to teach sophisticated Europeans. (Stewart, 1963, pp. 119, 121; cited in Kay, 2002, pp. 245–246)

Nietzsche would not have had a problem with rank-ordering races, but he would have dismissed the yearning for "pristine" or "original" nature. Living in a European landscape tilled and managed by humans for thousands of years, he had little interest in "wilderness," partly because he assumed that there was no land untouched by human hands.

Racist and anti-immigrationist comments made years ago by some American members of Earth First!, as well as the resurgence in Europe of far-right wing groups concerned about the relationship between blood purity and environmental well-being, confirm the conviction of many moderns that concern about the well-being of "nature" is sometimes bound up with reactionary social attitudes, including "ecofascism" (Biehl, 1995; Geden, 1996; Olsen, 1999; Staudenmeier, 1995; Zimmerman, 1995). Recently, Mark Sagoff has demonstrated that in speaking of invasive species, many scientists and environmentalists use the same vitriolic, fear-mongering, Other-hating language used by early-twentieth-century Americans who warned that the degenerate, semihuman masses (mostly Eastern European Jews and Southern European Catholics) were threatening to displace an America composed of white American Protestants (Sagoff, 1999).[3]

If Nietzsche were magically transported to the year 2008 and asked to explain the psychological and/or sociocultural roots of environmental problems such as global warming, acid rain, and species extinction, he would be unable to do so without a crash course in contemporary natural and social science, as well as in twentieth-century history. As his knowledge increased, Nietzsche would discover that the genetic revolution in Darwinism, as well as comparative and empirical anthropological research, undermined central aspects of the doctrines of race and breeding that were common in his era. Moreover, given the astonishingly evil purposes to which National Socialism put such racial doctrines, he might even renounce some dimensions of his aristocratic antimodernism. If Nietzsche could confront with real comprehension today's ecological problems in light of the events of the past century, I suggest, he would not write what he wrote more than a century ago.

A little earlier, we spoke of Nietzsche's attack on the ascetic ideal, its attendant slave morality, and the degenerate scientific modernity that shares such morality, even after having slain the Biblical God. Despite all this, however, Nietzsche made clear that ascetic man was far more *interesting*, morally *profound*, and ultimately more *promising* than the blond beasts, to whom we are nevertheless indebted for having used their violence to establish societies that were gradually taken over by violence-condemning and antiaristocratic ascetic priests and philosophers. Agreeing in some respects with those who complain that man is enslaved and debilitated by modern society, Nietzsche excoriated Rousseau for ascribing moral goodness to primitive humans (*BT*, § 2, 19; *UM* III, § 4; *HAH* I, §§ 216, 463; *D*, Preface, § 3; *TI*, 552), whereas in fact early human life was characterized by horrendous violence, unmediated resurrection of which Nietzsche did *not* recommend.

Instead of *reverting* to the murderous assaults justified by the blonde beasts' master morality, which was far too close to the "morality" governing other animals "red in tooth and claw," Nietzsche sought to *transcend* man as he is: herd man, maggot man, ascetic man, insipid socialist man, peace-loving man, and even—dare I say it? —*environmentalist* man. Insofar as Nietzsche's historical scheme exemplifies a three-phase movement—premodern, modern, and postmodern—his scheme shares the same Gnostic eschatology animating the work of Hegel, Feuerbach, and Marx (Voeglin, 2000). According to Nietzsche, the "danger of dangers" is that man will allow the ascetic morality at work in socialism and democracy to prevent attainment of "the *highest power and splendor* actually possible to the type 'man'" (*GM*, Preface, § 6). Anticipating and helping to make possible the attainment of this kind of human being are *central* themes in Nietzsche's thought. By bringing master and slave morality into constructive confrontation with one another (*GM*, I, § 16), by channeling instinctual energy—rather than either immediately giving in to it or else suppressing it—into the process of human self-overcoming, people willing to experiment may help to give rise to higher man, "the Roman Caesar with the soul of Christ" (*WP*, § 983).

Lest we get carried away here, however, let us recall that Nietzsche affirmed that higher men would be both willing to make use of others and even do violence against them, all of which would be justified insofar as it furthers the goal of saving humankind from the despair and nihilism that he saw stemming from the death of God. While a new goal is needed to replace that provided by the otherworldly God and the ascetic ideal, Nietzsche often indicated that this goal—which would require total mobilization of human activity—would be to generate a few extraordinary human beings, whose noble traits and astonishing capacities would be so aesthetically pleasing that they would justify the suffering, struggle, and effort required for ordinary mortals to exist. In a moment, we will return to what is required of humankind—and the earth—to fulfill this new goal. First, however, let us consider how Nietzsche's concern about the need to *justify* human life tempers his critique of anthropocentrism.

II. How Modern Science (Unwisely) Deflates Anthropocentrism

Nietzsche observes that astronomers have punctured our arrogance by showing that we are merely animals living on the side of a dirt ball in the middle of nowhere. Just as an ant may think it is the goal of the forest, so we think we're the goal of the universe! (*WS*, § 14). Indeed, it is an arrogant, monstrous, and insipid pose to regard man as the *measure* of all things (*GS*, § 346). Elsewhere, however, Nietzsche asserts that humans can no more avoid evaluating, measuring, judging, than they can avoid exploiting, dominating, and oppressing. Man may not be the measure of all things, but what man does *is* to measure, to give value to himself, others, and the world. For humans, there are no immediate perceptions or absolute truths but only perspectives, that is, vantage points that let us evaluate things in ways that enhance our *power* as individuals or as members of cultures. According to Nietzsche's naturalistic epistemology, such cognitive and evaluative activity serves above all the goal of survival of the species. In the opening lines of *The Gay Science*, we read:

> Whenever I contemplate men with benevolence or with an evil eye, I always find them concerned with a single task, all of them and every one of them in particular: to do what is good for the preservation of the human race. Not from any feeling of love for the race, but merely because nothing in them is older, stronger, more inexorable and unconquerable than this instinct—because this instinct constitutes *the essence* of our species. (*GS*, § 1)

Yet, highlighting the importance of instinctual self-preservation seems to contradict Nietzsche's view that life seeks not mere preservation or survival but instead ever greater *power*. This may explain why, at the end of the above-cited passage, Nietzsche adds "our herd" immediately after "our species." Man as he is up to now, *herd* man, makes survival his priority, but the anticipated *higher* man will seek the highest concentration of spiritual power, which will require that he see most deeply and resolutely into the abyss of nihilism and despair opened up by the death of God (*BGE*, § 56). Confronting such truth, however, is clearly not for everyone; the vast majority of people, including intellectuals, can endure only so much of it (*BGE*, §§ 39, 43). People need art, poetry, myth, religion, deceptive strategies, illusions, and noble lies of all sorts to avoid the black despair that follows from realizing that ultimately their lives are meaningless (*HAH* I, § 33; *GS*, § 357). Our organism is not prepared for the unvarnished truth that we are accidental byproducts of an accidental universe but instead depends on the lies of common-sense metaphysics (*GS*, § 110). Science itself cannot provide values, goals, or purposes after having taken them all away (*GS,* §§ 7, 373).

In the *Genealogy*, Nietzsche famously argues that in its quest for truth at any cost, science shows itself as the secret ally of the ascetic ideal that Enlightenment science supposedly renounced. Nietzsche asks: "Does anyone really believe that the defeat of theological astronomy represented a defeat for that [ascetic] ideal?" (*GM* III, § 25). On the contrary, we read, science promotes man's *self-belittlement* by destroying faith in his own "dignity and uniqueness," "his irreplaceability in the great chain of being . . ." Natural science has turned man into "an *animal*, literally and without reservation or qualification . . ." (*GM* III, § 25). Nietzsche continues: "Since Copernicus, man seems to have got himself on an inclined plane—now he is slipping faster and faster away from the center into—what? into nothingness? . . . Very well! Hasn't this been the straightest route to—the *old* [ascetic] ideal?" (*GM* III, § 25). Nietzsche presses his critique: "*All* science . . . has at present the object of dissuading man from his former respect for himself, *as if this had been nothing but a piece of bizarre conceit*" (*GM* III, § 25; my emphasis). Nietzsche, however, believed that human dignity and self-respect are *not* mere conceits but instead conditions necessary for the vast majority of human animals to exist without falling into suicidal despair. Very few, the lonely ones, are capable of saying "yes" to life when they sail out upon the horizonless sea, the infinite universe disenchanted by the death of God.

Here, I am reminded of Stanley Rosen's claim that there is an exoteric and an esoteric side to Nietzsche (Rosen, 1989). The exoteric Nietzsche writes not to the masses but to free thinkers grappling with the fall of God and the rise of scientific naturalism. Free thinkers may find life-affirming satisfaction in the proposal that humankind is capable of producing great living artworks, in the form of extraordinary exemplars of our species. The esoteric Nietzsche, however, writes perhaps only for himself. Consider the subtitle of *Thus Spoke Zarathustra*: "A Book for All and None." Nietzsche recognizes that even his own goal of generating great human beings is but another noble lie, one that may also sustain our species in centuries ahead. One who sees deeply and resolutely enough, however, realizes that *all* phenomena are ultimately expressions of the completely impersonal will. Humans, even the greatest, are merely epiphenomena of monstrous strivings that care and know nothing about us meager mortals. This reading downplays Nietzsche's contentions that the Will to Power is *multiple* and that humans can transform (via culture) the mineral, vegetal, animal drives at work in us (see Parkes' excellent book *Composing the Soul*, 1994). As if attempting to establish meaning for human existence in an almost completely impersonal world bereft of a Creator were not a sufficiently daunting task, Nietzsche raises the stakes by positing the horrifying claim that everything recurs *eternally*. Even the bravest, hardest, and most resolute individuals have difficulty in affirming life in the face of this claim. So far as we know, only one person managed to do so: Zarathustra, Nietzsche's fictional hero. In contrast to Nietzsche, even free thinkers and intellectuals must posit intermediate goals—great human accomplishments in the sciences and arts, personal career achievements, family well-being, leisure time activities—that provide the necessary balm that draws the veil of *lethe* over human meaninglessness. Attempting to restore human self-respect shredded by the Enlightenment's dialectical chainsaw

(Horkheimer and Adorno, 2002 [1944]), the *exoteric* Nietzsche describes man as the most interesting, courageous, and promising animal.

Many environmentalists would point out that this position resembles all too closely the anthropocentric idea of human exceptionalism. If Nietzsche is right, humans are not *merely* animals after all! In contrast, some radical ecologists describe humans as the lowest possible animals, such as vermin, or even as a cancer that should be eliminated. Nietzsche himself spoke contemptuously of "maggot" man, so such vocabulary would not bother him. What *would* bother him, however, is the claim—advanced even by such a well-known environmental ethicist as Paul Taylor—that the earth would be unaffected by human annihilation except insofar as this would enable earth to heal itself after millennia of human abuse (Taylor, 2001). Nietzsche would regard such an assertion as passive nihilism, the new Buddhism yearning for nothingness, oblivion, and self-extinction. Daniel Conway remarks that for Nietzsche, "The will to nothingness represents the final will of a declining people or epoch, as decadent human beings embrace self annihilation as the sole remaining goal capable of stimulating their enfeebled wills."[4] Is not the yearning for self-annihilation also visible in those Earth Firsters who called for eliminating layers of civilization and for a return to hunter-gatherer times when men were more innocent, neither desirous nor capable of threatening the biosphere? How might Nietzsche have evaluated a book popular among some environmentalists, *Ishmael*, named after a *talking ape* who depicts the past ten thousand years of human history as a regrettable mistake insofar as agriculture moved us away from living according to nature's cycles? (Quinn, 1992).

Drawing on Nietzsche, we could say that environmentalists who do not adequately *qualify* the claim that the human being is an animal are not only blind to its extraordinary capacities, but also help to justify human domination of nature. After all, if humans are merely animals, and if animal life is defined by the struggle for survival, then humans can be *expected* to expand their populations at the expense of other species. Slipping a moral claim into this naturalistic position, one could say that humans have every *right* to dominate nonhuman beings. Environmentalists reply that conceiving of humans as animals knocks us off our lofty pedestal and forces us to take into account the interests of our kin, whether plant or animal. It is not self-evident, however, that naturalism leads people to feel compassion for or take into account the interests of their animal (and plant) kin. True enough; the mid-nineteenth-century humane movement began in England, perhaps inspired partly by Darwin's revolutionary claims. Yet, those same claims were also put to use not only by social Darwinists to justify racist positions but also by industrialists who use the social Darwinist idea of "struggle for survival" to dismiss "sentimental" concerns about destruction of the land by railroads, airports, highways, factories, farms, suburbs, and cities.

Naturalism is closely tied to natural science, which analyzes phenomena under the assumption that they are strictly mechanical objects lacking interiority, that is, feeling, striving, or consciousness. Nietzsche agreed with naturalism that otherworldly religious categories are *not* explanatory, but he also showed contempt for *mechanistic* naturalism (*BGE*, §§ 21, 36; *GS*, § 373), because it ignores purposiveness and will, central instances of the *interiority* that Nietzsche ascribed to everything in a way that seems consistent with a variety of pan-psychism. Retaining a place for consciousness, soul, and spirit in *his* naturalism, Nietzsche ascribed to plants and animals an interiority that is overlooked *in principle* by the sciences that focus solely on mechanical behavior. In effect, he assumed that the basic "stuff" of reality was not matter but energy, which is always associated with a *perspective*, the "new infinity" (*GS*, § 374). For something to be means for it to be energy whose drive for power is guided by a perspective. As our previous discussions have indicated, however, the fact that Nietzsche acknowledges that all phenomena have interiority does not mean that he would agree with biocentric egalitarianism. A truly "high spirituality" knows that its mission is "to maintain the *order of rank* in the world, among things themselves—and not only among men" (*BGE*, § 219). Just as he had no compunction about enslaving, exploiting, and harming *human* beings so long as such behavior can be *justified*, so he assures us, Nietzsche also recognized that humans could justify dominating life on earth in pursuit of a crucial human end.

III. Man as the Evaluating Animal Par Excellence

Nietzsche personally was *not* pleased by the prospect of human domination of the planet. For him, dominating oneself (and at times even other humans) for the sake of self-overcoming was one thing; brutal dominion over animals, for example, was another. (On mistreatment of animals, see for example *HAH* I, §§ 36, 53.) Nevertheless, if my argument is correct, he saw no way around some form of human dominion over life on earth, especially in the coming centuries. Hence, he criticized as disingenuous *sentimental* attitudes toward nature because they ignore that people have *always* exploited the natural world (*D*, § 286; *BGE*, § 259). Nietzsche knew that humans could *not* have become intelligent, moral animals without relying on the work, food, and products provided by our animal cousins. Injury, appropriation, overpowering of what is alien and weaker, all these are *essential* to life, not its corruptions or imperfections. People should be *honest* about this, he tells us (*BGE*, § 259). Some poets claim to sense something "greater" lurking behind natural phenomena, but Nietzsche asserts that such sense is merely a residue of early human fear that something really was lurking behind trees and rocks: saber-toothed tigers, wolves, and other predators! (*D*, § 142). For Nietzsche, nature is relentless, pitiless, and indifferent to the concerns of any species; indeed, nature is another word for the infinite and constantly shifting perspectives of the Will to Power. Nature is no model for art, Nietzsche insists, because it has too many gaps, distortions, and infelicities. To see what "is" is *inartistic*! The artist and the poet, rather, improve and expand upon what is given (*TI*, "What Germans Lack," 7). Even sober scientists remain "artists in love," "burdened with those estimates of things that have their origin in the passion and loves of former centuries." Consider that mountain or that cloud: "What is 'real' in that? Subtract from it the phantasm and very human *contribution*, my sober friends! If you *can*!" (*GS*, § 57).

We project upon nature not only beauty and rationality, but also moral value. But, Nietzsche warns against projecting moral significance onto the back of amoral nature! (*D*, § 3). Surely he would criticize many of today's Greens, who not only promote utilitarian ideals (such as sustainability of exploitation), which he scorned, but who also adhere to Malthusian and ascetic notions about nature's scarcity, insufficiency, and limits. In contrast to such ascetic ideals, Nietzsche held that nature is given to lavishness, squandering, overabundance, violence, and exploitation, all in the service not merely of survival but of generating lucky hits—new types, new species—that keep the evolutionary game moving forward. He would also conclude, I believe, that environmentalists are in many cases ascetics who fail to posit an adequate *goal* for future humanity. He would ask: *So what* if we manage to preserve the biosphere so life can go on. Why *should* it "go on"? Of course, only the human animal can ask such a question, but Nietzsche is persuaded that the current answers to which we cling are crumbling.

For Nietzsche, man is a poet who has invented the "whole eternally growing world of valuations, colors, accents, perspectives, scales, affirmations, and negations" (*GS*, § 301). Hence, "Whatever has *value* in our world now does not have value in itself, according to its nature—nature is always value-less, but has been *given* value at some time, as a present—and it is *we* who gave and bestowed it" (*GS*, § 301). Later on, however, he scoffs at inventing values that supposedly exceed the value of the actual world and at putting existence on the scales and "find[ing] it wanting" (*GS*, § 346). Moreover, sounding like Emerson, he suggests at times that as humankind's spiritual insight grows, so does the space around him, such that "his world becomes more profound" (*BGE*, § 57), revealing glory hidden from the masses. The experience of such a tiny minority of people, however, can scarcely be expected to shape the behavior of the vast numbers of humankind who strive to control their environment.

The tension present in Nietzsche's assessment of the human treatment of nature is visible in the following passage from the *Genealogy*: "*Hubris* is our whole position regarding nature, our assaulting nature with the help of machines and heedless technological and engineering inventiveness . . ." (*GM* III, § 9). Although apparently agreeing with environmentalism's critique of the domination of nature, this passage occurs in a specific context, namely, discussion of the fact that what once was evil is now regarded as *good*. Introducing the above-quoted passage, Nietzsche writes: "[M]easured even by the standards of the ancient Greeks, our entire modern being [*Sein*], *insofar as it is not weakness but power and consciousness of power* [my emphasis], has the appearance of sheer *hubris* and godlessness. . . ." A little later, he remarks that from the ancient Greek perspective our attitude toward God and even to ourselves is *hubris*,

> for we experiment with ourselves in ways that we would never permit our-
> selves to experiment with animals and . . . we cheerfully vivisect our souls.
> . . . We assault ourselves nowadays, no doubt of it, we nutcrackers of the
> soul, ever questioning and questionable, as if life were nothing but crack-
> ing nuts; and thus we are bound to grow day-by-day more questionable,
> *worthier* of questioning; perhaps also worthier—of living? (*GM* III, § 9)

Despite the implicit critique of animal experimentation voiced here, Nietzsche makes clear that moderns regard the industrial mobilization of nature not as vio-lation but instead as the most efficient way to enhance not just human survival but human power and consciousness of power. What once seemed hubristic and thus evil now seems to be appropriate and good. To be sure, Nietzsche invidiously contrasted what he regarded as the rather crude and domineering modern mode of power-seeking with the spiritualized power acquired by great individuals in the process of overcoming themselves. Nevertheless, the modern will to power has legitimacy not only because it is an enactment of *will* but also because it may contribute to what Nietzsche regards as higher, more spiritual forms of power in the higher men arising from the turmoil of modernity.

IV. Nietzsche's Embrace of Progress, Rightly Defined

Having formerly attempted to revitalize in Germany the spirit of tragedy, Nietz-sche later concluded that European humankind has no historical alternative to going forward with the project of industrial modernity. "We are faltering, but we must not let it make us afraid and perhaps surrender the new things we have gained. Moreover, we *cannot* return to the old, we *have* burned our boats; all that remains is for us to be brave, let happen what may.—Let us only *go forward*, let us only make a move! Perhaps what we do will present the aspect of progress. . . ." Here, "progress" is defined as a positive development in human evolution (*HAH* I, § 248). In *Twilight of the Idols*, Nietzsche contrasts such authentic progress with the usual *modern* conception of "progress"—utilitarianism, rationalism, social justice, democracy, capitalism, socialism—as a degeneration of the instincts, as a weakening that should be hastened to allow for the emergence of a new, more life-affirming phase of human existence (*TI*, "Skirmishes," 43). In the *Genealogy* he returns to what he regards as genuine *progressus*, the convoluted evolution-ary process

> which always appears in the shape of a will and a way to *greater* power
> and is always carried through at the expense of numerous smaller pow-
> ers. The magnitude of an "advance" can even be measured by the mass of
> things that had to be sacrificed to it; humankind in the mass sacrificed

to the prosperity of a single *stronger* species of humanity—that *would* be an advance. (*GM* II, § 12)

A little earlier we read that all organic events involve a "subduing, a *becoming master*, and that all subduing and becoming master involves a fresh interpretation, an adaptation through which any previous 'meaning' and 'purpose' are necessarily obscured or even obliterated" (*GM* II, § 12). I interpret this passage as saying that the higher men must find a way to interpret industrial modernity *not* as ordinary progressives do, namely, as technological domination of nature for the sake of material prosperity and democratic rights for the laboring class, but instead as the condition necessary for the emergence of a new life-affirming goal for humankind: production of a few great human beings who are ends in themselves but who also provide the masses beings in whom they can take pride and venerate. Paradoxically, then, even though democracy is in one respect a sign of human decay and diminution (*BGE*, § 203), in another respect it promotes emergence of a higher type. "*The very same conditions* that will on the average lead to the levelling and mediocratizing of man—to a useful, industrious, handy, multi-purpose herd animal—are likely *in the highest degree* to give birth to exceptional human beings of the most dangerous and attractive quality" (*BGE*, § 242; emphasis added).[5] European democratization "is an involuntary arrangement for the cultivation of *tyrants*—taking that word in every sense, including the most spiritual" (*BGE*, §§ 242, 258; see also *WS*, § 275).

In fall, 1887, Nietzsche writes that according to an "economic justification" of virtue, "The task is [to] make humankind as useful as possible" by outfitting it with "machine-virtues" that make humans like unfailing machines (*SW* 12:10 [11]). "If we just have that unavoidably imminent total economic management of the earth, then humankind can find its best meaning as machinery in [economic] service: as a gigantic clockwork [*Räderwerk*], composed of ever-growing superfluity of all dominating and commanding elements; as a whole of tremendous force, whose individual factors represent *minimal forces,* minimal *values*" (*SW* 12:10 [17]; *WP*, § 866). Nietzsche regards this mechanistic dwarfing of humankind, however inevitable it may be, as a regressive (and dreadful?) phenomenon, one that requires considerable justification. Hence, he posits—but can by no means demonstrate—that there will arise a "countermovement" in the form of "the precipitation [*Ausscheidung*] of a luxury surplus of humankind: it aims to bring to light a stronger species, a higher type that arises and preserves itself under different conditions from those of the average human. My concept, my metaphor for this type is, as one knows, the word 'Overman'" (ibid.).

A few years earlier, Nietzsche had described modern democratic humanity not as cog in the monstrous economic machine but instead as a skillful actor. Nietzsche bemoaned the fact that "[T]he individual becomes convinced that he can do just about everything and *can manage almost any role*, and everybody experiments with himself, improvises, makes new experiments, enjoys his experiments, and all nature ceases and becomes art" (*GS*, § 356). Curiously, however, modern humanity's traits are very much like those that Nietzsche himself praises, especially the will to experiment on oneself. The apparent problem with such men, Nietzsche says, is that they crowd out the great "architects," those endowed with the strength to build, the courage to make plans, and the genius for organization. "For what is dying out is the fundamental faith that would enable us to calculate, to promise, to anticipate the future in plans of such scope, and to sacrifice the future to them—namely, the faith that the human being has value and meaning only insofar as it is *a stone in a great edifice*; and to that end the human being must be *solid* first of all, a 'stone'—and above all not an actor!" (*GS*, § 356). Is it possible, however, that democratic humanity's experimentalism and flexibility will allow it to engage in a mode of conformity unimaginable in previous societies? Will the invisible hand of democratic industrialism generate higher types "behind the backs" of the flexible actors? Will they unwittingly, or possibly even *willingly*, become solid stones? Will the industrial proletariat, the armies of the nation states, and multinational entrepreneurs make possible a scale of planetary domination hitherto undreamt of? Is *this* what is heralded by Nietzsche's Overman?

V. Heidegger's Reading of Nietzsche as the Thinker Heralding Technological Modernity

Readers will recognize that the last question animates Heidegger's controversial interpretation of Nietzsche. I believe, however, that my interpretation of Nietzsche can be justified by reference to Nietzsche's texts alone, independently of the debatable interpretative framework offered by Heidegger's critique of Western metaphysics. Around 1930, Heidegger was electrified by reading Ernst Jünger's book *Der Arbeiter*, which argued in effect that the total mobilization occurring in industrial modernity was generating a new human *Typus*, hard, dangerous, elemental, instinctual, far-seeing, cunning, organic construction, half-steel, half-flesh (Heidegger, 1998 [1955], 1972 [1954]; Zimmerman, 1990). This concentrated, flexible, courageous, and intelligent raw material rejoiced in aligning its energies with those of others of its type, the worker-soldiers bent on transforming the planet into a titanic factory that would make possible something truly extraordinary. *This* was how the Will to Power manifested itself in technological modernity, so at least Jünger and Heidegger concluded.[6] Heidegger reads Nietzsche's conception of being as Will to Power as the culmination of twenty-five hundred years of Western metaphysics. Critics have correctly pointed out that Heidegger glosses over texts that contradict his effort to force Nietzsche to lie in the Procrustean bed of the history of being. Nevertheless, given what I have been arguing, Heidegger's reading is more plausible than some critics contend.

To be sure, Nietzsche's embrace of industrial-democratic modernity was equivocal. For instance, even while speculating about the extent to which democracy might contribute to the goal of producing higher types, he preferred that great individuals take the lead in reshaping humankind and the earth. In this respect, he prefigured what Jeffrey Herf has called early-twentieth-century Germany's "reactionary modernism," according to which cutting-edge technology is used by an authoritarian society to achieve global dominion (Herf, 1984). Praising Napoleon for having made it possible in Europe for "the *man* [*der Mann*]" to become "master over the businessman [*Kaufmann*] and philistine," Nietzsche writes that the French warrior may have brought back the decisive slab of antique granite necessary to unite Europe in an *affirmative* sense, thereby making her "mistress of the Earth" (*GS*, § 362). In *Beyond Good and Evil*, we read: "The time for petty politics is over: the very next century will bring the fight for the dominion of the earth—the *compulsion* to large-scale politics" (*BGE*, § 208). This passage occurs at the end of a discussion of failure of European will, weakened by hybridization. Europe must unite so as "*to acquire one will* by means of a new caste that would rule Europe, a long, terrible will of its own that would be able to cast its goals millennia hence. . . ." Who would *constitute* this new caste? Nietzsche's higher men? The Overman? Jünger's worker-soldier?

A slightly more benign characterization of total human planetary domination is described years earlier in *The Wanderer and His Shadow*. There, Nietzsche argues that different people thrive (or are stunted) in different climates. Humanity must first discover empirically which regions of the earth have curative capacities and which give rise to degeneration and then transplant nations, families, and individuals "for as long and continuously as is needed for our inherited physical infirmities to be conquered. *In the end, the whole earth will be a collection of health resorts . . .*"(*WS*, § 188; my emphasis). In the very next section, Nietzsche writes:

> That which in senile short-sightedness you call the overpopulation of the earth [!] is precisely what proffers the more hopeful their greatest task: humankind shall one day become a tree that overshadows the whole earth bearing many milliards of blossoms that shall all become fruit for one another, and the earth itself shall be prepared for the nourishment of this tree. . . . The task is unspeakably great and bold: let us see to it that the tree does not *untimely* rot away! . . . What we must do . . . is to *look in the face* our great task of *preparing* the earth for the production of the greatest and most joyful fruitfulness—a task for reason on behalf of reason! (*WS*, § 189)

I detect no irony in these remarks, which are consistent with Nietzsche's overriding concern: promoting the self-overcoming of herd humanity for the sake of a higher type, in this case, a type characterized by mutual service, which is about as idealistic as Nietzsche ever becomes. In *Unfashionable Observations* (*UM*), Nietzsche remarked that humankind should make its own goal that at which plants and animals aim: production of powerful and superior *specimens*.

Humankind "must search out and produce those favorable conditions in which those great, redeeming human beings can come into being" (*UM* III, § 6). Here, Nietzsche assumes, contrary to many of his own remarks, that ordinary people, members of the herd, are capable of such discernment and willing to act on it. Nietzsche goes on to say that only in genuine, unselfish love does the soul "desire to look beyond itself and to search with all its might for a higher self that lies hidden somewhere" (*UM* III, § 6). To achieve the goal of generating great human specimens requires planetary alteration, which is consistent with the overriding *importance* that Nietzsche accords to the human animal:

> [T]he existence on earth of an animal soul turned against itself [ascetic man], taking sides against itself, was something so new, profound, unheard of, enigmatic, contradictory, and *pregnant with a future* that the aspect of the earth was essentially altered. . . . From now on, man is *included* among the most unexpected and exciting lucky throws in the dice game of Heraclitus' "great child," be he called Zeus or chance: he gives rise to an interest, a tension, a hope, almost a certainty, as if with him something were announcing and preparing itself, as if man were not a goal but only a way, an episode, a bridge, a great promise. (*GM* II, 16)

It would, I think, be difficult for environmentalists to interpret these passages as anything but anthropocentric except insofar as Nietzsche envisions that contemporary *anthropos* will overcome himself and generate something higher—perhaps even a planetary master capable of encouraging nonhuman beings to prosper. Long before such a noble prospect could emerge, however, humans would have to organize, manage, and cultivate the planet in order to nourish the growth and development of the *human* tree. The organic metaphor should not prevent us from seeing that planetary organization would require the enormous arrangements made possible by industrial technology. Nietzsche sees risk here, of course, but *not* the risk that such technology would destroy the biosphere, for this prospect never crossed his mind. The risk would be that, despite committing itself to something as great as overcoming itself, the moral animal might botch the job so badly that humans might regress to ape-like status. Even this, however, he could regard as an instance of nature's tendency to squander itself, sometimes absurdly (*TI*, 14).

How would Nietzsche have assessed today's environmentalists, who seem so timid and fearful in the face of possible climate change or species loss? Would he have regarded them as siding with Malthus and Darwin rather than with the bold and violent ones envisioning a new and even more extraordinary phase of human existence that is a dimension and even an expression of terrestrial life? Would Nietzsche have preferred that we roll the dice with industrial modernity to see what it might, even unintentionally, bring forth? Would he have admired the globalizing entrepreneur whose self-interested actions often bring to the market products that prove valuable to many or the allegedly selfless, small-is-beautiful Green? If apprized of the potential power of genetic engineering, which has been made possible by science at work in liberal democracy, would he look to it as a way to generate exalted exemplars of our species without the painful and often horrendous ascetic practices hitherto necessary to generate such exemplars? Would he insist that utilitarian-democratic social forces be prevented from guiding decisions about how and how widely to use genetic engineering? What poetic categories would he like to see put into play during the coming centuries when humankind redesigns the planet? What are the stakes in *this* version of a Nietzschean "politics of nature"?[7]

Works Cited

Acampora, Ralph R. 1994. "Using and Abusing Nietzsche for Environmental Ethics." *Environmental Ethics* 16: 87–194.

Biehl, Janet. 1995. "'Ecology' and the Modernization of Fascism in the German Ultra-Right." In *Ecofascism. Lessons from the German Experience*, ed. Janet Biehl and Peter Staudenmeier. San Francisco: AK Press.

Conway, Daniel W. 1998. "The Politics of Decadence." In *Nietzsche and Politics*, Spindel Conference 1998, ed. Jacqueline Scott, *The Southern Journal of Philosophy* 37, Supplement, 25.

Gasman, Daniel. 1971. *The Scientific Origins of National Socialism: Social Darwinism in Ernst Haeckel and the German Monist League*. New York: Science History Publications.

Geden, Oliver. 1996. *Rechte Ökologie: Umweltschutz zwischen Emanzipation und Faschismus*. Berlin: Elefanten Press.

Hallman, Max. 1991. "Nietzsche's Environmental Ethics." *Environmental Ethics* 13: 99–126.

Heidegger, Martin. 1972. *What Is Called Thinking?* Trans. J. Glenn Gray. New York: Harper Torchbooks.

———. 1998. "On the Question of Being." Trans. William McNeill. In Martin Heidegger, *Pathmarks*, ed. William McNeill. New York: Cambridge University Press.

Herf, Jeffrey. 1984. *Reactionary Modernism: Technology, Culture, and Politics in Weimar and the Third Reich*. New York: Cambridge University Press.

Horkheimer, Max, and Theodor W. Adorno. 1947 (transl. 2002). *Dialectic of Enlightenment*. Ed. Gunzelin Schmid Noerr and trans. Edmund Jephcott. Stanford: Stanford University Press.

Kay, Charles E. 2002. "False Gods, Ecological Myths, and Biological Reality." In Charles E. Kay, ed., *Wilderness and Political Ecology: Aboriginal Influences and the Original State of Nature*. Salt Lake City: The University of Utah Press.

Kevles, Daniel J. 1985. *In the Name of Eugenics: Genetics and the Uses of Human Heredity*. New York: Knopf.

Kuhl, Stefan. 1994. *The Nazi Connection: Eugenics, American Racisms, and German National Socialism*. New York: Oxford University Press.

Manes, Christopher. 1990. *Green Rage*. Boston: Little Brown.

Naess, Arne. 1989. *Ecology, Community, and Lifestyle*. Trans. and ed. David Rothenberg. New York: Cambridge University Press.

Olsen, Jonathan. 1999. *Nature and Nationalism: Right-Wing Ecology and the Politics of Identity*. New York: St. Martin's Press.

Parkes, Graham. 1994. *Composing the Soul: Reaches of Nietzsche's Psychology*. Chicago: University of Chicago Press.

———. 1998. "Staying Loyal to the Earth: Nietzsche as an Ecological Thinker." In *Nietzsche's Futures*, ed. John Lippitt. Basingstoke: Macmillan.

Quinn, Daniel. 1992. *Ishmael: A Novel*. New York: Bantam/Turner Book.

Rosen, Stanley. 1989. "Nietzsche's Revolution." In *The Ancients and the Moderns: Rethinking Modernity*, ed. Stanley Rosen. New Haven: Yale University Press.

Sagoff, Mark. 1999. "What's Wrong with Exotic Species?" *Institute for Philosophy and Public Policy*. http://www.puaf.umd.edu/IPPP/fall1999/exotic-species.htm.

Scott, Jacqueline. 2003. "On the Use and Abuse of Race in Philosophy: Nietzsche, Jews, and Race." In *Race and Racism in Continental Philosophy*, ed. Robert Bernasconi and Sybol Cook. Bloomington: Indiana University Press.

Stack, George. 1992. *Nietzsche and Emerson: An Elective Affinity*. Athens: Ohio University Press.

Staudenmeier, Peter. 1995. "Fascist Ecology: The Green Wing of the Nazi Party and Its Historical Antecedents." *Ecofascism: Lessons from the German Experience*. San Francisco: AK Press.

Stewart, O. C. 1963. "Barriers to Understanding the Influence of the Use of Fire by Aborigines on Vegetation." *Proceedings Tall Timbers Fire Ecology Conference*, 2, 117–126.

Taylor, Paul. 2001. "The Ethics of Respect for Nature." In *Environmental Philosophy: From Animal Rights to Radical Ecology*, ed. Michael E. Zimmerman, et al. Upper Saddle River, N.J.: Prentice Hall, 76–97.

Voeglin, Eric. 2000. *Modernity without Restraint*. Ed. Manfred Henningsen. Vol. 5 of *The Collected Works of Eric Voegelin*. Columbia: The University of Missouri Press.

Zimmerman, Michael E. 1983. "Toward a Heideggerian *Ethos* for Radical Environmentalism." *Environmental Ethics* 5: 99–131.

———. 1990. *Heidegger's Confrontation with Modernity*. Bloomington: Indiana University Press.

———. 1993. "Rethinking the Heidegger–Deep Ecology Relationship." *Environmental Ethics* 15: 95–224.

———. 1994. *Contesting Earth's Future: Radical Ecology and Postmodernity*. Bloomington: Indiana University Press.

———. 1995. "The Threat of Ecofascism." *Social Theory and Practice* 21: 207–308.

Notes

1. On another occasion, I would like to argue that in *The Birth of Tragedy* Nietzsche referred to Raphael's painting *The Transfiguration* not merely because it exemplified the classical Greek yearning for the Apollinian dream world, but also because Nietzsche himself yearned for a spiritual transfiguration in which the glorified body (represented by Christ in Raphael's painting) would occur in the very world occupied by the suffering masses below. The *only* figure in Raphael's painting who looks up at the transfigured Christ is an epileptic, with whom Nietzsche may have well identified himself: the wounded healer whose pre-seizure aura reveals to him

human possibilities hidden to the frightened masses incapable of affirming *this* life.

2. For an insightful account of how right-wing ideologues used—and abused—Nietzsche's thought, see Roger Woods, *The Conservative Revolution in the Weimar Republic* (New York: St. Martin's Press, 1996).

3. Donna Haraway has made a strong case for why environmentalists (and, so I would add, perhaps especially those looking to Nietzsche for inspiration) must keep in mind the potential, but not inevitable, connection between the politics of nature and the politics of race. See for example, "Universal Donors in a Vampire Culture: It's All in the Family: Biological Kinship Categories in the Twentieth-Century United States," in *Uncommon Ground*, ed. William Cronon (New York: Norton, 1995).

4. Conway also argues that Nietzsche finally saw no alternative to moving forward with modernity's potentially reinvigorating project. For an excellent account of the problems involved in Nietzsche's idea of "returning to nature," see Daniel W. Conway, "Returning to Nature: Nietzsche's *Götterdämmerung*," in *Nietzsche: A Critical Reader*, ed. Peter R. Sedgwick (Cambridge, Mass.: Blackwell, 1995), pp. 31–52.

5. Lawrence Lampert comments that Nietzsche imagined that the "global process of homogenization" would provide conditions needed to generate a few exceptional people. See "'Peoples and Fatherlands': Nietzsche's Philosophical Politics," in *Nietzsche and Politics*, Spindel Conference 1998, ed. Jacqueline Scott, *The Southern Journal of Philosophy* 37, Supplement, 43–63.

6. On Heidegger's relation to Jünger, see Michael E. Zimmerman, *Heidegger's Confrontation with Modernity*, Division One (Bloomington: Indiana University Press, 1990).

7. I am very grateful to Ben Crowe, Michael Eldred, Graham Parkes, Frank Schalow, and Teresa Toulouse for offering helpful criticism of various iterations of this essay. I wish *particularly* to thank Graham Parkes, who generously corresponded with me, despite his disagreement with my reading of Nietzsche. Remaining shortcomings are my responsibility.

Chapter Ten

Assassins and Crusaders

Nietzsche after 9/11

Gary Shapiro

Nietzsche describes his four *Unzeitgemässe Betrachtungen* as *Attentate*, assassination attempts. The first of these, his self-described "duel" with David Friedrich Strauss, published in 1873, begins with the question of war and time. It is *untimely* or *out of season* insofar as it challenges the smugness of the cultural philistines who take Germany's victory in the Franco-Prussian War to be a testament to the superiority of German culture. As those in the United States might have learned after the end of the Cold War and after the first Gulf War, "a great victory is a great danger," and we might substitute the name of another nation state—or an emerging globalizing empire—when Nietzsche speaks of "the defeat, if not the extirpation, of the German spirit for the benefit of the 'German Reich'" (*UM* I, § 1). Assassination is always untimely, an instrument of war and a response to war. Assassination interrupts the steady, sedentary time of the state.

It has never been easy to marginalize Nietzsche's talk of war and his often violent rhetoric, which was misappropriated by the Nazis, and that misappropriation then deployed as a means for marginalizing him as a thinker. At least since Walter Kaufmann's 1950 book, however, it has become more difficult to see Nietzsche as the evil genius who legitimized the idea of a Germanic master race. More recently scholarship has taken an increasingly nuanced approach to the question of Nietzsche's politics. While acknowledging his advocacy of the transnational "good European," his critique of the supremacy of the state, and even the possibility of deploying certain possibilities in his thought in the service of poststructuralist feminism, it has asked rightly, whether his praise of war and warriors can be said to be merely rhetorical (this would be an odd claim with regard to a thinker for whom language is so crucial).[1] Today "after 9/11" these questions are reminiscent of the attempts of the "West" to understand the stakes of the "war on terror." (All of these marked phrases are problematic, as I think will emerge from an exploration of Nietzsche's own penetrating meditations on time, his odd calendrical fantasies, and his uncanny, if highly sketchy, articulation of a coming global conflict for which an exemplary precedent is the struggle between Christianity and Islam. If I proceed to use these and similar phrases without marking them, I trust that the reader will understand that this is done in anticipation of such problematization.)

The question of how to take Nietzsche on war bears a striking parallel to the dispute about the meaning of *jihad* within Islam: is it to be understood primarily as an internal, spiritual struggle to live, think, and feel in accordance with the divine will, or does it name a struggle on all fronts, necessarily involving military combat and terrorism, to eliminate all forms of infidelity and directed, at its extremes, to the establishment of a global caliphate under a radical form of Islamic law? Nietzsche, of course, was no scholar of Islam, but he had read more of its history than those who have fashioned the West's recent "war on terror," sometimes described as a "crusade," sometimes said by George W. Bush to be guided by divine inspiration.[2] As we will see, Nietzsche was familiar with both some of the leading scholarship of his day on early Islam and its battles, both military and theological, as well as the semilegendary notions and fantasies of the Orientalism that was the ideological support of nineteenth-century European imperialism. It is striking, reading Nietzsche now in the wake of 9/11, war in Afghanistan and Iraq, and general concern with radical Islam, to see how much of Nietzsche's attention, especially in the last two years of his writing, was directed to thinking about the fate of Europe and Christianity within a broad historical and geographical perspective in which Assassins and Crusaders are two of the most prominent players and Europe's apparent victory over Islam is taken to be one of the reasons for launching a new "war to the death" against Christianity. The last phrase is taken from the "Decree (*Gesetz*) Against Christianity," which Nietzsche originally appended to *The Antichrist* and which Colli and Montinari have restored in their edition (*SW* 6.254).[3] Together with the concluding paragraphs of that work, the "Decree" implies that Nietzsche has no war with Islam, whose culture is the subject of his extravagant praise. Of course Nietzsche was writing at a time when the tottering Ottoman Empire seemed no longer to offer any threat to the expanding imperial powers of Europe. While his predictions of a century of great wars might be taken in the broadest terms to prefigure the three World Wars (including the Cold War), he could not have suspected that at the beginning of the twenty-first century the great war in prospect would appear to be one between the West and resurgent Islam. Yet Nietzsche increasingly borrowed figures and examples from Europe's conflict with Islam to attempt to make sense of the geopolitical past and future. What follows is a preliminary sketch of some aspects of that attempt, an attempt that could lead Nietzsche toward the end of *The Antichrist* to celebrate the motto he attributes to Friedrich the Second: "War to the knife with Rome! Peace, friendship with Islam" (*AC*, § 60). I find this sketch disturbing, as I find much of Nietzsche's politics disturbing. Yet I think we can learn something about Nietzsche as well as about Crusaders and Assassins, past and present, by beginning to explore the uncanny resonances of these figures that appear at the margins of his texts. We are told that "everything is different after 9/11." This may be too facile a judgment; even worse, it may provide ideological cover for new imperial expansion and the further degradation of liberal democracy. Nietzsche also had ideas about breaking time in two and starting anew; the "Decree" proposes a new calendar to begin on the date of its composition or proclamation (the former September 30, 1888); it may be that his illusions about a new time scheme can teach us something about our own fantasies and fears (which is not to say that either is totally devoid of truth, for do we not speak justly in some contexts of thought before and after Nietzsche?).

Since Germany is not so far a major player in the first great war of the new millennium, the one said to have been declared on September 11, 2001, and known by this date, so Nietzsche's name has not yet been invoked on the side of either the friends or the enemies of what are taken to be the identical causes of the West, democracy, freedom, and sexual equality. On the surface Osama bin Laden offers a striking example of Nietzsche's ascetic priest, who provides a meaning for the suffering of his flock. From the standpoint of radical Islam, as preached by bin Laden and Syed Qutub, a prominent recent theorist of violent *jihad*, the only virtue is total submission in this life, a submission predicated on the belief that all the deficiencies of this world will be compensated by the glories of the next.[4] There is no limit to the self-sacrifice called for by such submission; hence the supreme virtue of the suicide bomber or martyr. Yet this ascetic priest does not "alter the direction of *ressentiment*" by telling the faithful that they are the ones responsible for their own suffering.[5] There is an other, an evil enemy, a Satan, a society of infidels. This motivates a nomadic war machine with a spirit very different from the inward-turning nineteenth-century Protestantism and its secular variants that were the primary provocation of Nietzsche's critique. And rather than making their peace with the state, like most organized forms of Christianity, the radical Islamists are doctrinally committed to a total, global, theocratic community, the *umma*; along the way toward its realization, they countenance only temporary tactical truces with infidel powers. It has been suggested that the 9/11 hijackers and their allies could be characterized as nihilists, not simply as religious fanatics. Certainly, for Nietzsche the extreme otherworldliness involved in what we suppose to be the would-be martyrs' vision of paradise would itself be nihilism. And we can imagine Nietzsche, the "old philologist" whose analysis of Christianity benefits from the higher criticism of the Bible that flourished in the nineteenth century, being wickedly entertained by some recent critical readings of the Qur'an, according to which the "seventy dark-eyed virgins" promised to martyrs in the gardens of the afterlife is a misreading of "seventy white raisins," a rare delicacy in the Arabian peninsula.[6] Yet Nietzsche might once again be brought in as the intellectual godfather of the current war. Perhaps someone will discover that Western converts like John Walker Lindh or Richard Reid read Nietzsche's *Antichrist*, in which he says "Islam is a thousand times right in despising Christianity: Islam presupposes men [*Männer*]" (*AC*, § 59).

Someone, somewhere, will drag out Nietzsche's scattered comments in which he regrets Europe's turning away from the crypto-Islamism of German emperor Friedrich the Second, speaks with approval of the military genius of Muhammad, and at the end of *The Antichrist* denounces Christianity because

> it cheated us again out of the harvest of the culture of *Islam*. The wonderful world of the Moorish culture of Spain, really more closely related to *us*, more congenial to our senses and tastes than Rome and Greece, was *trampled down* (I do not say by what kind of feet). Why? Because it owed its origin to noble, to *male* instincts, because it said Yes to life even with the rare and refined luxuries of Moorish life. (*AC*, § 60)

Nietzsche's nostalgia for the loss of Andalusia evokes that of bin Laden's today as recorded on one of his video declarations of war. Neither acknowledges that it was internal conflict in Islam, spearheaded by Moroccan fundamentalists, that contributed at least as much as any Christian offensive to the dissolution of Moorish Spain. In this passage Nietzsche goes on to denounce the Crusades in a spirit that the ideologists of the September 11 attack would find appealing. Let us note parenthetically that Nietzsche does not praise all wars. If "it is the good war that hallows every cause," then it also seems clear that a war against a higher form of culture is not a good war and that what makes a good war good is not military success, ferocity, looting, rapine, and destruction. "Really," Nietzsche says,

> there should not be any choice between Islam and Christianity, any more than between an Arab and a Jew. Either one *is* a chandala, or one *is not*. "War to the knife against Rome! Peace and friendship with Islam"—thus felt, thus *acted*, that great free spirit, the genius among German emperors, Friedrich the Second. (*AC*, § 60)

Nietzsche seems to have derived his (late) view of Jews as chandalas or untouchables from reading Louis Jacolliot's annotated (and untrustworthy) translation of the Indian Law of Manu. His use of Jacolliot's eccentric thesis is peculiar, since the former claims that both Jews and Arabs were descended from chandalas driven out of India.[7]

Where did Nietzsche find the resources for his vision of Islam and the ideal caliphate of Andalusia? It was of course a marginal fantasy running throughout Western history, the idea of a counter-world of tolerance and cosmopolitan learning, a world symbolized by Granada and the Alhambra. When Nietzsche longs for a great architecture, one that builds for the ages and lays the foundation for a great culture, he may be thinking of these monuments. It is this world that is frequently invoked today as offering a very different version of Islam than the one of political and military *jihad* with biological, chemical, and nuclear weapons that the West fears now; it is an alternative to the image of radical Islam associated with September 11. So Nietzsche's enthusiasm for this cultural memory of Islam does not necessarily suggest that he would take the side of today's Islamic warriors. As early as March 1881 he had proposed to his old friend Gersdorff that they spend a year or two together in Tunis. It is not perhaps altogether accidental that Nietzsche had been somewhat alienated from this friend as a result of his marriage. But he writes, "I want to live among Muslims for a good long time, especially where their faith is most devout; in this way I expect to hone my appraisal and my eye for all that is European" (*B* 6.68; March 13, 1881). Nietzsche expresses the need for a marginal perspective on Europe. As here, many of Nietzsche's references to Islam are colored by a tone that is either antifeminist, homoerotic, or both. Later he will write to Paul Deussen, praising his work on Indian philosophy and speaking of his own "trans-European eye."[8]

The involvement with Islam and war goes further. In an unnerving passage in *On the Genealogy of Morality* Nietzsche refers to the original Assassins. This is perhaps his most explicit engagement with the possibility of a terrorist apparatus and its philosophical roots.

> When the Christian crusaders in the Orient encountered the invincible order of the Assassins, that order of free spirits *par excellence*, whose lowest ranks followed a rule of obedience the like of which no order of monks has ever attained, they obtained in some way or other a hint concerning that symbol and tally-word reserved for the highest ranks as their *secretum*: "Nothing is true, everything is permitted."—Very well, *that* was *freedom* of spirit; in *that* way the faith in truth itself was abrogated. (*GM* III, § 24)

Here we have a bit of geophilosophy in miniature. Nietzsche believes—more or less accurately—that the Assassins, or properly the Nizari Ismailis, a branch of the Shia, had liberated themselves from the morality of truth and developed a culture of self-discipline that set itself goals no longer human, all-too-human. According to stories relayed by Marco Polo and others, the Assassins were organized in ultrahierarchical fashion and the "soldiers" of the movement would gladly sacrifice their own lives at the command of their master, "the old man of the mountain." In one story, several disciples threw themselves to their deaths from high towers simply so that the "old man" could demonstrate the obedience of his troops. Notice that this war-machine (in the term of Deleuze and Guattari) is very different from the contemporary European "free spirits" with whom Nietzsche contrasts them in this same passage. Those half-hearted thinkers are still caught up in the religion of truth that claims their ascetic allegiance. The free spirits do not have the daring, the imagination, to cast it aside and pursue other projects. They do not envision other possibilities of becoming but are content to remain within the sedentary boundaries of the state, which they would like to alter just a little bit, replacing the church with the religion of science. But if *everything is permitted*, then what is permitted includes grand experiments in overcoming the human. It is the transhuman, posthuman, or *Übermensch* who looms on the horizon, if only today's free spirits could understand what was once the *secretum* of the Assassins, to whom Nietzsche could be linking himself in describing his books as assassination attempts. He also suggests that the Crusaders, whom he will denounce in *The Antichrist* and elsewhere, may have sensed at some deep, unconscious level the insight of the Assassins and carried it back to Europe with them. That suspicion is reflected in the shadowy legends of the extreme hierarchy, secret doctrines (like metempsychosis), and practices of the Knights Templar, as fictionalized in Klossowski's Nietzschean novel, *The Baphomet*.[9]

Following a genealogy with which Nietzsche was probably familiar, some have traced these connections back to the original Zoroaster or Zarathustra. Writing in *The New York Times* three months after 9/11, the historian Marina Warner said that we should understand the guiding ideology of Al Qaeda not as Islamic fundamentalism but as a resurgence of Zoroastrianism, that is, the teachings of the original Persian Zarathustra[10]; it is that extreme dualism that Nietzsche's version of the sage has come to renounce. Zoroastrianism so understood is a kind of gnosticism that sees an absolute opposition between a good and an evil principle. Such dualism lends itself to esotericism, so that the good stands in unmediated contrast with the evils and confusion of the world. This sets up the possibility of a transition from a secret truth that lays down rigid moral injunctions and prohibitions to the *secretum* of the Assassins: "nothing is true, everything is permitted." In a note of 1884 Nietzsche writes "Fundamental principle: So far as the public good goes, the Jesuits are right, and in the same way the order of the Assassins; and similarly the rule of the Chinese" (*SW* 11.101). And in the same year, he links the students of Brahma, those who take vows in temples, and the Assassins as exhibiting "the practice of obedience," and remarks on "the divinization of the feeling of power among the Brahmans: it is interesting that it arose in the warrior caste and only later was passed on to the priests" (*SW* 11.208–209). In *Zarathustra* it is the Shadow who says, "'Nothing is true, all is permitted,' thus I spoke to myself" (*SW* 4.340). In this context the Shadow is giving voice to a melancholy confession: he has followed Zarathustra into the most daring reaches of thought, but has turned into nothing but a ghost or shadow. He is *only* a shadow because he spoke only to himself, not like the Brahmans, Assassins, and Jesuits, to an organized order.

Let us look more carefully at *Genealogy* III, § 24, where Nietzsche contrasts the Assassins and the free spirits. He refers to the notorious formula of the *secretum* as a *Kerbholz-Wort*, or tally-word. The term is unusual enough in German to have received a detailed commentary in Maudmarie Clark's and Alan J. Swensen's notes to their translation of *On the Genealogy of Morality*. As they point out, it is Nietzsche's coinage, deriving from the rather rare *Kerbholz*. I quote at some length from their commentary, since Nietzsche's language has implications for how we are to understand his repetition of the Assassins' formula:

> The German word *Kerbholz* now survives only in the idiom: *etwas auf dem Kerbholz haben* (literally: "to have something on one's tally"), which now has a moral rather than a legal meaning—to have a sin or crime on one's conscience. The *Kerbholz* or "tally" [originally a stick notched to keep score or track of a debt, e.g. drinks consumed] was generally split lengthwise across the notches or "scores" and each party involved in the transaction was given one half. The correspondence between the two halves could then be used to confirm the size of the debt and the identity of the creditor.[11]

As Clark and Swensen note, Nietzsche uses *Kerbholz-Wort* one more time (his only other usage) in a notebook of 1885 to 1887 (previous to the composition of the *Genealogy*) when he writes: "'Paradise is under the shadow of swords'—also a symbolon and *Kerbholz-Wort* by which the souls of noble and warlike descent betray themselves and recognize each other."[12] Again, like the *secretum* of the Assassins, this sentence is placed in quotations. The external source, if there is one, has not been identified. However, as explained below, it could very well derive from Nietzsche's reading or imagination of the Assassins, since a basic part of their legend has to do with the promise of entrance into paradise for those who obeyed the master of the order. Some of the essential ingredients of the legend, then, that emerge in *Genealogy* III, § 24, are that the Assassins form a hierarchical order, demanding and achieving absolute obedience, whose degrees are marked by initiation into secret teachings, that the highest teaching involves the notorious secret *Kerbholz-Wort*, and that some inkling of this secret teaching was probably transmitted to the Crusaders. Clark and Swensen remark that Nietzsche's use of *Kerbholz-Wort* "is another example of a moral phenomenon evolving from an economic one."[13] The context renders this observation highly ironic, since the point of the *secretum* is the supermoral one that "everything is permitted." Yet while the usual reading of this passage takes Nietzsche to be authorizing a kind of unbridled individualism, it is precisely the obedience of the order and the startling, spectacular results that such obedience can achieve that are the focus of the legend to which Nietzsche alludes. The Assassins are not "existentialists" in the vulgar sense of individuals choosing their own way of life without regard to custom or authority but a disciplined order undertaking dramatic projects of political power and social transformation.

Following his citation of the Assassins' secret, Nietzsche inserts one of those ellipses by which he aims at provoking rather than pronouncing thought and turns to emphasizing the distinction between his reading of the famous sentence and the attitude of contemporary European free spirits:

> . . . Now *that* was *freedom* of the spirit, *with that*, belief in truth itself was *renounced*. . . . Has any European, any Christian free spirit ever lost his

way in this proposition and its labyrinthine *consequences*? Does he know
the Minotaur of this cave *from experience*? . . . precisely in their belief in
truth they are more firm and unconditional than anyone else.

European free spirits are identified here, it seems, as *Christians*, which at first
seems paradoxical, since the typical free spirit, as Nietzsche presents such, identifies herself as an atheist or agnostic. But as the argument of the *Genealogy*
proceeds, Nietzsche's point becomes clearer. Christianity believes in Truth, and
that belief is transmitted to the free spirits who imagine themselves in rebellion
against it. They oppose Christianity in the name of one of its highest values. They
are Christians despite themselves. Since it is the relation between Assassins and
Crusaders that introduces this reflection, implicit here is the thought that not all
religions, not even all monotheisms, are committed to Truth in this sense. Islam,
at least, was able to give rise to a different perspective. The proposition and its
unspoken "labyrinthine *consequences*" remain unthought by the European free
spirits. We could suggest that these consequences involve not only surrendering
belief in the Truth, but also passivity in the face of the Truth, what Nietzsche goes
on to call "philosopher's abstinence . . . fatalism of '*petits faits*' . . . renunciation
of all interpretation," in short, a nihilistic positivism, one that would certainly
preclude the adventurous possibilities of "everything is permitted." Given the opposition between the order of the Assassins and the unreflective individualism
of the free spirits, we can surmise that the latter are Christian in an additional
(Nietzschean) sense: they continue to believe, if not in the literal immortality of
the soul, then at least in the autonomy of the individual as the source of action
and value. The Assassins, in legend and in Nietzsche's allusion, were not so limited. Zarathustra's Shadow can repeat the verbal formula, but in his weakness
he fails to work through its daring consequences and ends in the self-confessed
impotence of his song "Among Daughters of the Desert" (*SW* 4.379–85). Since
Nietzsche associates the Shadow with a degenerate understanding of the Assassins' *Kerbholz-Wort*, we can read his parody of European Orientalist poetry as the
passive nihilist version of the sensual paradise with willing maidens promised to
the lower orders of the faithful. The Shadow, then, is a mere free spirit, an impotent
European individualist. He can repeat the verbal formula of the Assassins, but
he fails to understand that it is a *Kerbholz-Wort* rather than a *Grundsatz*. It is not
a principle, or not merely a principle. It is rather, or also, a symbol by which the
adepts reveal and recognize one another. In this respect it is worth thinking of
its similarities to the teaching of eternal recurrence, which appears in Nietzsche's
notebooks of 1881 as a thought to be understood for its political implications; he
notes that through the new teaching (including the self-education of its teachers)
"in this way a new ruling caste forms itself" (*SW* 9.497).

Somewhere Nietzsche had heard of the Assassins, whose reputation entered European literature as early as the twelfth century and was given currency
in the nineteenth in a relatively popular and sensational German account by the

Austrian Orientalist Joseph von Hammer-Purgstall, *History of the Assassins*.[14] In the eleventh and twelfth centuries the Nizari had established themselves in the mountain stronghold of Alamut, at 10,200 feet in the highlands of Persia, and from there they captured other fortresses in a series of surprise raids. The group grew out of a strain within the Ismaili tradition, itself a Shia heresy, which foresaw a form of Islam that would be freed from doctrine, prayer, and ritual. As Nietzsche's passage indicates, they were famed for a complex internal organization that allowed the grand master to transmit orders to highly disciplined cells. In Marco Polo's description, based on travels ten years after the final defeat and dispersal of the movement by the Mongols, the grand master was said to have used hashish to put his recruits to sleep; they would awake in his fabulous garden and be attended by beautiful women. This taste of paradise was then used to motivate them in their murderous missions with the promise that they could always return to the garden as miraculously as they had entered it for the first time. The traditional Western etymology of *Assassins* derives from the hashish that they supposedly smoked in order to work themselves up into a state of supreme fervor. The accuracy of this legend has been contested, quite sensibly, on the grounds that hashish is not good for discipline. It seems likely that the term was applied by outsiders to suggest that the Assassins were as mad as hashish addicts. After a series of startling successes over a period of sixty or seventy years, the Assassins were finally defeated by the Mongols around 1260 and all or almost all of their own books and records were destroyed. During their heyday the constant threat of secret attack and the absolutely fearless quality of their warriors spread terror throughout the territory from Persia to Syria. One estimate is that there were about 150,000 of the Ismaili "Assassin" sect scattered throughout northern Syria, Persia, Oman, Zanzibar, and India. The combination (actual or legendary) of hierarchical organization, fighters ready and willing to sacrifice themselves, terror and propaganda (they called themselves the new propagandists), drugs, hidden mountain strongholds, and a heretical use of Islamic tradition seems to have rooted itself in Western Orientalism. Also significant is the fact that the Assassins were eventually defeated and dispersed by another nomadic force, the Mongols, who swept aside everything in their path.

We can tentatively reconstruct some of the sources from which Nietzsche may have gained some knowledge or hearsay concerning the Assassins. He refers to August Müller's *Der Islam in Morgen- und Abendland*, a massive history published in 1885.[15] Müller gives a relatively straightforward account of the rise and fall of the Assassins (given the prejudices of his time), including their complex relations with the Crusaders, which included temporary alliances. He also had great respect for the scholarship of Julius Wellhausen, from whose writings he drew in his analysis of Judaism and early Christianity; Nietzsche knew and quoted from Wellhausen's writings on the theological-political history of early Islam.[16] In the fall of 1887 he copies these notes from Wellhausen's studies of Islam:

"In Islam community in battle is at the same time sacramental community: whoever takes part in our prayers and eats the meat of the battle is a Muslim." "A command of the cult transforms itself into a command of the *culture*." (*SW* 12.531)

Most intriguing is the question of whether he knew Von Hammer-Purgstall's *History of the Assassins*, for it includes a reverential treatment of Zarathustra/Zoroaster and the oldest Persian kingdoms, a quasi-philosophical analysis of the Assassins as nihilist revolutionaries, and an attempt to awaken Europe to what the author saw as the imminent danger posed by secret societies that were ideologically and perhaps organizationally descended from the Assassins, especially the Freemasons. While there seem to be no explicit references to the *History of the Assassins* in Nietzsche's writings, we should note that this book, published first in 1818, went through a number of editions and was translated into several languages; it was a mainstay of nineteenth-century Orientalism and played an important role in the anti-Masonic hysteria of the time. Only around 1848 did the specter haunting Europe begin to change its name from the Masons to the communists, but then, for von Hammer, both the Assassins and the Masons were revolutionaries, communists, and nihilists.

Reading von Hammer after Nietzsche, we might be struck by some of these aspects of his narrative: He begins by praising the ancient kingdom of the Persians and the religion of Zoroaster, which in its "primeval purity" offered no support for rebellion. But some later Zoroastrian sects "preached universal liberty and equality, the indifference of all human actions, and community of goods and women." When the Persian Empire was destroyed by Islamic Arabs they "sought the ruin of Islamism, not only by open war, but also by secret doctrines and pernicious dissensions."[17] Von Hammer describes the emergence of various cults, culminating finally in the Assassins of Alamut. All of these are characterized by hierarchical orders among the Ismailite Shia in which adepts proceed through various degrees of secrecy. In one of the latter stages it becomes clear that philosophy takes precedence over all positive religion. Von Hammer translates the teaching of the final stage in a number of ways that closely resemble Nietzsche's *secretum*: "nothing was sacred and all was permitted," "to believe nothing and to dare all," "all was doubtful and nothing prohibited."[18] He delights in telling stories of the bloody and grotesque exploits of the group, especially its grand masters, in their pursuit of power, which eventually extended over much of present-day Iran, Iraq, and Syria. Von Hammer relates that the Assassins conspired with the Crusaders when it suited their purposes and were capable of the most devious forms of disguise and betrayal. He reminds us of the resemblance of the Assassins to the Jesuits and Masons (Nietzsche associates Jesuits and Assassins also), and he describes the Ismailis as "nestled, like birds of prey, among the rocks" of their mountain stronghold, a metaphor that recalls many of Nietzsche's.[19]

(For example, in relating the composition of *Zarathustra* in *Ecce Homo*, he tells us that the "decisive chapter that bears the title 'On Old and New Tablets' was composed on the most onerous ascent from the station to the marvelous Moorish eyrie [*Felsennest*], Eza" [*SW* 6.341]. Zarathustra's legislation is associated not only with his own unnamed [Persian?] mountain but with one of Islam's former rocky strongholds in Europe.) One of the most interesting chapters of the story of the Assassins tells of the grand master Hassan, son of Mohammed. While the order typically kept up the appearances of Islamic faith and obedience among the population and the lower degrees of the order, Hassan openly preached their secrets, ordered feasting on Ramadan, and attempted to introduce a new calendar beginning with his reign.[20]

If Deleuze is right in seeing Nietzsche as a nomadic philosopher, then his theory and practice of war may owe something, at least on a symbolic level, to his vision of the war of Christianity and Islam and to the war within Islam waged by the Assassins. But here we should not forget that there is an apparent tension in Nietzsche's praise of Islamic Andalusia and his possible sympathy with the Assassins. Nietzsche knew that there was a hierarchical system among the Assassins that was tied to levels of initiation. He saw the group as practicing an esoteric teaching, a *secretum*. This could give some force to Geoff Waite's thesis in *Nietzsche's Corps/e* that his work should be construed as an esoteric form of warfare.[21] But on Waite's view, Nietzsche's polemic is primarily directed against socialism and democracy. The associations with Islam and the Assassins, like much of Nietzsche's writing, suggest that the struggle is primarily with religion, specifically with Christianity. Of course Nietzsche will sometimes link these together, as in the notorious passage of *Twilight* where he spells out one form of the warrior ideal:

> The human being who has *become free*—and how much more the *spirit* who has become free—spits on the contemptible form of well-being dreamed of by shopkeepers, Christians, cows, females, Englishmen, and other democrats. The free human being [*Mensch*] is a warrior. (*TI*, "Skirmishes," 38)

Deleuze and Guattari, building on Nietzsche, argue that thinkers like Hegel and Marx fail to understand the nomads and specifically the nomadic war machine. Hegel, Marx, and almost all of western political philosophy has seen war as a conflict between states rather than between a state and forces of the outside. To the extent that these thinkers recognize the nomadic, or warrior, as such, they must make them primitive stages, long surpassed or existing only as fossils. Nevertheless, there is an aesthetic longing in Hegel's discussion of the epic, Homeric world in his *Aesthetics* and in Marx and Engels' sketches of hunter-gatherers. The failure to understand the nomadic ("nonstate agents" in official U.S. parlance) leads to initial and continuing bewilderment as U.S. mainstream news analysts attempt to comprehend Al Qaeda and similar organizations. We can learn more about the structure of the conflict from films about terrorist conspiracies than from political philosophers like John Rawls or Robert Nozick, more from a few conservative political theorists and journalists like Samuel Huntington with his war of civilizations or Robert Kaplan with his talk of "the coming anarchy" than from Habermasian critical theory.

When Nietzsche declares war on Christianity he does so in a context shaped by admiration for Islam and the Assassins whose tally-word, he says, was "Nothing is true, everything is permitted." The last formula, in his text, is not a license for individualism, arbitrary whim, or vulgar existentialism. It is a formula of military discipline. The last paragraph of the main text of *The Antichrist* promises a writing on the walls and a revision of the calendar based on Nietzsche's declaration of war on Christianity.

> Wherever there are walls I shall inscribe this eternal accusation against Christianity upon them—I can write in letters which make even the blind see. . . . And one calculates *time* from the *dies nefastus* on which this fatality arose—from the *first* day of Christianity! *Why not rather from its last?—From today?*—Revaluation of all values! (*AC*, § 62)

As we now know, this passage was followed immediately by the "Decree Against Christianity," which proposes a "day one" (replacing September 30, 1888) marking the war against Christianity.

Deleuze has written of the profound structure that underlies this phantasm of the splitting of time in *Difference and Repetition*. He contrasts the Cartesian *cogito* and the Kantian "I think." The *cogito* determines the I as a thinking being whose identity is dependent upon God. Kant saw that only the bare form of temporality was implied by the "I think," and so consequently "time signifies a fault or a fracture in the *I* and a passivity in the self."[22] Rational psychology must go the way of rational theology. Hölderlin and Nietzsche are the true heirs of Kant, rather than Fichte and Hegel. The time is out of joint and necessarily marked by a caesura. This "caesura, of whatever kind, must be determined in the image of a unique and tremendous event, an act which is adequate to time as a whole."[23] So Nietzsche's interruption of time, whether in the thought of eternal recurrence or in the introduction of a new calendar, is to be understood as a "symbolic image" of time out of joint.

It is worth noting that Nietzsche's challenge to rethink time with the thought of eternal recurrence is "untimely," that it goes contrary to the measuring of time, its *Zeitmass*, insofar as it coincides with the global standardization of time that was put into effect by the railroads and ratified by governments in the early 1880s.[24] Nietzsche, perhaps the first railway philosopher, raises the question "who will be the lords of the earth?" in a context where it means, among other things, who will set the earth's time and calendar. Geophilosophy must also be chronophilosophy. The striated space and time of the global transportation system is challenged by the time of the earth, the animal, the horizon, and the sun. It is Nietzsche's anti-Copernican revolution.

War-time, the war against Christianity *and its false reckoning of time*, is time in the wake of God's death. In the parable of the madman (*GS*, § 125), time is out of joint because the true news of God's death, like the light from distant stars, is still on its way to the traders in the marketplace. What they do not see, in their all too easy and all too human atheism, is that the date of their *Wall Street Journal* is out of date and that the market is about to be engulfed in war. Nietzsche's war-time is the time in which "I is another," in which the Antichrist(ian) repeats the tragic age of the Greeks in its post-Christian and post-Cartesian difference.

The declaration of war, the "Decree Against Christianity," perhaps removed by his sister and early editors, was restored finally by Colli and Montinari. During his last year Nietzsche was obsessed with the question of law giving and found inspiration in Jacolliot's book *The Religious Lawgivers*, with its translation of the Law of Manu and its running commentary with comparisons to Moses and Muhammad. The "Decree," which was to form the last page of *The Antichrist*, could be the text of a poster to be put up in public places. (It was found in Nietzsche's papers glued to the last pages of *The Antichrist*; Colli and Montinari argue that it was intended to be the last page of that work.) It declares that priests should be imprisoned, that "every participation in a religious service is an attack on public morality," that Protestantism is worse than Catholicism and liberal Protestantism its worst variety, that all preaching of chastity or denigration of sexuality is to be condemned, that eating with a priest is forbidden, and that the words used in positive senses in the Bible like *God* and *redeemer* should be understood as insults. It is impossible to determine what in this decree is parody and what is meant in total seriousness. Nietzsche, who constantly tells his readers that he expects the most subtle, philologically attuned ear for his writings, offers something in the style of a comic book, a set of directives as shockingly simplified, if not more so, than the instructions and videotapes of the suicide bombers. However, I want to focus now, in the wake of September 11, and so in the era that takes its name from that date, on the line just below the title of the "Decree Against Christianity." That line reads "Proclaimed on the first day of the year one (on September 30, 1888) of the false time scheme." Of course the parallelism is not exact. Bin Laden and associates did not announce a new time scheme; they presumably accept the traditional Islamic calendar. Some of his pronouncements refer to events "eighty years ago," possibly the Balfour Declaration. In the months following September 11, there was speculation by intelligence services and journalists about whether that attack and feared future attacks were geared to some religious or esoteric calendar.[25]

Let us compare these two September dates: September 11, 2001, and September 30, 1888. Of course the last is expressed in what Nietzsche calls the old, false system of reckoning time. It should be day one, year one, of a time that has been newly divided in two—a new common era. Nietzsche's day one is put forward as an affirmative date, yet to the extent that it recognizes a prior time with which it contrasts itself, the question arises whether it can be completely affirmative. For the war against Christianity time must be recalibrated with a new calendar, one unindebted to the enemy's system of values. But like Christianity and Islam, Nietzsche's calendar splits the history of humanity into two, unlike the Jewish calendar which begins with the creation of the world and so has nothing anterior to its basic date. Nietzsche's new way of reckoning time is tied up with wars and battles, like 9/11. In the Jewish and Christian imaginary, which Nietzsche probably shared on this point, there is a tendency to think of early Islam as defined by its wars. But the Islamic calendar begins with the Hijra, understood as an act of complete submission: Muhammad saves the faith and its revelation by leaving Mecca for Medina. Since Nietzsche praises the Islamic war on Christianity he may have felt some kinship with what he took to be its associated way of dividing time into two parts. And like Jewish and Islamic dates, when presented in Christian or in secular contexts, Nietzsche gives the other time scheme as a point of reference.

The use of September 11 as a watershed, although it is a military date, the beginning of a war, has a very different sense than any of these other primal dates. When used in politics and the media, it too has an absolute before and after. Before we were innocent and unsuspecting; after we are vigilant and fighting back. George W. Bush declared war on terrorism on that date, and it is the date of "Let's roll," flight 93 passenger Todd Beamer's answer to the "Allah Akbar" of the hijackers over Pennsylvania. September 11 is a date that in this context is thought to be *thrust upon us*. It is recorded in the prevailing calendar because it is an offense to that calendar (Christian, Jewish, and secular Americans will certainly not refer to it as the sixth day of Jumada II, 1422 A.H., its Islamic date). In this dating system, those who were attacked let themselves be defined by the aggressions of the other. Some, of course, will suggest that there is a certain subterfuge in this, whether conscious or unconscious. They might suggest that it is American or Israeli aggression, globalization, or the corrupt regimes of Egypt and Saudi Arabia, propped up by the West, that bear some major responsibility for September 11. The extreme form of this view is the one according to which the attacks were planned by the United States or Israel. That is absurd, although it would be supremely foolish to understand September 11 without attending to its geopolitical context.

What I am attempting to focus on is the question of the date as a way of naming an event, dividing time, and marking the initiation of a war, a war that seems to open up a new kind of future, a war, as "we" are repeatedly told, that will be unlike all other wars, the war of the new millennium, the war of the future. The obviously parochial character of the before and after 9/11 system is marked by the fact that it seems almost impossible to use it, at least in an American context, without the use of the first person plural: it is "our" date. Those in the United States might think of December 7, 1941, "a day that will live in infamy," as Franklin Roosevelt said. But this became the war with the Axis powers and World War II. Because we could name the nation-states of Germany, Japan, and their satellites and allies as enemies, the war did not have to be defined in terms of a date. September 11 remains so far the date that *names* the current war, because the enemy is otherwise nameless. This also opens up the possibility, noted by many observers, that there will be no way of marking the end of the war, since it cannot be defined in terms of the defeat and surrender of any sovereign state(s), as the end of World War II was marked by V-E and V-J days or the conclusion of the Cold War by the fall of the Berlin Wall or the dissolution of the Soviet Union. It stands in for a war against evil, sometimes characterized by George Bush as "the evil one" (bin Laden) or as the "axis of evil" (Iran, Iraq, North Korea) but most generally as a "war on terror."

The United States military adventure in Iraq could be seen as an attempt to superimpose a traditional war against a sovereign state on the intrinsically indefinite calendar of the war on terror, but the misguided character of this attempt is evident from the staged character of the toppling of Saddam Hussein's Baghdad statue and of George W. Bush's announcement on May 1, 2003, of the cessation of "major combat operations" in Iraq. Here, Nietzsche the philosophical expert on masks and costumes, would find himself in one of his occasional alliances with Marx. The spectacle of Bush arriving in flight outfit and making his declaration under the banner "MISSION ACCOMPLISHED" on the deck of an aircraft carrier lends itself to Marx's analysis of historical masquerade in *The 18th Brumaire of Louis Bonaparte:*

> The tradition of all the dead generations weighs like a nightmare on the brain of the living. And just when they seem engaged in revolutionizing themselves and things, in creating something that has never yet existed, precisely in such periods of revolutionary crisis they anxiously conjure up the spirits of the past to their service and borrow from them names, battle cries and costumes in order to present the new scene of world-history in this time-honored disguise and this borrowed language.[26]

Marx would have been amused by the borrowing of "names, battle cries and costumes" in the spectacles by which government and media attempt to say simultaneously both that everything is different and that a traditional victory has been accomplished. And Marx was no doubt more acute than Nietzsche at seeing through the illusions of the calendar, as his ironizing of the French revolutionary calendar in the title of *The 18th Brumaire* demonstrates.

Nietzsche, however, is the better analyst of the language of good and evil that drives the current war effort by both contemporary Assassins and Crusaders. The rhetoric of evil is reactive. September 11 is the sign of our victimization by the evil ones; we, in contrast, must be good. It is the mirror image of Al Qaeda's calendar of good and evil in which it is dates like those of the Crusades themselves, the Spanish expulsion of the Moors, or the Balfour Declaration that mark corresponding events. *On the Genealogy of Morals* proposes a contrast between a sovereign language of "good and bad" and the reactive moral discourse of "good and evil." The struggle against evil necessarily tends toward a metaphysical and theological hypostatization of evil and a similar faith in the transcendent purity of those who reactively designate themselves as the good. So Nietzsche would understand why the explicit appeal to theology by bin Laden and his kind is increasingly matched by parallel presidential invocations of "the Almighty" and by Christian apocalyptic fantasies centered on the Middle East. Even in Nietzsche's "Decree," which goes far in the direction of mimicking that which it opposes, Christianity is referred to as "depravity [*Laster*]" rather than as evil, and there is no suggestion of its total obliteration.

Is it not remarkable that the declaration of *The Antichrist* is directed only against Christianity, not against the other Abrahamic monotheisms and not against religion as such? Of course we are familiar with Nietzsche's comments in *Beyond Good and Evil* and elsewhere about how the philosophical legislator can and should make use of religion. So the limitation to Christianity here may appear as strategic. Nietzsche can declare himself the disciple of Dionysus, hope for an alliance between officers of the March Brandenburg and Jewish bankers, and side with Muslims resisting the Crusades. Since Islam did enter into armed conflict with Christianity and was its main geopolitical rival for at least one thousand years, say until the lifting of the siege of Vienna, on September 12, 1683, we can see why Nietzsche might have felt some sympathy with it.[27] Add to this the idealized version of Andalusian culture that he had absorbed, and it becomes intelligible how he could see a certain affinity with its *jihad* against Christianity.

In spring 1888, Nietzsche, apparently fresh from his reading of Jacolliot, produces this theological-political schema:

> What a yes-saying Aryan religion, the product of the *ruling* class looks like:
>   the Lawbook of Manu
>
> What a yes-saying semitic religion, the product of the *ruling* class looks like:
>   the Lawbook of Muhammad; the Old Testament, in its earlier parts
>
> What a no-saying semitic religion, the product of the *oppressed* class looks like: According to Indian-Aryan concepts:
>   the New Testament—a chandala religion
>
> What a no-saying Aryan religion looks like, having developed among the ruling class:
>   Buddhism
>
> It is completely reasonable that there is no religion of the oppressed Aryan races: for that is a contradiction: a master race is either in charge or goes to ruin. (*SW* 13.380–381)

The schema is a useful guide to Nietzsche's meditations on the psychological and historical significance of the great religions. The Assassins, in his understanding (and in the nineteenth-century views that he adopted) clearly stand outside all of these forms, for they used religion rather than practicing it. He would have had no sympathy with those who welcome death because they believe they are following a divine command and expect immediate translation to paradise. For Nietzsche, the Assassins were this-worldly and employed death and sacrifice for the sake of this-worldly ends. So far we have no reason to think that groups like Al Qaeda operate on the basis of a *secretum* like the one that tradition attributes to the masters of Alamut. We can only speculate about the ends that Nietzsche might have found appropriate for Assassins of the future, and we would probably be right to view them with horror and alarm.

Nietzsche's unremitting hostility to the Crusaders is quite another story. Crusaders are above all stupid, he says, as when he sketches a rhyme that speaks of "goats, geese, and other Crusaders" (*SW* 10.94; cf. 10.542, 630; 13.550). In those last pages of *The Antichrist*, Nietzsche explains the Crusades as the appropriation by the Christian church of the German military machine. Yes, they wanted booty (*Beute*), he says, in other words the medieval equivalent of oil and pipelines. The basic structure of the event is the deployment of a paid army in the service of ascetic Christianity:

> The German knights, always the "*Schweizer*" [Swiss soldiers, guard] of the Church, always in the service of all the bad instincts of the Church—but *well paid*. . . . It is precisely with the aid of German swords, German blood and courage, that the Church has carried on its deadly war against everything noble on earth! (*AC*, § 60)

It is no longer the medieval Church and the German knights that play these roles. In the war in Iraq that began in 2003, we can substitute for these terms a born-again president, governing with the support of apocalyptic fundamentalists, career armies, and contractors lured by the booty. Unlike the Crusades, we do not know the outcome. Indeed, the current Assassins (bin Laden and allies) tell us that the war is a continuation of their struggle with the Crusaders. Nietzsche and Heraclitus would not have been surprised.

May 1, 2004 (first anniversary of George W. Bush's declaring the end of "major combat operations" in Iraq)

Notes

1. See *Nietzsche, Godfather of Fascism?* Ed. Jacob Golomb and Robert S. Wistrich (Princeton: Princeton University Press, 2002) for a series of recent essays on this topic, with references to the literature since the 1930s.
2. For a review of Nietzsche's knowledge of Islam and further references, see Ian Almond, "Nietzsche's Peace with Islam: My Enemy's Enemy Is My Friend," *German Life and Letters*, January 2003, pp. 43–55.
3. For a translation of the "Decree," see Gary Shapiro, *Nietzschean Narratives* (Bloomington: Indiana University Press, 1989), p. 146; for the textual background see the editors' commentary in Friedrich Nietzsche, *Sämtliche Werke: Kritische Studien-*

ausgabe (*SW*), ed. Giorgio Colli and Mazzino Montinari (Berlin: de Gruyter, 1980), vol. 14, pp. 450–453.

4. See, e.g., Syed Qutub, *Milestones* (Lahore: Kazi, n.d.).
5. The Shia, who hold themselves responsible for the betrayal and death of Ali, are another story; the Assassins were a sect that arose among the Ismailite branch of the Shia.
6. *The New York Times*, March 2, 2002, p. A1.
7. Louis Jacolliot, *Les législateurs religieux: Manou, Moïse, Mahomet* (Paris: A. Lacroix, 1876). I am indebted to my colleague Thomas Bonfiglio for discussions of this strange text. Jacolliot was a judge in French India who wrote on diverse subjects, including the occult sciences and his experiences as a big game hunter. He claims to have witnessed scenes of levitation by spiritual adepts in India.
8. Letter to Paul Deussen, January 3, 1888; Nietzsche, *Sämtliche Briefe*, ed. Giorgio Colli and Mazzino Montinari (Berlin: de Gruyter, 1986), vol. 8, p. 222. Abbreviated as *B*.
9. Pierre Klossowski, *The Baphomet*, trans. Sophie Hawkes and Stephen Sartarelli (Hygiene, CO: Eridanos Press, 1988)
10. December 16, 2001.
11. Nietzsche, *On the Genealogy of Morality*, trans. Maudmarie Clark and Alan J. Swensen (Indianapolis: Hackett, 1998), editors' note, p. 163.
12. *SW* 12.75.
13. Clark and Swensen, p. 163.
14. See Bernard Lewis, *The Assassins: A Radical Sect in Islam* (New York: Oxford University Press, 1987), pp. 12–13, for the reference to Joseph von Hammer-Purgstall's *Geschichte der Assassinen aus morgenländischen Quellen* (Stuttgart: 1818); *The History of the Assassins,* trans. Oswald Charles Wood (New York: Burt Franklin, 1967 [reprint]; references below are to this edition). Von Hammer's book, as Lewis notes, was meant as a cautionary work warning against the dangers of secret societies in Europe, such as the Freemasons. Only in recent years has there been a serious scholarly history of Ismaili practice and doctrine, including what is called Nizari Ismailism of the Alamut period, due largely to the Center for Ismaili Studies in London, financed by the Aga Khan, whom most of the world's Ismailis acknowledge as their leader and to whom they pay tribute. For a recent and comprehensive history, see Farhad Daftary, *The Ismailis: Their History and Doctrines* (New York: Cambridge University Press, 1990), especially ch. 1, "Western Progress in Ismaili Studies," pp. 1–31, and ch. 6, "Nizari Ismailism of the Alamut period," pp. 324–434.
15. August Müller, *Der Islam im Morgen- und Abendland* (Berlin: G. Grot'sche Verlagsbuchhandlung, 1885–87), 2 vols. Nietzsche cites Müller at *SW* 13.579 in one of his late notebooks of 1888 from the time when he was working on *The Antichrist*. In his commentary on the latter, Andreas Sommer notes that Nietzsche would not have derived his idealized vision of medieval Andalusia from Müller, who describes the complexity of the historical situation.
16. Nietzsche refers to Wellhausen's *Reste arabischen Heidentums* 11.352 (in *SW*). He studied and made excerpts from this book and from Wellhausen's *Skizzen und Vorarbeiten*, which deals with Islamic subjects; see *SW* 12. 530; 14.441, 747, 755.

17. Von Hammer, pp. 24–25.
18. Von Hammer, pp. 33, 61.
19. Von Hammer, pp. 106, 76.
20. Von Hammer, pp. 106ff.
21. Geoff Waite, *Nietzsche's Corps/e* (Durham, NC: Duke University Press, 1996).
22. Gilles Deleuze, *Difference and Repetition*, trans. Paul Patton (New York: Columbia University Press, 1994), p. 86.
23. Deleuze, *Difference and Repetition*, p. 89.
24. See Clark Blaise, *Time Lord: Sir Sandford Fleming and the Creation of Standard Time* (New York: Random House, 2002).
25. There is an interesting date in the Western calendar—the false time scheme for both Islam and Nietzsche—of September 12, 1683. This was the lifting of the siege of Vienna. The farthest military advance of the Ottoman Empire into the West was halted on that day. For two months the city of Vienna was under siege by the Ottoman forces, which at that time held what is now Greece, Bulgaria, Romania, Hungary, and most of the former Yugoslavia, as well as its base in Turkey and lands held to the east. A coalition of Polish, Bavarian, and Bohemian forces slowly came together, and the siege was broken on September 12. Over the next century the Habsburgs and Russia pushed back the western boundaries of the Ottoman Empire, which continued its decline until its dissolution in the general crisis of World War I. We might wonder if the terrorists could be thinking that an assault on the financial and political capitals of the United States could be revenge for the loss of three centuries ago. But the Islamic lunar calendar, whose year is eleven days shorter than the Christian one, and so more loosely connected with the earth's movement around the sun and the seasons, would find no obvious link between September 11, 2001, and September 12, 1683.
26. Karl Marx, *The 18th Brumaire of Louis Bonaparte* (New York: International Publishers, 1975), p. 15.
27. Perhaps it is time to give serious thought to understanding modern philosophy, roughly the standard Descartes to Kant and Hegel story, in terms of the European response to Islam. European states lived at least the first half of that period in struggle with a powerful civilization. The expulsion of the Moors (and Jews) from Spain in 1492 and the subsequent colonization of the western hemisphere marked a turn in the fortunes of the Christian states, one that reached an apparently definitive turning point with the lifting of the siege of Vienna on September 12, 1683. Could the classical rationalism of Descartes and Leibniz be seen not only as a response to the scientific revolution but as an attempt to bolster European reason against the threat of the oriental and Islamic other? And might the rise of German idealism culminating in Hegel's Eurocentrism be understood as the triumphalist ideology of a civilization that is confident of its political and military superiority as well as its cultural hegemony? In contrast Nietzsche's geopolitical vision, his "trans-European eye," suspects that the rise of Europe, "this little cape of Asia," is not necessarily permanent. One day Europe will survive, he suggests, simply in the form of a collection of thirty or so great books.

Chapter Eleven

The Convalescent

Geographies of Health and Illness

Stuart Elden

Nietzsche was not a well man. He was a sick man, an unhealthy man, and he thought there was something wrong with his liver. This illness, generally accepted to have been caused by syphilis but doubtless exacerbated by diphtheria and dysentery contracted while a paramedic in the Franco-Prussian war, forms a powerful context within which his works were composed. *Migraines, problems with his eyes.* Medical complaints led to his early retirement from the University of Basel in 1879, and much of the later part of his sane life was spent travelling around Europe from resort to resort, seeking alternatively solace and solitude. His experience is, he suggests, "the history of an illness and recovery" (*AOM*, Preface, § 6). *Violent stomach pains, lassitude.* Like the illness itself, the places in which he stayed form not just a backdrop to his work but also feature in his work as places for discussion. There are, for example, observations about Turin, Genoa, Venice, and Sils Maria, many of which are revealing in terms of his life story. *Nerves, cramps, and insomnia.* But these discussions of illness and location go beyond merely biographical interest, illuminating though that can be (see Krell, 1996a). Essentially, they do two things.

First, they demonstrate the way in which health and illness, disease and cure, function as modes of valuing and evaluating, metaphor and more, in Nietzsche's work. This use of medical terminology is revealing both for the approach and for showcasing the parallels between his own illnesses and those of modernity. *A sensation close to seasickness.* As early as 1873 Nietzsche was seeing the curative powers of good historical and philosophical study when he started, though

205

later abandoned, a treatise entitled *The Philosopher as Cultural Physician* (*Arzt der Kultur*; *SW* VII, pp. 545–547; see also *GS*, Preface), and throughout his career he used the German word *Heilmittellehre*, meaning healing through learning, specifically history. Nietzsche's *Über die Zukunft unserer Bildungsanstalten* (On the Future of our Educational Institutions) lectures recognise the dual disease and cure potential of education (*SW* I, 641–752). *Continual pain.* It is also perhaps worth remembering that one of the alternative and unused subtitles for *Twilight of the Idols* was "a moral code for physicians" (see Pasley, 1978).

> The various *cultures* are various spiritual climates each of which is especially harmful or healthful to this or that organism. *History* as a whole, as knowledge of the various cultures, is *pharmacology* but not the science of medicine itself. The *physician* is still needed who will avail himself of this pharmacology to send each person to the climate favourable precisely to him—for a period of time or forever. To live in the present, within a single culture, does not suffice as a universal prescription: too many people of the highest utility who cannot breathe properly in it would die out. With the aid of history one can give them *air* and try to preserve them; men of retarded cultures also have their value.—This spiritual regimen is paralleled by a physical one through which, by a medicinal geography, mankind has to discover to what sicknesses and degenerations each region of the earth gives rise, and conversely what curative factors it offers: and then nations, families and individuals must gradually be transplanted for as long and continuously as is needed for our inherited physical infirmities to be conquered. In the end the whole earth will be a collection of health resorts. (*WS*, § 188)

What we find in this passage, with its heady mix of geography and health, history and medicine, is the blending of academic and lifestyle choices—it demonstrates the importance of philosophy as a way of life, an opening up of concrete possibilities. *Sweats and chills.* Arthur Danto has accordingly called *On the Genealogy of Morality* "a medical book: etiological, diagnostic, therapeutic, prognostic" (Danto, 1988, p. 19). Etiology is the philosophy, or study, of causation—the first step in any genealogical approach to a subject, where the emergence and descent of the phenomena being studied are traced. Those "judgements, judgements of value concerning life, for it or against it" that could never be "true" can, nonetheless, "have value only as symptoms" (*TI*, p. 474). *A semiparalysis that makes mute.* After a full diagnosis, an analysis to gain understanding and perspective, the therapeutic stage can begin (see also Krell, 1996b; Ansell-Pearson, 1997).

Second, as will be particularly dealt with here, the interest in geographies of health and illness showcases a broader concern with questions of the meanings of spaces and the spaces of meaning in both concrete and more abstract senses. Nietzsche regularly stresses the importance of location more broadly. We can find this in his analysis of the Bayreuth festival, the interiors of churches, Greek theatres, and the isolation of deserts—both actual and figurative. This emphasis on place comes particularly to the fore in *Thus Spoke Zarathustra*, which is carefully constructed in terms of oppositions between different places—mountains and sea, the cave and the town—and recurrent metaphors of under and over, height and depth. Zarathustra's long struggle with his role as prophet of the eternal recurrence is dramatically and spatially represented. *Retching, grinning, grimacing, and crying.* Throughout his work, these locations have a range of positive and negative connotations. Place is associated with health or illness: solitude, silence, and convalescence or crowds, noise, and infirmity.

I. Spatial Metaphors

It is noticeable that in Nietzsche's works spatial metaphors are often used to designate different moralities, different systems of thought, different ways of being (see Kofman, 1993). For example, in *The Antichrist* Nietzsche makes such an analysis of the nature of truth: "Truth and the faith that something is true· two completely separate realms of interest almost diametrically opposite realms— they are reached by utterly different paths" (*AC*, § 23). Throughout his work he makes references to the "morality of [an] environment" (*BGE*, § 186), bordered by boundary stones to mark out the territory, a "labyrinth of 'fixed ideas'" (*GM* II, § 22). Concepts are divided by "rigid mathematical lines" like a "templum" (a delimited, often religiously sanctified, space or area), or a "columbarium" (a Roman vault with niches for funeral urns). Similarly, we can visualise a beehive of concepts or a spider's web (*SW* I, pp. 881–882). *Dilated pupils, hyperaesthesia.* Nietzsche also talks of the philosopher's (Kant's) urge toward "classifications . . . tables of categories" (*GS*, § 348).

Nietzsche's "revaluation of values" is dedicated to "toppling boundary markers" (*GS*, § 4), as "one digs up morality when one digs up boundary stones" (*WS*, § 285). In *The Birth of Tragedy* he contrasts Apollo, the god of boundaries, with Dionysus (*BT*, § 9). On the other hand, his genealogical studies, as a necessary prelude to this philosophy of the future, serve to map them out. This can help us break out from the prisons of our convictions (*AC*, § 54). *No painkilling cures work.* Nietzsche's own philosophy, especially as seen in *Thus Spoke Zarathustra*, is clearly seen by him in this light, as a spatial inclusion/exclusion: "I draw circles around me and sacred boundaries; fewer and fewer men climb with me on ever higher mountains" (*Z* III, § 12, 19).

To move outside of these boundaries, Nietzsche uses two main metaphors. The first is that of flight, the conquest of space—new seas, mountains, wildernesses (see Luke, 1978). "He who will one day teach men to fly will have moved all boundary stones" (*Z* III, § 11, 2), says Nietzsche, and he makes several references to flight, to birds, in his works. One of the key passages is found at the end of *Daybreak*, where he talks of "brave birds which fly out into the distance," who "somewhere or other will be unable to go on and will perch on a mast or a bare cliff-face." However, there remains "an immense open space before them," they have not "flown as far as one *could* fly." Nietzsche closes this book with the promise that "*other birds will fly farther!*" (*D*, § 575). *A longing for death.* Flight is clearly linked here with the thought patterns of the original thinker, able to think outside the boundaries they are enclosed within (Hollinrake, 1982, p. 97). For great thinkers, the ability to move outside the boundary stones, to move outside the system, must be based on the experience of the system they are within: "anybody who has built a 'new heaven,' only mustered the power he needed through his *own hell*" (*GM* III, § 10).

The other spatial metaphor used is that of excavation. *On the Genealogy of Morality* can be read as a digging down below moral systems. While others are content with building structures on the ground (*D*, Preface, § 3), Nietzsche excavates below to uncover the underpinning foundations. *Slow pulse.* His preface to *Daybreak* shows this clearly: "in this book you will discover a 'subterranean man' at work, one who tunnels and mines and undermines" (*D*, Preface, § 1; compare Dostoyevsky, 1991). Foucault would later call this excavation of the foundations of a system an archaeology. Psychologically the excavation metaphor also holds, as consciousness is merely a surface (*EH*, "Clever," § 9; see also *BGE*, §§ 230, 289), and shows the influence that Nietzsche would later have on Freud: "it is a painful and dangerous undertaking . . . to tunnel into oneself and to force one's way down into the shaft of one's being by the nearest path" (*UM* III, § 1). *Thoughts, what thoughts.* Nietzsche sees in the figure of Luther another who looked beneath the surface into himself, saying he remained "an honest miner's son" who, shut up in a monastery, lacking "other depths and 'mineshafts' descended into himself and bored out terrible dark galleries" (*D*, § 88). Nietzsche also applies this subterranean reading to the German soul (*BGE*, § 244).

Nietzsche's main argument about community is related to his ideas about morality, as he argues that "to be moral, to act in accordance with custom, to be ethical means to practice obedience towards a law or tradition established from of old" (*HAH* I, § 96; see also *D*, § 9). Traditions and customs are "above all directed at the preservation of a *community*, a people" (*HAH* I, § 96). Community is, of course, an exclusion as well as an inclusion, a segregation. Transgressing the community's rules (Nietzsche uses the comparison of a debtor and creditor) leads to the transgressor's being "cast out" (*GM* II, § 9), leading to *Elend*, the common German word for misery, but which literally means "other country," banishment, exile. *Loneliness and constipation.* Space here functions both as metaphor and fact: the community often has both actual, physical boundaries and more figurative boundaries of custom and morality. As Nietzsche demonstrates, a community that grows in power no longer casts out the wrongdoers but shields them within, imprisons them (*GM* II, § 10).

II. Spatial Analyses

What we find here is a particular geography—issues of depth and height, the outside and inside, distance and nearness. Constraint is looked at as particularly dangerous; flight and transgression valorised. As I have argued elsewhere (Elden, 2001, pp. 49–51), Nietzsche goes beyond this interest in spatial metaphors to make some remarkable analyses of architecture and in particular the significance embedded in buildings (see *HAH* I, §§ 218, 276; *UM* II, § 3). In one of the most striking passages, Nietzsche claims that "the architect has always been under the spell of power. His buildings are supposed to render pride visible, and the victory over gravity, the will to power. Architecture is a kind of eloquence of power in forms—now persuading, even flattering, now only commanding. The highest feeling of power and sureness finds expression in a *grand style*" (*TI*, pp. 520–521). *Abysses of dejection.* This ideal is pursued in most detail in a reading of the Greek theatre (*BT*, § 8)—an analysis, which like much of the rest of that book, should make us think of Wagner, here particularly in relation to the Bayreuth theatre.

Nietzsche's break with Wagner happened around the mid-1870s. It is interesting to note the way in which Nietzsche uses space in his subsequent attack on him. The section titled "On the Flies of the Marketplace" in *Thus Spoke Zarathustra* has clear links with the festival, with the countryside and solitude of Sils Maria (in Switzerland, where Nietzsche often spent his summers) contrasting with the marketplace of Bayreuth: "Where solitude ceases the market place begins; and where the market place begins the noise of the great actors and the buzzing of the poisonous flies begins too" (*Z* I, § 12; see Kaufmann, 1974, p. 414). Later in the same work Nietzsche/Zarathustra pointedly tells the crowd: "I do not love your festivals either: I found too many actors there, and the spectators, too, often behaved like actors" (*Z* I, § 16; see *SW* XII, p. 553). *Contagion, pollution.* Nietzsche's developing contempt for the masses led him against the idea of the theatre as cultural spectacle, describing it as a cruder measure than art itself: "Wagner, too, did not change anything in this respect: Bayreuth is large-scale opera—and not even *good* opera.—The theatre is a form of demolatry in matters of taste; the theatre is a revolt of the masses, a plebiscite *against* good taste" (*CW*, Postscript).

In *The Gay Science* he makes the link between music and health clearly: "I no longer breathe easily once this music begins to affect me. . . . But does not my stomach protest, too? My heart? My circulation? My intestines? Do I not become hoarse as I listen?" On putting some of his objections about the theatre to a Wagnerian, Nietzsche reports the response: "Then you really are merely not healthy enough for our music" (*GS*, § 368). Rather than the damp North, "the steam of the Wagnerian ideal," Nietzsche declares "*il faut méditerraniser la musique*," music must be made Mediterranean, for the following reasons: "the return to nature, health, cheerfulness, youth, *virtue!*" (*CW*, §§ 2–3). Wagner is a neurosis, "a great corruption of music. He has guessed that it is a means to excite weary nerves—and with that he has made music sick" (*CW*, § 5). *Prolonged vomiting of phlegm.* It was not always this way. Aside from *The Birth of Tragedy*, that remarkable work that draws parallels between Greek tragedy and modern music-drama, Nietzsche also wrote the powerful "Richard Wagner in Bayreuth," where he stresses the relation of music to the lifting of spirits:

> When Brünnhilde is awoken by Siegfried; here [Wagner] attains to an elevation and sanctity of mood that makes us think of the glowing ice- and snow-covered peaks of the Alps, so pure, solitary, inaccessible, chaste and bathed in the light of love does nature appear here; clouds and storms, even the sublime itself, are beneath it. (*UM* IV, § 2)

> He plunges into daybreaks, woods, mist, ravines, mountain heights, the dread of night, moonlight, and remarks in them a secret desire: they want to resound. (*UM* IV, § 9)

Given Nietzsche's lifelong engagement with the Christian religion, it is not surprising that he offers some thoughts on the spaces of churches. Some comments are similar to others he makes on aspects of the religion, dismissive and hardly worthy of serious attention, such as "one should not go to church if one wants to breath *pure* air" (*BGE*, § 30), but others are more substantial. Nietzsche argues that the architecture of the churches symbolically relates to the faith of the religion, with "stairways of repentance," "sweet-smelling caves" with "falsified light" and "musty air," where "the soul is not allowed to soar to its height" (*Z* II, § 4). *Digestive fevers.* The symbolism of height within a church is clearly important to the interrelation of faith and power, with the architectural elements of the pulpit and the altar and the body movements of kneeling and standing. Nietzsche also looks at the way in which certain sacred places are forbidden to the uninitiated (*HAH* I, § 100).

Nietzsche associates the Christian religion with darkness, nooks, and corners, "an underworld kingdom, a hospital, a *souterrain* kingdom, a ghetto kingdom" (*AC*, § 17), which he links both to the church itself—"the breath of the architecture, which, as the abode of a divinity, reaches up into obscurity, in the dark spaces of which the divinity may at any moment make evident his dreaded presence" (*HAH* I, § 130)—and to the teachings of the religion—"public acts are precluded; the hiding-place, the darkened room, is Christian. The body is despised, hygiene repudiated as sensuality" (*AC*, § 21). In *On the Genealogy of Morality* the man of *ressentiment* has a mind that "loves dark corners, secret paths and back-doors" (*GM* I, § 10). The Christian religion is, for Nietzsche, the defining example of *ressentiment. Blood moving slowly.* Nietzsche continually makes references to the Christian religion's despising of the body and of drives and passions, arguing that it often demands the extirpation, the covering, the hiding of the passions (see, for example, *WP*, § 226: "They despised the body: they left it out of their account: more, they treated it as an enemy. It was their delusion to believe that one could carry a 'beautiful soul' about in a cadaverous abortion . . ."). Indeed, for Nietzsche, only the destruction of these buildings and what they stand for is enough, looking for a time "when the pure sky again looks through broken ceilings and down upon grass and red poppies near broken walls" (*Z* II, § 4), as he does "not see how we could remain content with such buildings even if they were stripped of their churchly purposes. The language spoken by these buildings is far too rhetorical and unfree, reminding us that they are houses of God and ostentatious monuments of some supramundane intercourse" (GS, § 280).

> We Europeans confront a world of tremendous ruins. A few things are still towering, much looks decayed and uncanny, while most things already lie on the ground. It is all very picturesque—where has one ever seen more beautiful ruins?—and overgrown by large and small weeds. The church is this city of destruction. (GS, § 358)

These passages show that Nietzsche realises that for his own "philosophy of the future" new buildings must be built, space must be used in new ways. *Serene crippledom.* "Quiet and wide, expansive places for reflection" are missing from our cities, "buildings and sites that would altogether give expression to the sublimity of thoughtfulness and of stepping aside" (GS, § 280). In 1882 he anticipates how things might turn out when he writes, "science has not yet built its cyclopic buildings; but the time for that, too, will come" (GS, § 7). This reading of a town, of buildings, is well shown when Nietzsche comments on Genoa, with "its villas and pleasure gardens and the far-flung periphery of its inhabited heights and slopes." The region, for Nietzsche, is "studded with the images of bold and autocratic human beings. They have *lived* and wished to live on: that is what they are telling me with their houses, built and adorned to last for centuries and not for a fleeting hour"; he sees "violence and conquest" in the eyes of the builders. The "whole region is overgrown with this magnificent, insatiable selfishness of the lust for possessions and spoils" and each "conquered his homeland for himself by overwhelming it with his architectural ideas and refashioning it into a house that was a feast for his eyes" (GS, § 291). *Raw from weeping.* A similar attitude is found when Nietzsche contrasts "quiet, aristocratic Turin" with "a small German town . . . [a] pinched and flattened, cowardly world" and "a German big city—this built-up vice where nothing grows, where everything, good or bad, is imported" (EH, "Clever," § 8). This distrust of the city is regularly referred to in his writings:

> A venerable specimen of very much older sensibility could certainly have been more easily preserved in remoter regions, in less travelled mountain valleys, in more self-enclosed communities: while it is improbable that such discoveries would be made in, for example Berlin, where people come into the world washed and scaled clean. (AOM, § 223)

The figure of solitude is much used in Nietzsche's works, partly at least because he spent so much time alone. In *On the Genealogy of Morality*, he talks of finding "deserts" to withdraw to, to become a hermit in, in order to think in solitude (GM III, § 8; see HAH, Preface, §§ 3–4). These deserts need not be "Syrian . . . a stage desert," mountains, "even a room in some crowded, run-of-the-mill hotel" can be a desert, can be "desolate enough." Nietzsche compares the Temple of Artemis, where Heraclitus withdrew to think, with what he calls his "nicest study," the "Piazza di San Marco" (*GM* III, § 8). Lars Gustafsson reads this as a place where Nietzsche is almost inviting us "to come and see him" (Gustafsson, 1988, p. 184), but this misses the point that though this is a large public square in Venice, undoubtedly busy and full of people, Nietzsche values its anonymity. The point is surely that the spatial characteristics of this square are conducive to Nietzsche's thoughts, that one can be alone even when other people are around. These spaces need not be large. In an important note on the role of the church, Nietzsche lists the things that it has spoiled. One of these is the cloister, a place of temporary isolation where external contact, including letters, is forbidden, but that allows the "deepest recollection and rediscovery of oneself" (*SW* XII, pp. 552–553). A *factum* of indescribable sadness. However, it is not solely man-made space that can be read in this way, as natural space also serves to shape: "In the writings of a hermit one always also hears something of the echo of the desolate regions, something of the whispered tones and the furtive look of solitude" (*BGE*, § 289).

III. The Spaces of Zarathustra

Throughout *Thus Spoke Zarathustra*, Nietzsche sets up "antithetical spatial images," such as height and depth, mountain and sea, and the important bifurcation of over and under, *ünter* and *über* (Hollinrake, 1982, pp. 90–108). Indeed, elsewhere, one of Nietzsche's most beautiful snapshots of his thought is the suggestion that "to elevate [*erheben*] men one has to be sublime [*erhaben*] oneself" (*CW*, § 6). As Hollinrake and Luke have pointed out, these spatial (dramatic) conceptions often mirror the philosophical content of Zarathustra's teachings, for example the tightrope walker between two towers (dramatic) with the idea of man as a bridge "between beast and *Übermensch*" (*Z*, Prologue, §§ 3–6; see Hollinrake, 1982; Luke, 1978; more generally Miller, 1995, chapter 7; Irigaray, 1991; Oliver, 1995).

The eternal return is the key teaching of Zarathustra and the key message of *Thus Spoke Zarathustra*. Within the work it functions as an important dramatic device, and the narrative is shaped around Zarathustra's thoughts, doubts, and teaching of this message. In Nietzsche's work as a whole the eternal return is mentioned in several places, the most important in *The Gay Science* (*GS*, § 341), where it appears as a test to be thought through, and though in some of his notes of the 1880s Nietzsche attempts a scientific proof (see *WP*, §§ 1053ff; Löwith, 1997), it certainly functions best as a dramatic idea, a test of a life and its living, through which it links with other key ideas of Nietzsche's, such as the *Übermensch*, the will to power, *amor fati*, and the revaluation of all values. *Obstinate headaches and nausea.*

Everything is kaput, my stomach so much so that it even refuses the sedatives—in consequence of which I have sleepless, terribly tormented nights and, a further consequence, a profound nervousness. (*Selected Letters*, p. 209)

Zarathustra's first problem with his "abysmal thought" is that any thought of the eternal return must involve the return of the small man, the rabble, which causes the nausea he struggles to fight for the next two parts. Zarathustra's own life with its attendant problems—and Nietzsche's own sufferings form a necessary backdrop and parallel—is not the thing he is unable to affirm, but the return of the mediocre is (Z II, § 6). As he confesses in a letter of the time, "in all my states of sickness I feel, with horror, a sort of downward pull toward the weakness of the rabble, the gentlenesses of the rabble, even the virtues of the rabble" (*Selected Letters*, p. 243). *Weakness of the gastric system.* This inability to fully affirm prevents Zarathustra from expounding the doctrine, forcing him into silence (Z II, § 20) and retreat to the cave and solitude. Here he confesses that he is aware of the thought: "I know it, but do not want to say it!" He knows the name of his "awesome mistress," but this is a name as yet unsaid and unknown to the reader (Z II, § 22).

In Part Three, Zarathustra struggles to come to terms with his thought, a thought he calls his "*ultimate* peak," his "hardest path" and "loneliest walk." The eternal return is first presented by Zarathustra in the form of a riddle, a "vision of the loneliest." In this riddle, Zarathustra is walking up a mountain path "not cheered by herb or shrub" with his archenemy the spirit of gravity, in the form of a dwarf, sitting on him, weighing him down. Zarathustra climbs slowly, making his ascent, praising courage, which he says can slay "even death itself, for it says, 'Was *that* life? Well then! Once more!'" (Z III, § 2, 1). *Intoxication, becoming more beautiful.* Just as Zarathustra is about to present the riddle, his abysmal thought, the dwarf jumps from his shoulders, freeing Zarathustra from the weight. The key dramatic presentation of the challenge is presented—the gateway with its two faces, the place where paths stretching toward eternity meet. Inscribed above is the single word *moment, Augenblick,* the blink of an eye. *The first glimpses of the sunlight of returning health.*

Zarathustra then asks whether it is possible for these two paths to contradict each other eternally and berates the dwarf for his answer, which though essentially correct for the doctrine (that "all truth is crooked, time itself is a circle") is without the weight and difficulty that Zarathustra attaches to it. Zarathustra suggests that all has passed along these paths before—the dwarf, the gateway, himself, and restating *The Gay Science* (§ 341), the slow spider in the moonlight—and will do so again and again for all eternity. *Every pain and every joy.* Zarathustra at this point starts speaking ever more softly and suddenly encounters a return from his own past, a howling dog that he remembers from his childhood, which swiftly changes into a scene that dramatises Zarathustra's nausea at this idea, a shepherd gagging on a heavy black snake.

This is clearly a fundamental challenge to linear notions of time but is also a theoretical test of the self-affirmation of the *Übermensch*. It is equally presented both in terms of health and geography. *All the heavens rejoice.* The struggle with this thought has been the cause of Zarathustra's nausea, and it is only at the end of the third part of the book that he is able to overcome his nausea and declare his love for the female figure of Eternity. In the penultimate chapter of the third part, Zarathustra meets Life, who realises he must leave her soon, but Zarathustra whispers into her ear something to which she replies, "you know that, O Zarathustra? Nobody knows that." Spring after Winter. It is clear that Zarathustra has informed her that he knows the *truth* of the eternal return. For Zarathustra, "life was dearer to me than all my wisdom ever was" (Z III, § 15, 2), but now both Life and Wisdom must be left behind as Zarathustra embraces his awesome mistress: "For I love you, O eternity!" (Z III, § 16, 1). This cry is repeated seven times: a dramatic presentation of the repetition of the return. In the fourth part Zarathustra discovers that his final trial is pity.

> O what years! What tortures of every kind, what solitudes and weariness with life! And against all that, as it were against death *and* life, I have brewed this medicine of mine, these thoughts with their small strip of *unclouded* sky overhead. (*Selected Letters*, p. 185)

As I have shown elsewhere (Elden, 2001, pp. 46–47), the entire book *Thus Spoke Zarathustra* is dramatically structured around a spatial return. At the top of the initial cycle we have Zarathustra's cave in the mountains; at the foot the town of man. Zarathustra goes down the mountain to the forest and from there to the town. He leaves the town in the middle of the night, back to the forest, where he sleeps until midday, looking back up to the mountains above. Although he does not return himself until the end of the first part, what we have is a spatial return—mountains, forest, town, forest, and mountains. *Dyspepsia, protracted sickness.* The movement of the sun parallels the movement of Zarathustra himself with its rise and its setting and then again rising to high noon.

At the beginning of the second part of the book we find Zarathustra withdrawn and in his cave again. Once more he heads down the mountain to the world of men, where he remains for the entire second half of the book, realising he must return toward the end of that book. Because he is in the Blessed Isles, this journey home takes the third part of the book, a spatial return that takes him on a long and indirect route, almost a denial of the final destination. But Zarathustra is able to cope with the thought of the return home, the spatial return, before the thought of the eternal return. *Sensory hallucinations.* On his way back, Zarathustra comes to the gate of a great city—"I am nauseated by this great city" (Z III, § 7)—and then reaches the town known as the Motley Cow, in which he had spent time earlier, where he realises he has "only two more days to go to reach his cave . . . his soul jubilated continually because of the nearness of his return home" (*Z* III, § 8). He eventually arrives in the chapter actually titled "The Return Home." Here he declares his love for its solitude: "Too long have I lived wildly in wild strange places not to return home to you in tears" (*Z* III, § 9).

While in his cave, Zarathustra again cannot face the thought of the eternal return, and there follow some lengthy chapters of denial. *Face flushed and tongue furred.* Finally there is the key chapter "The Convalescent," where he shelters, indeed hides, back in the cave. Here too he complains of his nausea, and it is his animals that force him to confront both the outside world—"step out of your cave: the world awaits you like a garden"—and the doctrine itself:

> Everything goes, everything comes back: eternally rolls the wheel of be-
> ing. Everything dies, everything blossoms again: eternally runs the year
> of being. Everything breaks, everything is joined anew; eternally the same
> house of being is built. Everything parts, everything greets every other
> thing again; eternally the ring of being remains faithful to itself. In every
> now, being begins; round every Here rolls the sphere There. The centre is
> everywhere. Bent is the path of eternity. (*Z* III, § 13)

Zarathustra is still in denial because of the recurrence of the small man, the man of whom he is weary. But his animals are having none of this: "For your animals know well, O Zarathustra, who you are and must become: behold, *you are the teacher of the eternal return*—that is your destiny" (*Z* III, § 13, 2). Zarathustra comes to deal with this, and it is in the following pages, at the very end of the third part, that he affirms the return without regret or limit. *Sing a new song to me.* The fourth part, originally intended to be a continuation of the first three, rather than a close, similarly has a journey of departure and return (on this part, see Higgins, 1987).

IV. Convalescence and Madness

Nietzsche describes *The Gay Science* as a book of gratitude, "the gratitude of a convalescent—for *convalescence* was unexpected." Written in 1886, this is a description of how he felt in 1881–1882, "all at once attacked by hope, the hope for health, and the *intoxication* or *drunkenness* [*Trunkenheit*] of convalescence" (*GS*, Preface, § 1). Convalescence is *Genesenden*, the convalescent is *die Genesung*—recovery, being delivered of something, recuperation, the return home. Convalescence, *con* together with *valescere*, to grow strong, to get well. The wanderer's recovery, the return? (see Heidegger, 1991, II, 21).

> For Nietzsche's nomadism proved to be cyclical. He spent his winters on
> the Mediterranean, first in Genoa, then in Nice, and his summers in the
> mountains of the Upper Engadine, almost always in Sils-Maria. Only dur-
> ing the final winter of his productive life did he move inland, to Turin,
> as though combing the hills of Aosta for the most archaic of seas. (Krell
> and Bates, 1997, p. 121)

In an unpublished note from the autumn of 1887, Nietzsche notes that "when one is sick, one should crawl away and hide in some 'cave': that is what's reasonable, only that is the animal way" (*SW* XII, p. 394). *A dreadful burden. Chronic misery.* His own response was both to follow and disregard this advice.

> Just as a physician places his patient in a wholly strange environment so that he may be removed from his entire "hitherto" . . . so I, as physician and patient in one, compelled myself to an opposite and unexplored *clime of the soul*, and especially to a curative journey into strange parts. . . .
> (*AOM*, Preface, § 5)

Nietzsche controls his environment, that much is clear. He watches everything he eats—the German spirit comes from "distressed intestines"—and is strict in drinking—"a single glass of wine or beer in one day is quite sufficient to turn my life into a vale of misery," enjoying only water, especially spring water, no coffee, and "a little but strong" tea (*EH*, "Clever," § 1). "In all these matters—in the choice of nutrition, of place and climate, of recreation—an instinct of self-preservation issues its commandments, and it gains its most unambiguous expression as an instinct of *self-defence*" (*EH*, "Clever," § 8).

And yet, he does "not want to take leave ungratefully from that time of severe sickness whose profits I have not yet exhausted even today" (*GS*, Preface, § 3). It is "from such abysses, from such severe sickness, also from the sickness of severe suspicion, one returns *newborn*, having shed one's skin, more ticklish and malicious, with a more delicate taste for joy, with a tenderer tongue for all good things, with merrier senses, with a second dangerous innocence in joy, more childlike and yet a hundred times subtler than has ever been before" (*GS*, Preface, § 4; see *GS*, § 382). We find a similar way of thinking in another one of the prefaces that he wrote in 1886 to his earlier books, this time to *Human, All-Too-Human. Fingers freezing, eyes burning.* Nietzsche describes the passage from the illness through convalescence to the "*great* health" he now claims to enjoy (*HAH*, Preface, §§ 4–5; see Krell, 1996b, p. 206). This great health is "an as yet undiscovered country whose boundaries nobody has surveyed yet" (*GS*, § 382). But, "what unprecedented shudders! What happiness even in the weariness, the old sickness, the relapses of the convalescent!" (*HAH*, Preface, § 5). *Strabismus and myopia.* If this is overblown in terms of his physical health, it is more accurately paralleled in the way his mid-period works are a sign of mental convalescence, a period where he progressively rids himself of the twin sicknesses of Schopenhauer and Wagner.

Sickness then, for Nietzsche, "is a powerful stimulant, only one has to be healthy enough for it" (*SW* XIII, p. 535). If this seems paradoxical, note the way in which Nietzsche continually stresses the importance of life taken generally. Illness then is not something that only operates as a lack of health, and certainly not a lack of life. It too is a form of life (Kofman, 1993, pp. 52–53; see *WP*, §§ 47, 812; *GM* III, § 14; *EH*, "Wise," § 2). In Kofman's remarkable phrase, "illness is a *relève* for health," illness is a relief from health, but also an elevation from it (1993, p. 53, see p. 164 n. 39). In playful mood, Nietzsche asks, "why is it that health is not as infectious as sickness—in general but especially in matters of taste? Or are there epidemics of health?" (*WS*, § 129). *Collapse, delirium.*

Various interpretations or diagnoses can be imposed upon Nietzsche after 1889: "paraphrenia, dementia praecox, paranoia, schizophrenia" among them (Klossowski, 1997, p. 239). *The world is transfigured.* But as Klossowski compellingly argues, all these are external impositions, thoughts from the outside (for a reading of the psychiatrists, including Karl Jaspers, who have tried to analyse Nietzsche after the event, see Krell, 1996b, pp. 202–203). It seems appropriate to leave things there. *Progressive paralysis.* As his health descends into terminal illness, his geographies close in around him, and he rarely leaves the room and his sister's care. And finally a stroke. *The stone, the desert, death.*

Medical Note

I have taken much general information from Hayman, 1980; Krell, 1996a, 1996b; and Klossowski, 1997. As Krell notes, "whereas Klossowski raises the question of Nietzsche's thought as a periodic battle with migraine, I wish to relate his thought to the matter of infection" (1996b, p. 201; see Klossowski, 1997, especially p. 24). I have also made use of Nietzsche's letters (1986; 1969), and the first part of *Ecce Homo*, "Why I Am So Wise," for the various ailments and symptoms. The final sentence is based on *Dionysus Dithyrambs*, SW XII, p, 387.

Works Cited

Ansell-Pearson, Keith. 1997. *Viroid Life: Perspectives on Nietzsche and the Transhuman Condition*. London: Routledge.

Danto, Arthur. 1988. "Some Remarks on *The Genealogy of Morals*." In Robert C. Solomon & Kathleen Higgins (eds.), *Reading Nietzsche*. Oxford: Oxford University Press.

Dostoyevsky, Fedor. 1991. *Notes from the Underground*, translated by Jane Kentish. Oxford: Oxford University Press.

Elden, Stuart. 2001. *Mapping the Present: Heidegger, Foucault, and the Project of a Spatial History*. London/New York: Continuum.

Gustafsson, Lars. 1988. "Dr. Nietzsche's Office Hours Are Between 10 and 12 AM." In Robert C. Solomon and Kathleen Higgins (eds.), *Reading Nietzsche*. Oxford: Oxford University Press.

Hayman, Ronald. 1980. *Nietzsche: A Critical Life*. London: Weidenfeld & Nicolson.

Heidegger, Martin. 1991. *Nietzsche*, translated by David Farrell Krell, Frank Capuzzi & Joan Stambaugh. 4 vols. San Francisco: HarperCollins.

Higgins, Kathleen Marie. 1987. *Nietzsche's Zarathustra*. Philadelphia: Temple University Press.

Hollinrake, Roger. 1982. *Nietzsche, Wagner, and the Philosophy of Pessimism*. London: George Allen and Unwin Ltd.

Irigaray, Luce. 1991. *Marine Lover of Friedrich Nietzsche*, translated by Gillian C. Gill. New York: Columbia University Press.

Kaufmann, Walter. 1974. *Nietzsche: Philosopher, Psychologist, Antichrist*. 4th ed. Princeton, NJ: Princeton University Press.

Klossowski, Pierre. 1997. *Nietzsche and the Vicious Circle*, translated by Daniel W. Smith. London: Athlone.

Kofman, Sarah. 1993. *Nietzsche and Metaphor*, translated by Duncan Large. London: Athlone Press.

Krell, David Farrell. 1996a. *Nietzsche: A Novel*. Albany: State University of New York Press.

Krell, David Farrell. 1996b. *Infectious Nietzsche*. Bloomington: Indiana University Press.

Krell, David Farrell, and Donald L. Bates. 1997. *The Good European: Nietzsche's Work Sites in Word and Image*. Chicago: University of Chicago Press.

Löwith, Karl. 1997. *Nietzsche's Philosophy of the Eternal Recurrence of the Same*, translated by J. Harvey Lomax. Berkeley: University of California Press.

Luke, F. D. 1978. "Nietzsche and the Imagery of Height," in Malcolm Pasley (ed.), *Nietzsche: Imagery and Thought*. London: Methuen.

Miller, J. Hillis. 1995. *Topographies*. Stanford: Stanford University Press.

Nietzsche, Friedrich. 1969. *Selected Letters of Friedrich Nietzsche*, edited and translated by Christopher Middleton. Chicago: University of Chicago Press.

Nietzsche, Friedrich. 1986. *Sämtliche Briefe: Kritische Studienausgabe*, edited by Giorgio Colli and Mazzino Montinari. 8 vols. Munich: Deutscher Taschenbuch.

Oliver, Kelly. 1995. *Womanising Nietzsche: Philosophy's Relationship to the Feminine*. London: Routledge.

Pasley, Malcolm. 1978. "Nietzsche's Use of Medical Terms," in Malcolm Pasley (ed.), *Nietzsche: Imagery and Thought*. London: Methuen.

Index